"Ayman Ibrahim has provided English speakers with an excellent guide to learning written Arabic. There are thorough explanations in English with many more clear tables than in comparable textbooks. Exercises encourage translation from Arabic to English and English to Arabic. Excerpts from the Qur'an and the Bible in Arabic are an original feature that will appeal to students of religious studies. I wish this book had been available when I first learned written Arabic."

—*Mark Beaumont*, research associate at London School of Theology, formerly senior lecturer in Islam and Mission

"This textbook fills an important niche for those beginning the study of Arabic. Ayman Ibrahim introduces the student to a wide variety of everyday as well as less common vocabulary within clear, well-structured lessons and exercises. Highly recommended for the classroom and self-directed students, *Basics of Arabic* surpasses other currently available textbooks."

—*Sandra Toenies Keating*, professor of theology, Providence College

"*Basics of Arabic* provides the student with an accessible step-by-step introduction to the Arabic language with ease but with grammatical rigor. Ayman Ibrahim gradually introduces the language with minimal grammatical jargon, allowing the student to move from one topic to the next without getting overwhelmed."

—*George A. Kiraz*, Gorgias Press, Editor-in-Chief

"In *Basics of Arabic*, Ayman Ibrahim has provided in one place an innovative and user-friendly grammar and workbook for the beginning student of Arabic. Carefully laid out, visually appealing, and studded with helpful charts, vocabulary lists, and exercises, the book's twenty lessons expertly guide the student from the basics of the Arabic alphabet through to the intricacies of Arabic verbs and sentences. A truly unique and welcome feature of the book is that it draws examples and exercises from the Arabic Bible and the Qur'an, as well as from everyday life in the Arabic-speaking world. Highly recommended!"

—*Matthew J. Kuiper*, Missouri State University

"This is a delightful introduction to Modern Standard Arabic. The presentation is orderly and well paced. The overview of the verbal system is a model of clarity. Uniquely, the vocabulary items mastered by students include an essential assortment of religious terms shared by Arabic-speaking Muslims and Christians. While designed for use with a teacher, the text is also appropriate for self-study and as a supplementary grammar in a course on proficiency of Arabic. A student who masters the material in this book will have a solid foundation with which to continue the study of Arabic and an ability to read religious and nonreligious literature in standard Arabic."

—*John C. Lamoreaux*, Department of Religious Studies, Southern Methodist University

BASICS of
ARABIC

BASICS *of* ARABIC

A COMPLETE GRAMMAR, WORKBOOK, AND LEXICON

AYMAN S. IBRAHIM

ZONDERVAN ACADEMIC

Basics of Arabic
Copyright © 2021 by Ayman S. Ibrahim

ISBN 978-0-310-09328-2 (hardcover)

Requests for information should be addressed to:
Zondervan, *3900 Sparks Dr. SE, Grand Rapids, Michigan 49546*

Unless otherwise indicated, Scripture quotations are those of the authors.

Any internet addresses (websites, blogs, etc.) and telephone numbers in this book are offered as a resource. They are not intended in any way to be or imply an endorsement by Zondervan, nor does Zondervan vouch for the content of these sites and numbers for the life of this book.

All rights reserved. No part of this publication may be reproduced, stored in a retrieval system, or transmitted in any form or by any means—electronic, mechanical, photocopy, recording, or any other—except for brief quotations in printed reviews, without the prior permission of the publisher.

Cover design: LUCAS Art & Design
Typesetting: Miles V. Van Pelt

Printed in the United States of America

To my beloved brother and esteemed friend
with whom I enjoyed many wonderful conversations in Arabic.
You are dearly missed, *habibi*.

Tony Maalouf
(1955–2020)

Table of Contents

Acknowledgments .... *xv*

Introduction .... *xvii*

Abbreviations .... *xix*

LESSON ONE — 1

    Alphabet: General and Transliteration — 1

    Single Letters — 1

    Connecting Letters Together — 3

    Exercises — 6

LESSON TWO — 8

    Additional Letters — 8

    The *Tā' Marbūṭah* (تاء مربوطة) ة or ـة — 8

    The *Alif Maqṣūrah* (ألف مقصورة) ى — 9

    The *Hamzah* (همزة) ء — 10

    Vocabulary — 11

    Exercises — 12

LESSON THREE — 13

    Arabic Vowels — 13

    Short Vowels — 13

        The *Fatḥah* (فتحة) — 13

        The *Ḍammah* (ضمة) — 14

        The *Kasrah* (كسرة) — 14

        An Important Note on Short Vowels — 15

    Long Vowels — 15

        Alif (ا) — 16

        Wāw (و) — 16

        Yā' (ي) — 18

    Sukūn (سُكون) — 19

    Shaddah (شَدّة) — 20

Maddah (مَدَّة)	21
Vocabulary	22
Exercises	24

LESSON FOUR — 25

Arabic Syllables	25
Diphthong	28
Arabic Definite Article (الـ)	29
Sun and Moon Letters	29
Tanwīn (تَنوين)	31
Vocabulary	35
Exercises	38

LESSON FIVE — 39

Parts of Speech: Words in Arabic	39
Arabic Sentences	40
Nominal Sentences	40
Verbal Sentences	42
Inflection: Declension and Conjugation	44
Arabic Case System	45
Nominative Case (مَرْفوع)	46
Genitive Case (مَجْرور)	47
Accusative Case (مَنْصوب)	48
Declinable and Indeclinable	48
Vocabulary	49
Exercises	52

LESSON SIX — 53

Particles	53
Arabic Prepositions (حُروف الجَرّ)	53
The Particles of Conjunction (حُروف العَطْفِ)	55
Vocabulary	58
Exercises	61

LESSON SEVEN — 62

Nouns (الأسْمَاء) — 62
- *Separate Subject Pronouns* (ضَمائِرُ الرَّفْعِ المُنْفَصِلَةُ) — 62
- *Gender in Nouns* — 64
- *Number in Nouns* — 67

Vocabulary — 72

Exercises — 74

LESSON EIGHT — 77

Adjectives (الصِفات) — 77

Arabic Cardinal Numbers (الأرْقَام) — 81

Vocabulary — 82

Exercises — 86

LESSON NINE — 88

Demonstratives (أَسْمَاء الإشارَة) — 88
- *Demonstratives as Adjectives* — 89
- *Demonstratives as Pronouns* — 91

Vocabulary — 93

Exercises — 95

LESSON TEN — 97

The *Nisbah* Adjective (النِّسْبَة) — 97
- *Nouns Ending with* Alif *or* Tā' Marbūṭah — 99
- *Nouns Ending with* Alif-Hamzah — 100
- *Dual and Plural Forms with the* Nisbah *Adjectives* — 102

Vocabulary — 103

Exercises — 104

LESSON ELEVEN — 106

Possessive Pronouns (ضَمائِرُ المُلْكِيّة) — 106

The *Iḍāfah* Construct — 112

Interrogative Particles (حُروفُ الاستِفْهام) — 115

Vocabulary	117
Exercises	120

LESSON TWELVE — 123

Introduction to Arabic Verbs (الأفعال)	123
Verb Roots	123
Al-Awzān (الأوْزان)	126
Vocabulary	129
Exercises	131

LESSON THIRTEEN — 133

Arabic Verbs: Categories	133
The Past Tense (الفِعْل الماضي)	133
The Verb and Its Subject (الفِعْلُ والفاعِلُ)	147
Vocabulary	151
Exercises	154

LESSON FOURTEEN — 157

Verbs and Their Accusative Direct Objects	157
Past Passive (الماضي المَجْهول)	159
Vocabulary	166
Exercises	167

LESSON FIFTEEN — 169

Past Tense Verbs: Negation and Other Forms	169
Past Tense with the Particle قَدْ	169
Negating Past Tense	169
The Substitute of the Verb's Doer (نائِبُ الفاعِلِ)	171
Arabic Participles (اسْمُ الفاعِلِ واسْمُ المَفْعولِ)	176
Nouns of Intensiveness and Exaggeration (اسْمُ المُبالَغَة)	179
Vocabulary	182
Exercises	185

LESSON SIXTEEN — 187

- Present Simple Verbs — 187
- Present Active Tense (الفِعْلُ المُضارِع) — 187
- Present Passive Tense (المُضارِع المَجْهول) — 198
- Vocabulary — 201
- Exercises — 202

LESSON SEVENTEEN — 205

- Future Simple Tense (الزَّمَنُ المُسْتَقْبَل) — 205
- Negating Present Tense — 207
- Negating Future Tense: Introducing Subjunctive Mood — 208
- Another Way to Negate Past Tense: Introducing Jussive Mood — 214
- Negating Nominal Sentences — 217
- Vocabulary — 219
- Exercises — 220

LESSON EIGHTEEN — 223

- The Imperative Verb (فِعْلُ الأمرِ) — 223
- Cutting and Connecting *Hamzah* (هَمْزَةُ الْقَطْعِ وهَمْزَةُ الْوَصْلِ) — 225
- Un-nunated Nouns (المَمْنوعُ مِنْ الصَّرْفِ) — 227
- Arabic Adverbs — 232
- Vocabulary — 236
- Exercises — 239

LESSON NINETEEN — 241

- Sound and Weak Verbs — 241
- Basic Categories in Sound and Weak Verbs — 242
  - *Hamzated* Verbs — 243
  - Geminate Verbs — 246
  - Assimilated Verbs — 248
  - Hollow Verbs — 253
  - Defective Verbs — 256
- Vocabulary — 257
- Exercises — 259

LESSON TWENTY — 262

Verbs Forms — 262

- Form 1 فَعَـلَ — 263
- Form 2 فَعَّـلَ — 263
- Form 3 فاعَلَ — 264
- Form 4 أَفْعَـلَ — 265
- Form 5 تَفَعَّـلَ — 266
- Form 6 تَفاعَلَ — 267
- Form 7 اِنْفَـعَـلَ — 268
- Form 8 اِفْتَـعَـلَ — 269
- Form 9 اِفْعَـلَّ — 269
- Form 10 اِسْتَـفْعَـلَ — 269

Verbal Noun (المَصْدَر) — 270

Vocabulary — 273

Exercises — 277

Glossary of Vocabulary and Expressions — 279

Acknowledgments

My thanks should first go to Nancy Erickson, Executive Editor at Zondervan Academic, for persevering with me throughout the process to complete such a detailed book. She believed in this book and has always been enthusiastic for it. Thanks also to Joshua Kessler, Marketing Director at Zondervan. He was the first member of Zondervan with whom I talked about an Arabic textbook.

My sincerest gratitude and deepest appreciation go to the talented and thorough Mrs. Lamis Maalouf, who reviewed this book and provided outstanding comments. Her meticulous observations improved the text tremendously. If anything is remotely good in this grammar, it is probably because of a remarkable observation or a brilliant comment she made. Thanks also to the skillful Miles V. Van Pelt, who typeset the entire book. He took the many Arabic and English words I wrote and placed them wonderfully and beautifully in an artful and organized way.

I am also grateful for my Southern Seminary students, whose love for learning Arabic inspires me. Their comments and questions added a clear value to the content of the book. My utmost thanks and gratitude go to my very best friend, my wife, without whose encouragement and support my published works would not exist. She is my Arabic-speaking journey partner, whose love for Arabic is only second to her love for me.

To all, *shukran*.

Introduction

Welcome to the study of Arabic! *Ahlan wa sahlan*! *Marḥaban*!

Arabic is the language of the Quran. Muslims view it as the most beautiful language, because it is used in their scripture. The Arabic of the Quran is classical. It includes unique vocabulary, some of which is rarely used today. Classical Arabic is also used in the earliest Muslim writings, including Muhammad's biography and the early histories and narratives. Muslims recite the Quran and their ritual prayers in Classical Arabic.

The contemporary version of Arabic is Modern Standard Arabic, which is used in newspapers and on official TV programs in over twenty-two Arabic-speaking countries. This form of Arabic is the focus of this book. It is commonly known as *al-fuṣḥā* (الفُصْحَى).

This is an introductory book that aims to help students take their first steps toward exploring the modern use of this unique, beautiful, and multifaceted language. A student can begin this book with no knowledge of Arabic, then move smoothly toward learning nouns and verbs, and finally reach the threshold of further advanced studies in Arabic. Along the way, important Arabic phrases are introduced in order to encourage students to practice with their Arabic-speaking friends.

Basics of Arabic is intended for use with peers and under a teacher's instruction, so that students may practice speaking. However, it is also designed in a way that can serve self-learners. Although language learning can present particular difficulties due to the necessity of incorporating advanced material at the beginning, this grammar attempts to order the learning process as logically as possible. In a nutshell, after the alphabet, nouns and adjectives are introduced, some verbs are interspersed, particles are tackled, and then verbs and their various forms and tenses are explained.

The book can be divided into two somewhat equal parts: nouns and verbs. Lessons One through Eleven focus on nouns, adjectives, demonstratives, and particles. Lessons Twelve through Twenty cover verbs, their tenses, conjugations, and forms. The lessons related to nouns also include initial remarks concerning verbs. In addition, in the vocabulary section in some noun lessons, a few verbs are included, specifically to feed inquiring minds of some students, as well as to explain the use of verbs alongside nouns.

The student of *Basics of Arabic* will become familiar with numerous Arabic words. Each lesson following the initial alphabet ends with a set of vocabulary words.

Many new words are introduced in the lesson itself, along with their translations. In some lessons, we reoffer the translation of words that were mentioned previously. This is because seeing words often, pronouncing them repeatedly, and recognizing them in sentences help students tremendously. The more senses you use to learn Arabic words, the better. Read, write, and pronounce the words aloud. Practice the memorization with a friend so that you listen to the words as well.

Some religious terms are commonly used by students. In an attempt to help students practice in their own contexts, plenty of nouns from the Bible and the Quran are included in this grammar. The goal is to help students use Arabic daily with words that are familiar. In fact, it is sometimes beneficial for students to read the Arabic passages of religious texts they know by heart. This is one reason why in the examples and exercises here Arabic texts of famous biblical and quranic passages have been included.

Since significant attention is paid here to vocabulary and grammar, at the end of the book a glossary of vocabulary and expressions is provided. The glossary has more than 900 Arabic words, arranged alphabetically for easy access. *Basics of Arabic* includes twenty lessons. They aim to cover between 25 to 35 lectures, with each lecture ranging between 2 to 3 hours. The book is intended to cover two consecutive semesters of study. Some of the lessons are lengthier than others, especially those regarding verbs (12–20).

As with vocabulary, each lesson ends with a set of exercises. While many examples are offered in the lesson itself, there is a significant benefit from applying what you learn as you practice. The exercises are straightforward. They follow the pattern of the examples offered in each lesson. Additionally, exercises aim to connect the vocabulary that has been learned to the examples that have been studied in order to encourage creativity in forming new sentences. Some of the exercises serve as interesting puzzles that you might enjoy. While no exercise is intended to be tricky, an item for advanced students who seek an additional challenge is often added. However, every exercise can be solved using the material presented in the lesson itself. The goal is to help—and challenge—you rather than to discourage or frustrate you.

In the early lessons of *Basics of Arabic*, transliteration of the Arabic words is provided in order to help students learn how to pronounce the language. This is necessary, in the beginning, for learning purposes. Thus, in Lesson One the transliteration system is introduced in order to show students how to use it. Transliteration will be provided until Lesson Six, when the amount of transliterated words will decrease in order to encourage students to read and write in Arabic. After Lesson Eight, transliteration will no longer be regularly provided. In later lessons, however, when it is crucial to understanding, transliteration for some words will be included.

To the student—whenever you learn a new word, try to learn a sentence in which you can use this word. Use the word in conversation with others. Repeat it. Perhaps this is challenging during the first few lessons, but by the end of the first semester, you should be forming and using your own Arabic sentences. Write out your own vocabulary cards. Once you reach the verbs, your practice should enter a completely different dimension—creating complete sentences, using them, modifying them, and repeating them. The words you do not use repeatedly will be forgotten. Make it a daily habit to practice Arabic, to memorize new vocabulary, and to create new sentences. Think of learning Arabic as exercising a muscle—the more you use it, the better results you will get.

Finally, I hope this book gives you a good introduction to Arabic. I have seen many students enjoy learning Arabic from this material, and many of them sought advanced studies of Arabic afterwards. It was my hope to make this material interesting and accessible. Now that you have begun your journey, I wish you the very best as you explore one of the most beautiful languages on earth.

Again, *ahlan wa sahlan* to Arabic!

Abbreviations

m	masculine
f	feminine
s	singular
d	dual
p	plural
ms	masculine singular
mp	masculine plural
fs	feminine singular
fp	feminine plural
md	masculine dual
fd	feminine dual

Lesson One

Alphabet: General and Transliteration

Arabic has 28 letters in the alphabet. Let's study the alphabet, first as single, isolated letters, and then as interconnected letters.

Single Letters

Letter Name	Arabic Form	Transliteration	Sound
alif	ا	ā	like "a" in far, bar
bā'	ب	b	like "b" in better
tā'	ت	t	like "t" in table
thā'	ث	th	like "th" in thanks
jīm	ج	j	like "j" in Jesus
ḥā'	ح	ḥ	like "h" but with throat friction
khā'	خ	kh	think of German "ch" in Bach
dāl	د	d	like "d" in dynamic
dhāl	ذ	dh	think of the strong "th" in though
rā'	ر	r	like "r" in rabbi, but often rolling
zāy	ز	z	like "z" in zoo
sīn	س	s	like "s" in school
shīn	ش	sh	like "sh" in shark
ṣād	ص	ṣ	emphatic "s"; more on this below
ḍād	ض	ḍ	emphatic "d"; more on this below

ṭāʼ	ط	ṭ	emphatic "t"; more on this below
ẓāʼ	ظ	ẓ	emphatic "z"; more on this below
ʿayn	ع	ʿ	guttural *ayn*, deep throat friction
ghayn	غ	gh	think of the French "r" like "gh"
fāʼ	ف	f	like "f" in free, full
qāf	ق	q	emphatic "k"; more on this below
kāf	ك	k	like "k" in kilo, or "c" in cat
lām	ل	l	like "l" in love
mīm	م	m	like "m" in Matthew
nūn	ن	n	like "n" in north
hāʼ	ه	h	like "h" in hello
wāw	و	w	consonant: as "w" in well
wāw	و	ū	vowel: as "u" in June, "oo" in tool
yāʼ	ي	y	consonant: like "y" in year, yes
yāʼ	ي	ī	vowel: like "ee" in meet, greet

We will use transliterations in the early lessons to help students figure out pronunciations; however, by the fourth lesson you are expected to attempt reading Arabic without transliterations.

Attempt to write the alphabet. Begin from right to left. From the initial listening of the alphabet, you can notice various matters.

First, we have several emphatic letters: ص, ض, ط, ظ, and ق. These emphatics are pronounced with the back of the tongue raised slightly: ṣād, ḍād, ṭāʼ, ẓāʼ, and qāf, respectively. Each of them is a counterpart of an unemphatic letter. Compare these emphatics to the unemphatics س, د, ت, ذ, and ك, respectively, which are pronounced as sīn, dāl, tāʼ, dhāl, and kāf. However, we should also note that some Arabs do not include ق in the emphatics.

Second, from the table note that the letters و and ي can function as consonants and vowels, with different pronunciations. Third, there are three letters that are unique to Arabic: the ḥāʾ ح, the ʿayn ع, and the ḍād ض. Since they have no similarities in English, your only way to learn them is to listen to them pronounced repeatedly. The more you listen to them pronounced, the better you excel in mastering them. The ḥāʾ ح is similar to constricted fricative English "h," while the ʿayn ع is purely Arabic and sometimes explained as the sound of an opera singer when voicing a high note, or precisely as the outward throat breathing when vomiting. As for the ḍād ض, it is a counterpart of the English "d," yet with the tongue filling the upper part of your mouth.

Now we turn to connecting these letters.

Connecting Letters Together

In Arabic we write from right to left. Each letter has four forms: alone, in the beginning, in the middle, and at the end of a word.

When letters are connected to form words, the letters generally change shape in order to link to the preceding and following letters.

Read the following chart from right to left: the letter, its initial, medial, and final forms. To help you recognize the similar forms, a blank row divides the letters into groups.

Final	Medial	Initial	Letter
ـا	ـا	ا	ا
ـب	ـبـ	بـ	ب
ـت	ـتـ	تـ	ت
ـث	ـثـ	ثـ	ث
ـج	ـجـ	جـ	ج
ـح	ـحـ	حـ	ح
ـخ	ـخـ	خـ	خ
ـد	ـد	د	د

Lesson One

Final	Medial	Initial	Letter
ـذ	ـذ	ذ	ذ
ـر	ـر	ر	ر
ـز	ـز	ز	ز
ـس	ـسـ	سـ	س
ـش	ـشـ	شـ	ش
ـص	ـصـ	صـ	ص
ـض	ـضـ	ضـ	ض
ـط	ـطـ	طـ	ط
ـظ	ـظـ	ظـ	ظ
ـع	ـعـ	عـ	ع
ـغ	ـغـ	غـ	غ
ـف	ـفـ	فـ	ف
ـق	ـقـ	قـ	ق
ـك	ـكـ	كـ	ك
ـل	ـلـ	لـ	ل
ـم	ـمـ	مـ	م
ـن	ـنـ	نـ	ن
ـه	ـهـ	هـ	ه
ـو	ـو	و	و
ـي	ـيـ	يـ	ي

You notice that there are consonants that look alike (similar strokes), though they have different dots. Also, there are six letters which do not connect with following letters:

ا د ذ ر ز و

Practice writing the interconnected letters. Remember that Arabic is read from right to left so your letters strokes should also be written from right to left. As you write, practice pronouncing the letter. The more you rehearse, the easier it will be as you proceed in your learning.

Exercises

Exercise 1.1

Identify the letters below, and try to read each word aloud. Write the words out in the blank spaces.

ثاب	تاب	باب
قام	صام	عام
جور	سور	صور
مال	قال	شال
قار	صار	ضار
نير	سير	بير

Exercise 1.2

Attempt to transliterate the words in exercise 1.1 (although we will study more later, especially regarding the letters *alif*, *wāw*, and *yā'*). Here is the answer key:

thāb	ثاب	*tāb*	تاب	*bāb*	باب
qām	قام	*ṣām*	صام	*ᶜām*	عام
jūr	جور	*sūr*	سور	*ṣūr*	صور
māl	مال	*qāl*	قال	*shāl*	شال
qār	قار	*ṣār*	صار	*ḍār*	ضار
nīr	نير	*sīr*	سير	*bīr*	بير

Exercise 1.3

Identify the letters of each word in the following biblical passage.[1] Write it in the blank space.

أبانا الذي في السماوات ليتقدس اسمك ليأت ملكوتك لتكن مشيئتك كما في السماء كذلك على الأرض.

(Note that the letters أ, ئـ, and لا are new for you. We will study them in the next lesson.)

Identify the letters of each word in the following quranic verse. Write them in the blank spaces:

بسم الله الرحمن الرحيم.

الحمد لله رب العالمين.

Now let's move one step further. Look at the following sentence:

السحابة السوداء في السماء. السحابة تحجب الشمس عند أقصى الأفق قبل لحظة الغروب.

You will notice some letters which do not appear in the list we gave for the alphabet. Consider, in particular, the words السحابة, السوداء, السماء, أقصى, الأفق, and لحظة. Arabic has more letters. They are unique and very important to learn. Let's turn to examine these additional letters.

---

1. All Arabic verses are from the *Arabic Version of the Bible*, eds. Eli Smith and Van Dyck, trans. Nasif al-Yaziji, Boutros al-Bustani, and Yusuf al-Asir (Cairo: Bible Society of Egypt, 1865).

Lesson Two
اِثْنَان

Additional Letters

In addition to the letters we studied in Lesson One, we encounter several other letters as we read and write Arabic. In this lesson we will study three additional letters in particular.

The *Tā' Marbūṭah* (تاء مربوطة) ة or ـة

The letter *tā' marbūṭah* never occurs in the middle of a word. It always comes at the end.

Generally, we can think of it as a combination of the letters *hā'* and *tā'* (ـه + ت) or simply as a form of the regular *tā'* ت, with the exception that it only occurs at the end of a word.

There are two ways to write the *tā'marbūṭah*, depending on the letter which precedes it. When connected with a previous letter, it is written ـة; if not connected, it is ة.

Remember that we have six letters which do not connect with following letters (e.g., ر ، ز ، د ، ذ). Here you should be introduced to the comma in Arabic. We write it as ،, immediately following the word.

See these examples on the *tā' marbūṭah* (and note the Arabic comma):

بقرة، حياة، صورة

كلمة، سلطة، منحة

In the first group (three words), the *tā'marbūṭah* is not connected to the letter preceding it and is written ة. In the second group, the *tā'marbūṭah* is linked to the letter which precedes it and appears as ـة.

In short, the rule is as follows: If the preceding letter does not connect to the *tā'marbūṭah*, then it is written ة. If it connects, we write it ـة.

The pronunciation and transliteration of the *tā'marbūṭah* require explanation.

Since it is basically a form of a *tā'*, you might expect it to be pronounced and transliterated as a soft "t." Indeed, this is somewhat true; however, Arabs tend to soften the end of any given word. Thus, they pronounce the *tā'marbūṭah* as "a" or "ah" instead of "t," unless the *tā'marbūṭah* occurs at the end of a word, which forms a construct pronounced "at."

Consider Some Examples:

One meaning for the word حارة in Arabic is "lane." It is pronounced as *ḥārah*, not *ḥārat*. If we are speaking of a construct (e.g., the lane of the road), we will pronounce—and transliterate—it as *ḥārat al-ṭarīq* (*al-ṭarīq* = the road).

To summarize, the *tā'marbūṭah* is generally pronounced as "ah" unless in a construct, which is pronounced "at."

Another example is the word سادة, which means "masters," and is pronounced as *sādah* (not *sādat*), unless we want to speak of "the masters of something." Then it is *sādat*.

These two examples are merely a sample. After we understand the vowels and their transliterations, we will be able to develop more examples.

Two Final Remarks:

Note #1: The *tā'marbūṭah* will be very important as we discuss feminine nouns (Lesson Five).

Note #2: This will be explored later, but for now take a hint. When we use suffixes on words ending with a *tā'marbūṭah*, we change the *tā'marbūṭah* into a regular *tā'* then add the suffix (Lesson Seven).

The *Alif Maqṣūrah* (ألف مقصورة) ى

Like the *tā'marbūṭah*, the *alif maqṣūrah* only occurs at the end of a word. It looks like a dot-less *yā'* (compare ي to ى).

In Arabic an *alif maqṣūrah* (ألف مقصورة) simply means a restricted, constrained, or shortened *alif*. Some refer to it as *alif layyinah* (ألف لينة), denoting a flexible *alif*. Although it looks like a *yā'* without the two dots beneath it, we treat it as an ending *alif*.

It is pronounced as "aa" or "ā" and transliterated as *ā* (we will reemphasize this when we discuss long vowels).

See These Examples:

راضي

راضى

The first (راضي) reads *rāḍī*, the second (راضى) *rāḍā*.

عادي

عادى

The first (عادي) reads *ᶜādī*, the second (عادى) *ᶜādā*.

Two Important Notes:

Note #1: When we study the vowels, we will discuss more options for words ending with the *alif maqṣūrah*.

Note #2: This is a note which will be explored later, but take a hint for now. When we use suffixes on words ending with an *alif maqṣūrah*, we change the *alif maqṣūrah* into a regular *alif* or a *yāʾ*, then add the suffix (Lesson Seven).

The *Hamzah* (همزة) ء

The *hamzah* is not included as part of the alphabet, although it is a letter. This is the glottal stop in Arabic. The pronunciation of the Arabic *hamzah* is like the stop sound you make *before* certain English words, such as "anti," "amnesty," "above," or "apple." It is the sound of the glottal stop at the beginning of the word "Iowa."

The *hamzah* (همزة) is usually written by itself on the line as ء. See these words: ماء ، وفاء ، سماء. The last letter in each of them is a *hamzah*.

The *hamzah* can be anywhere in a word, not only at the end. However, in most cases it is attached to the letters *alif*, *wāw*, or *yāʾ* (ا ، و ، ي), which are the three long vowels which we will study shortly. When associated with any of the three letters, the *hamzah* appears as follows:

أ ، إ ، ئـ ، ئ ، ـئ ، ـؤ ، ؤ

Note that there should be no space between a word or letter and its following comma. A space is added here only for clarification.

Vocabulary

These vocabulary words are merely a sample. We need to study vowels in order to write them properly. However, we give them here as an introduction, and once we learn the Arabic vowels, we will be able to memorize more words. Attempt to read the words. The transliteration may help.

Translation	Transliteration	Word
no	lā	لا
yes	naᶜam	نعم
I am	anā	أنا
what?	mādhā?	ماذا؟
mommy	māmā	ماما
daddy	bābā	بابا
door	bāb	باب
Sarah	sārah	سارة
he said	qāl	قال
peace	salām	سلام
water	mā'	ماء
sky or heaven	samā'	سماء

Exercises

Exercise 2.1

Identify each letter in every word by reading it aloud. Circle each *hamzah*. Attempt to pronounce the words. Again, note the way we write the comma in Arabic. Pay attention that we do not leave a space between the comma and its preceding word.

أسلم، أراد، أبى، أبي، أحبار، أن

إرميا، إسلام، إبراهيم، إسماعيل، إسحاق

مؤمن، مؤلف، بؤرة، رؤية

مائدة، بئر، سائر

Exercise 2.2

Examine the following sentences, and identify each *tā' marbūṭah*, *alif maqṣūrah*, and *hamzah*.

كان هناك فتى صغير يدعى علي، وقد كان فلاحاً. في يوم من الأيام، وفي أثناء سيره على شاطئ البحر، وجد فتاة جميلة حسناء. كانت الفتاة ترتدي أحلى الثياب.

Note how we write the period (full-stop) in Arabic. Again, note that there is no space between a word and its following comma or period.

Now let's turn to the various kinds of vowels in Arabic. This should open the way for us to read and practice more pronunciation.

Lesson Three

Arabic Vowels

In this lesson we study the Arabic vowels. In Arabic, there are short vowels and long vowels, three of each.

Short Vowels

The three short vowels are as follows:

fatḥah	فتحة	َ	بَ
ḍammah	ضمة	ُ	بُ
kasrah	كسرة	ِ	بِ

They always follow a consonant—the *ḍammah* and *fatḥah* are written above it, while the *kasrah* is written underneath.

Arabs usually do not add the short vowels when they write as the vowels are commonly understood from the context and grammar of a sentence. However, this can be confusing for non-Arab beginners. Therefore, we will add the short vowels in most cases throughout this book.

Now let us examine how the short vowels look and sound and how to transliterate them.

The *Fatḥah* (فتحة)

Note the *fatḥah* (فتحة) in the following words:

مَـرْيَـم، سَـلام، طَـريق، مَـحبوب، تَـرجَـمَـة، حَـلـيف، يَـسـوع

The *fatḥah* (فتحة) is the diagonal stroke written above the consonant. The *fatḥah* (فتحة) follows the consonant and is pronounced after it. It always looks the same and is pronounced like the "a" in "tag" and "bag," or sometimes like the "u" in "bug." We always transliterate the *fatḥah* (فتحة) as an "a."

See the following words and their transliterations:

baraka	بَـرَكَ
ḥasana	حَـسَـنَ
saraqa	سَـرَقَ

The *Ḍammah* (ضمة)

Note the *ḍammah* (ضمة) in the following words:

لُـقمان، بُـرهـان، قُـضاة، مُـلـوك، مُـحَـمَـد، عُـمَـر

The *ḍammah* (ضمة) takes the shape of a small و *wāw* (like an apostrophe) written above the consonant and follows it. It is pronounced like the "u" in "put." It is a short vowel which always looks the same and is transliterated as a "u."

See the following words and their transliterations:

marqus	مَـرقُـس
ʿumar	عُـمَـر
shughl	شُـغَـل

The *Kasrah* (كسرة)

Note the *kasrah* (كسرة) in the following words:

بِـركة، مِـحنة، مِـن، شِـرك، فِـرَق

The *kasrah* (كسرة) is a diagonal stroke written below a consonant. It resembles the *fatḥah*, but it is placed below the consonant and follows it. The *kasrah* (كسرة) is a short vowel, pronounced like the "i" in "with," "in," or "pit." We always transliterate it as "i."

See the following words and their transliterations:

birkah	بِـركة
miḥnah	مِـحنة
min	مِـن
shirk	شِـرك
firaq	فِـرَق

An Important Note on Short Vowels:

A familiarity with the meaning behind the names of the short vowels will help students to comprehend their functions. The word *fatḥah* (فتحة) comes from the verb *fataḥa* (فتح), which means "to open." Using a *fatḥah* opens the letter up by establishing the sound "a," which is produced by opening the mouth. The word *ḍammah* (ضمة) comes from the same root as the Arabic verb *ḍamma* (ضَمّ), indicating an act of closing in or wrapping up. Thus, when we use a *ḍammah*, we close our lips to make the sound of "oo" in "book." Similarly, the word *kasrah* (كسرة) comes from the verb *kasara* (كَسَرَ), which indicates breaking down and refers to the breaking down of a letter by using the "i" sound after it.

Since we have studied short vowels, we can now write their Arabic words fully and properly:

فَتْحَة، ضَمّة، كَسْرَة

You notice two marks ْ and ّ that we have not yet studied. We will do so shortly.

Long Vowels

A long vowel is a stretching or lengthening of a short vowel. It sounds like the short vowel but longer in pronunciation. Unlike short vowels, long vowels are not marks above or underneath the letters. Instead, long vowels are actual letters which correspond to the lengthening of the sound of short vowels. While the short vowels are represented as a, u, and i, long vowels are accomplished by lengthening these letters, which become aa, uu, and ii, transliterated as ā, ū, ī, and represented by three Arabic letters: *alif*, *wāw*, and *yā'*. Thus, while the three short vowels appear as signs above or below the consonants carrying them (فَتْحَة، ضَمّة، كَسْرَة), the three long vowels are simply the letters *alif* (ا), *wāw* (و), and *yā'* (ي).

Lesson Three

Alif (ا)

The letter ا (*alif*) is a long vowel, transliterated as *ā* and pronounced as a long "aa," such as in "ma'am," "man," and "Sam."

Notice the long *alif* in the following words:

bāb	باب
māmā	ماما
bābā	بابا
ᶜāmil	عامل
kāmil	كامل

It is important to examine the difference in pronunciation between the long *alif* and the short vowel *fatḥah* (فَتْحَة). The long *alif* corresponds to the *fatḥah*, but is longer in pronunciation. Think of the "a" sound in Sam (long) and contrast it with the "a" sound of the letter "u" in buck (short).

Try to distinguish *tam* and *tām* (more like *taam*):

تَم

تام

The same goes with the following three pairs:

مَلِك	مالِك
سَجَد	ساجَد
رَكِب	راكِب

Wāw (و)

The second long vowel in Arabic is و (*wāw*).

It is notable that و can be a long vowel or a consonant.

When it is a long vowel, we transliterate it as *ū* and pronounce it as the "oo" in "spoon" or "moon." When it represents a consonant, we transliterate it as *w* and pronounce it as such (e.g., the word وَلَد is transliterated as *walad*).

See the long vowel و in the following words:

fūl	فـول
ʿūd	عـود
maḥmūd	مَـحـمـود
suʿūd	سُـعـود
lūṭ	لـوط

We should note here that when the و is a long vowel, there is a short vowel *ḍammah* (ضَـمَّة) associated with its preceding consonant; however, this short vowel is usually assimilated in the long vowel *wāw* and we rarely need to add it. For instance, the above words should be written as فُـول، عُـوُد، مَـحْـمُـود، سُـعُـود، لُـوط, but we write them as فـول، عـود، مَـحـمـود، سُـعـود، لـوط, because the long vowel is stronger in the pronunciation and the corresponding short vowel is obvious. Thus, in this book we will only identify the long vowel and will not include the short vowel on the preceding consonant.

For the letter و as a consonant, see the following words:

waraq	وَرَق
walad	وَلَـد
wādī	وادي
walīd	وَلـيـد
waḥīd	وَحـيـد

Note that *wāw* as a consonant often appears at the beginning of a word (or at the beginning of a syllable, which we will discuss in the next lesson).

In some words the letter و appears both as a consonant and as a vowel. Consider the following words:

wurūd	وُرود
wufūd	وُفود
wuʿūl	وُعول
wuʿūd	وُعود
wuṣūl	وُصول

In these five words, the first و is a consonant, while the second is a vowel.

Yāʾ (ي)

The third, and final, long vowel is the ي (yāʾ).

Like the letter و (wāw), the ي can be a vowel or a consonant. As a long vowel, it is transliterated as ī and pronounced "ee" as in "seed," "feed," or "sheep." When it represents a consonant, we transliterate it as y and pronounce it as such (e.g., the word يَدان is transliterated as yadān).

See the long vowel ي in the following words:

jamīl	جَميل
ʿīd	عيد
farīd	فَريد
ṭawīl	طَويل
samīr	سَمير

For the letter ي as a consonant, see the following words:

yanbūʿ	يَنبوع
yasūʿ	يَسوع

yaʿmal	يَعـمَـل
yūsuf	يـوسُف
yāshir	يـاشِر

In some words, the letter ي appears both as a consonant and as a vowel. See the following words:

yamīn	يَمـين
yaqṭīnah	يَـقـطـينة
yaṣīr	يَصـيـر
yuʿīq	يُـعـيـق

Just as we mentioned with *wāw*, there is a special rule for the *yā'*. In the case of a long vowel *yā'* ي, a short vowel *kasrah* should appear underneath the preceding consonant. However, like the *ḍammah* before the long *wāw*, the *kasrah* before the long *yā'* is assimilated and usually not written.

For instance, if you look at the example words given above for the long vowel *yā'*, instead of جَمـيـل، عِـيـد، فَـريـد، طَـويـل، سَمِـيـر, we will simply write جَمـيـل، عـيـد، فَريـد، طَـويـل، سَمـيـر.

Now we have studied short and long vowels. What about the absence of a short vowel? What about the doubling of consonants? Each of these has a specific description in Arabic.

In the next section, we will study the absence of a vowel (it is called *sukūn*), the doubling of a consonant without vowels in between (called *shaddah*), and the *alif maddah* (which is a *hamzah* + a long vowel *alif*).

Sukūn (سُكون)

In the absence of a vowel, a consonant receives a mark called a *sukūn* (سُكون), which is a small circle above it (ْ). The consonant which receives a *sukūn* (سُكون) is called a *sākin* (ساكن), which means "static" or "calm." We do not transliterate the *sukūn* (سُكون). Shortly, we will discuss Arabic syllables and indicate that the *sukūn* represents the end of a syllable.

Lesson Three

Highlight the سُكون (sukūn) in the following words and attempt to read them. The transliterations will help.

injīl	إِنْجِيل
amthāl	أَمْثَـال
ḥukm	حُكْم
zahr	زَهْر
bint	بِنْت
shuʿbah	شُعْبَة
ʿushb	عُشْب
majd	مَجْد

Shaddah (شَدَّة)

In some words the same consonant occurs twice with a *sukūn* in between. This structure includes a consonant followed by a *sukūn*, followed by the same consonant. Instead of writing the consonant twice with a *sukūn* in between, we write the consonant only once and place a *shaddah* (شَدَّة) on top of it. The *shaddah* (شَدَّة) appears as a small "w" above the consonant and represents doubling (or the gemination, Arabic *tashdīd* تَشْدِيد) of a consonant. It indicates emphasis or the stressing of the consonant. Transliterating a consonant with a *shaddah* (شَدَّة) is thus doubling the consonant. In other words, if a consonant has a *shaddah* (شَدَّة), this indicates that there are two of this consonant. The *shaddah* (شَدَّة) is always associated with a short vowel (*fatḥah*, *ḍammah*, or *kasrah*), which is written above or below the *shaddah* (شَدَّة). Note that a *shaddah* (شَدَّة) cannot have a *sukūn* (سُكون) above it.

Identify the شَدَّة (*shaddah*) in the following words. Attempt to read the words. Pay attention to the doubling of the consonants in the transliterations:

makkār	مَكَّـار
karrām	كَرّام

سَجَّـاد	sajjād
جَبَّـار	jabbār
جَزَّار	jazzār
مُتَشَدِّد	mutashaddid
مَحَبَّة	maḥabbah

One last note on the شَدَّة (shaddah)—as we will indicate in the following lesson, a شَدَّة (shaddah) indicates the end of one syllable and the beginning of another; it can never occur in a middle of a syllable.

Maddah (مَدَّة)

When a *hamzah* (ء) is followed by long *alif*, we have what we call a *maddah* (مَدَّة) or *alif maddah* (آ). The term *maddah* actually stems from a root corresponding to the verb (*madda* مَدَّ), which means "to stretch." Thus, a مَدَّة (*maddah*) is a stretch in the *hamzah* due to the existence of a following long *alif*. The مَدَّة (*maddah*) appears as a tilde above an *alif* and indicates a stretched or lengthened glottal stop. Note that the مَدَّة (*maddah*) does not appear by itself and must come over an *alif*. Since *alif maddah* indicates a *hamzah* followed by a long *alif*, we will transliterate it as 'ā.

See the following words and identify the مَدَّة (*maddah*):

آمِين	'āmīn
آسِف	'āsif
آسَاف	'āsāf
قُرْآن	qur'ān
آل	'āl
آلاف	'ālāf

Here we transliterated the words as we pronounce them. However, it should be noted that in academic writing we do not indicate the initial *hamzah* in our transliteration. Thus, in scholarly work you find the words as *āmīn, āsif, āsāf, qur'ān, āl, ālāf*.

Lesson Three

Vocabulary

Translation	Transliteration	Word
darling, beloved	ḥabīb	حَبيب
my darling	ḥabībī	حَبيبي
peace	salām	سَلام
the peace	al-salām	السَّلام
on, upon	ᶜalā	عَلَى
on you (ms)	ᶜalayka	عَلَيْكَ
on you (fs)	ᶜalayki	عَلَيْكِ
on you (mp)	ᶜalaykum	عَلَيْكُم
peace be upon you	al-salāmu ᶜalaykum	السَّلامُ عَلَيْكُم
and peace be upon you	wa ᶜalaykum al-salām	وَعَلَيْكُم السَّلامُ
and	wa	وَ
pleased to meet you	tasharrafnā	تَشَرَّفْنا
heart	qalb	قَلْب
my heart	qalbī	قَلْبي
this (m)	hadhā	هَذا
this (f)	hadhihi	هذِهِ
a day	yawm	يَوْم
a book	kitāb	كِتاب
a boy	ṣabī	صَبي
a girl	fatāh (or fatāt)	فَتاة

a male	*dhakar*	ذَكَر
a female	*unthā*	أُنْثَى
a teacher	*mudarris*	مُدَرِّس
a school	*madrasah*	مَدْرَسَة
a student	*ṭālib*	طَالِب
an engineer	*muhandis*	مُهَنْدِس
an artist	*fannān*	فَنَّان
name	*ism*	اِسْم
my name	*ismī*	اِسْمي

One note on the transliteration of the word اِسْم—We transliterated it correctly as *ism*. However, this can be confusing since its first letter appears as an *alif*. You thought correctly, but the fact is that this *alif* is actually a combination of a *hamzah* followed by a *kasrah*. We will explain this kind of *hamzah* (called connecting *hamzah*) in Lesson Eighteen. Now, when we transliterate the word, we write '*ism*, but then we drop the initial *hamzah* in our transliteration. The result becomes *ism*.

Exercises

Exercise 3.1

In the following passage, circle each فَتْحَة، ضَمَّة، كَسْرَة، سُكون، شَدَّة، مَدَّة، تاء مربوطة، هَمْزَة، ألِف مَقْصورَة. The passage is from the Quran 3:45–49 and speaks of Jesus's mother and his miracles.

إِذْ قَالَتِ الْمَلَائِكَةُ يَا مَرْيَمُ إِنَّ اللَّهَ يُبَشِّرُكِ بِكَلِمَةٍ مِنْهُ اسْمُهُ الْمَسِيحُ عِيسَى ابْنُ مَرْيَمَ وَجِيهًا فِي الدُّنْيَا وَالْآخِرَةِ وَمِنَ الْمُقَرَّبِينَ. وَيُكَلِّمُ النَّاسَ فِي الْمَهْدِ وَكَهْلًا وَمِنَ الصَّالِحِينَ. قَالَتْ رَبِّ أَنَّىٰ يَكُونُ لِي وَلَدٌ وَلَمْ يَمْسَسْنِي بَشَرٌ قَالَ كَذَٰلِكِ اللَّهُ يَخْلُقُ مَا يَشَاءُ إِذَا قَضَىٰ أَمْرًا فَإِنَّمَا يَقُولُ لَهُ كُنْ فَيَكُونُ. وَيُعَلِّمُهُ الْكِتَابَ وَالْحِكْمَةَ وَالتَّوْرَاةَ وَالْإِنْجِيلَ. وَرَسُولًا إِلَىٰ بَنِي إِسْرَائِيلَ أَنِّي قَدْ جِئْتُكُمْ بِآيَةٍ مِنْ رَبِّكُمْ أَنِّي أَخْلُقُ لَكُمْ مِنَ الطِّينِ كَهَيْئَةِ الطَّيْرِ فَأَنْفُخُ فِيهِ فَيَكُونُ طَيْرًا بِإِذْنِ اللَّهِ وَأُبْرِئُ الْأَكْمَهَ وَالْأَبْرَصَ وَأُحْيِي الْمَوْتَىٰ بِإِذْنِ اللَّهِ وَأُنَبِّئُكُمْ بِمَا تَأْكُلُونَ وَمَا تَدَّخِرُونَ فِي بُيُوتِكُمْ إِنَّ فِي ذَٰلِكَ لَآيَةً لَكُمْ إِنْ كُنْتُمْ مُؤْمِنِينَ.

Now, identify the same items in this passage from the Gospel of Mark 1:1–5.

بَدْءُ إِنْجِيلِ يَسُوعَ الْمَسِيحِ ابْنِ اللَّهِ: كَمَا هُوَ مَكْتُوبٌ فِي الْأَنْبِيَاءِ: «هَا أَنَا أُرْسِلُ أَمَامَ وَجْهِكَ مَلَاكِي الَّذِي يُهَيِّئُ طَرِيقَكَ قُدَّامَكَ. صَوْتُ صَارِخٍ فِي الْبَرِّيَّةِ: أَعِدُّوا طَرِيقَ الرَّبِّ اصْنَعُوا سُبُلَهُ مُسْتَقِيمَةً». كَانَ يُوحَنَّا يُعَمِّدُ فِي الْبَرِّيَّةِ وَيَكْرِزُ بِمَعْمُودِيَّةِ التَّوْبَةِ لِمَغْفِرَةِ الْخَطَايَا. وَخَرَجَ إِلَيْهِ جَمِيعُ كُورَةِ الْيَهُودِيَّةِ وَأَهْلُ أُورُشَلِيمَ وَاعْتَمَدُوا جَمِيعُهُمْ مِنْهُ فِي نَهْرِ الْأُرْدُنِّ مُعْتَرِفِينَ بِخَطَايَاهُمْ.

Lesson Four
أَرْبَعَة

In this lesson we will study syllables, diphthongs, the definite article, and a special feature called *tanwīn*.

Arabic Syllables

A syllable is a continuous unit of pronunciation, an unbroken and uninterrupted flow of speech. An Arabic word is thus divided into syllables, with each syllable including one consonant (or more) and a vowel. Every word has at least one syllable. As a rule, a syllable cannot begin with a vowel. While there are various kinds of syllables in Arabic, two are most common.

Type One: Consonant (C) + Vowel (V)

Type Two: Consonant + Vowel + Consonant

Note that a vowel in a syllable can be short or long.

These types are labeled Type One (CV) and Type Two (CVC). Some describe these types as short and long, respectively, where the first type (the short syllable) is a single consonant followed by a single vowel (usually a short vowel). The long syllable is anything else, most commonly a consonant followed by a vowel and another consonant. Additionally, some call Type One (CV) an open syllable and Type Two (CVC) a closed one, because the consonant closes the syllable.

Some examples of Type One (CV) are as follows:

fa	فَ
fi	فِ
fu	فُ
fī	فِي

Some examples of Type Two (CVC) are as follows:

tāb	تـاب
mar	مَـر
rāʿ	راع
mash	مَـشـ
tūḥ	ـتوح

Now let's examine the following words and identify their syllables:

كِتـاب، مَـركِـب، شِـراع، مَـشـروع، مَـفـتوح

Do your best first, before we solve them here.

The word كِتـاب consists of a short syllable كِـ (CV) followed by a long syllable تـاب (CVC). The word مَـركِـب has two long syllables: مَـر plus كِـب. As for شِـراع, it consists of a short syllable شِـ followed by a long one ـراع. The word مَـشـروع has two long syllables: مَـشـ plus ـروع. Similarly, مَـفـتوح consists of two long syllables: مَـفـ plus ـتوح. The transliterations of the words are kitāb, markib, shirāʿ, mashrūʿ, and maftūḥ, respectively.

Note that a syllable can never begin with a vowel, a *sukūn*, or a *shaddah*. While a syllable can never begin with a *sukūn*, it can end with one. As for the *shaddah*, remember that a *shaddah* signifies the doubling of a specific consonant. If a consonant has a *shaddah*, we know that there are actually two of that letter. There can never be two consecutive consonants in one syllable without a vowel separating them—we either have CV or CVC. Since the *shaddah* represents two consonants, we will never find a *shaddah* in the middle of a syllable. A *shaddah* represents the end of one syllable and the beginning of another. Because a *shaddah* always serves as a hinge between two syllables, each *shaddah* is accompanied by a short vowel instead of a *sukūn*. When a *shaddah* is added to a letter, it must be accompanied by a short vowel.

Consider the following examples regarding syllables and the *shaddah*. Examine each word, and identify the syllables:

قَـصّـار

عَـدّاء

جَبَّــار

سَــجَّــادة

تَــشَــدَّد

Do your best first, before you study the answers below.

The word قَصَّـار consists of two long syllables: قَص (CVC) and صَار (CVC). The word عَـدَّاء also has two long syllables: عَد and داء. Similarly, جَبَّـار has two long syllables: جَب and بَار. As for سَجَّـادة, it consists of a long syllable سَج, followed by a short syllable جَ, then a long syllable دَة. The word تَشَـدَّد has three syllables: a short one تَ, followed by a long syllable شَد, then another long syllable دَد. Attempt to transliterate these words. Pay attention that a *shaddah* represents the doubling of a specific consonant.

Here are the transliterated words:

qaṣṣār	قَصَّـار
ʿaddāʾ	عَدَّاء
jabbār	جَبَّـار
sajjādah	سَجَّـادة
tashaddad	تَشَـدَّد

To conclude the study of Arabic syllables, here is an advanced note to feed the inquiring minds of some students. This division into short and long syllables is helpful when one explores which syllable to stress or which syllable is accented. In Arabic, every syllable should be pronounced, but one syllable is stressed. So, unlike French, Arabic does not ignore the pronunciation of any syllable, even those which are unstressed. While it is true that in Arabic the issue of which syllable to stress is complex, for our purposes it will suffice to state that the basic rule is to stress the long syllable (CVC) closest to the end of a word. If there is no long syllable in a given word, then stress the third syllable from the end—a case often repeated in past simple tense verbs, which, in their basic root forms, consist of three short syllables in a row (Lesson Thirteen). In this case, we stress the first syllable among the three short syllables. However, one should acquire accentuation rather than memorize it. This is best accomplished by practicing Arabic with a native speaker.

Lesson Four

For some examples, consider the following words:

Transliteration	Arabic
ki.*tāb*	كِتاب
mar.*kib*	مَركِب
shi.*rāᶜ*	شِراع
mash.*rūᶜ*	مَشروع
maf.*tūḥ*	مَفتوح
sa.*lām*	سَلام
kha.laqa	خَلَقَ
sa.*rāb*	سَراب
ka.*lām*	كَلام

We stress the bold part of each word. In the transliterated words, only the stressed syllable is italicized.

Diphthong

In Arabic there are two diphthongs. The first diphthong consists of a *fatḥah* followed by a *wāw*, while the second consists of a *fatḥah* followed by a *yā'*. The letters *wāw* and *yā'* in diphthongs serve as consonants; therefore, we transliterate the two diphthongs as "aw" and "ay," respectively. Remember that the *wāw* and *yā'* can be either consonants or long vowels. In diphthongs they serve as consonants. See the diphthongs below:

Transliteration	Arabic
bayt	بَيْت
khawf	خَوْف
ṣawt	صَوْت
layl	لَيْل

ʿayn	عَيْـن
bayrūn	بَـيْـرون
ṣawm	صَـوْم
nawm	نَـوْم

We should note two important rules regarding diphthongs. First, the *wāw* and *yā'* in diphthongs always take a *sukūn*. In fact, one way to identify a diphthong is to locate a *wāw* or *yā'* that has a *sukūn* above it. Second, a diphthong closes a syllable with its preceding consonant, i.e., a long syllable (CVC).

Arabic Definite Article (الـ)

In Arabic the most common way to make a noun definite is to prefix it with *alif-lām* (الـ). We call the *alif-lām* (الـ) combination the definite article. There are other ways to make a noun definite (e.g., using a personal, demonstrative, or relative pronoun, or by the addition of a vocative particle يا), which will be studied later. In Arabic there is no indefinite article. The general way to transliterate the الـ (*alif-lām*) is *al-*, as the following examples demonstrate:

Transliteration	Arabic
al-walad	الـوَلَد
al-bint	البِنت
al-ghurfa	الـغُرْفَة
al-bayt	الـبَـيـت
al-khawf	الـخَـوف

Look at the الـ (*alif-lām*) as the definite article. You will never see the *alif* take a *hamzah*, i.e., the definite article can never be written as أل. It is always ال.

Sun and Moon Letters

While the definite article الـ is always transliterated *al-*, it should be noted that there is a special feature related to its pronunciation. Sometimes the sound of the definite article is strong and distinct, while at other times the sound of the *lām* is absent and

Lesson Four

appears to assimilate into the actual word. This feature is related to the so-called Sun and Moon Letters.

The Arabic alphabet has 28 letters. We classify them into two groups: Sun Letters (الحُروف الشَّمسيّة) and Moon Letters (الحُروف القَمَريّة). The classification into "sun" and "moon" letters is due to the Arabic pronunciation of the words "sun" and "moon" when connected to the ال (*alif-lām*). Say the following words out loud and try to discern the difference in pronunciation of the ال:

الـشَّمس

الـقَمَر

While the transliterations of these words are *al-shams* and *al-qamar*, respectively, what you hear is *slightly* different: *a-shshams* and *al-qamar*.

Thus, the ال in the word الـشَّمس seems to assimilate into the actual word; the *lām* is silent, and the first letter ش is not only pronounced immediately after the *alif*, but also seems to double, i.e., receives a *shaddah*. This is because the letter ش is a Sun Letter.

As for the ال in the word الـقَمَر, the matter is different. You hear both the ال and the actual first letter ق distinctly. The definite article (especially the *lām* in the ال) does not assimilate into the word—it is pronounced clearly.

The rule is as follows: the definite article ال assimilates into Sun Letters and results in doubling its sound (by adding a *shaddah*), while no assimilation occurs in the case of Moon Letters.

The 14 Sun Letters:

ت ث د ذ ر ز س ش ص ض ط ظ ل ن

The 14 Moon Letters:

أ ب ج ح خ ع غ ف ق ك م هـ و ي

Examples of words beginning with Sun Letters (focus on the letter immediately after the ال) are as follows:

الشَّمس، الشَّعر، الشِّعر، الشِّراع

التُّراب، التِّمساح، التَّاج

الثَّعلَب، الثَّلج، الثُّعبان

الدَّلو، الدُّبّ، الدَّرَج، الذُّباب

الرِّحْلَة، الرَّجُل

الزَّورَق، الزَّمان، الزِّلزال

الصَّليب، الضَّرير، الـطَّريق، الظَّرْف

الـلِّقاء، الـنَّور

In each of these examples, the definite article is assimilated into the word due to the existence of a Sun Letter at the beginning of the word. Thus, the *lām* in the ال loses its strong and distinctive sound.

Examples of words beginning with Moon Letters are as follows:

الأخ، الأُخت، الأُم، الأب

البَشَر، البـاب، البَرَكَـة

الجَدّ، الجِدار، الحَبيب، الحَليب، الخَروف

الفَرَس، الفارِس، القَلْب، الكَلْب، الكلام

المَطَر، المَرأة، الهَواء، اليَوم

In each of these words, the *lām* in the ال is not silent. The definite article is fully pronounced with its distinctive sound. We encounter this feature when the definite article precedes any of the Moon Letters.

As a final observation, consider the first four examples: الأخ، الأُخت، الأُم، الأب. Note the change in the shape of the letter *alif* when it comes after the definite article. We see لا, although لا is expected. While both are the same, we should note that when an *alif* comes after a *lām* they make what Arabic speakers call a *lām-alif*, which is written in an artistic form لا.

Tanwīn (تَـنوين)

It is common in Arabic to find at the end of *indefinite* nouns (or adjectives) a double *fatḥah*, double *ḍammah*, or double *kasrah*. This doubling is called *tanwīn* (تَـنوين), which refers to the *nūn* (نون) sound which is added at the end of the word. This *nūn* is only a sound; it is never written.

Note, first, that تَـنوين (*tanwīn*) only occurs at the end of a word, and second, it can only occur with indefinite words, i.e., nouns lacking ال. You will never find a word that has both the definite article and *tanwīn*. Grammatically, تَـنوين (*tanwīn*) is a term

Lesson Four

known as *nunation* and is represented by the adding of the sound *nūn* (نون) at the end of an indefinite noun.

Since we have three short vowels in Arabic, we have three kinds of تَنوِين (*tanwīn*):

1. *tanwīn fatḥah* (a double *fatḥah*) ً
2. *tanwīn ḍammah* (a double *ḍammah*) ٌ
3. *tanwīn kasrah* (a double *kasrah*) ٍ

Because *tanwīn* adds a نون (*nūn*) sound to the end of the word, the *tanwīn fatḥah* ً represents the sound *an*, *tanwīn ḍammah* ٌ *un*, and *tanwīn kasrah* ٍ *in*.

Tanwīn ḍammah ٌ and *tanwīn kasrah* ٍ are straightforward; you simply double the short vowel and make a *nūn* sound. See the following examples:

tanwīn kasrah ٍ		tanwīn ḍammah ٌ		Noun
jamalin	جَمَلٍ	jamalun	جَمَلٌ	جَمَل
malikin	مَلِكٍ	malikun	مَلِكٌ	مَلِك
shamsin	شَمسٍ	shamsun	شَمسٌ	شَمس
qamarin	قَمَرٍ	qamarun	قَمَرٌ	قَمَر
kitābin	كِتابٍ	kitābun	كِتابٌ	كِتاب
ra'sin	رَأسٍ	ra'sun	رَأسٌ	رَأس
bābin	بابٍ	bābun	بابٌ	باب

Note that all these words are indefinite, i.e., they do not have الـ. Note also that *tanwīn ḍammah* in the printed form does not resemble two *wāws* (وو). It appears as ٌ. However, in handwriting it is clearer and takes the shape of two *wāws*.

Unlike the straightforwardness of the *tanwīn ḍammah* ٌ and *tanwīn kasrah* ٍ, the *tanwīn fatḥah* ً has a unique twist: it is necessary to add an *alif* at the end of the word before placing the double *fatḥah* on the added *alif*. This additional *alif* is called *alif tanwīn*.

Here are the previous words—and some more—when attached to the *tanwīn fatḥah*:

jamalan	جَـمَـلاً
malikan	مَـلِـكاً
shamsan	شَـمْـساً
qamaran	قَـمَـراً
kitāban	كِـتـاباً
ra'san	رَأساً
bāban	بـاباً
rajulan	رَجُـلاً
qalaman	قَـلَـمـاً
baytan	بَـيـتاً
laylan	لَـيـلاً

Notice the added *alif* before the *tanwīn fatḥah* and the unique shape of the *lām-alif* (لا). Again, this is the common rule.

This rule applies to all words, except when the last letter in a word is *tā' marbūṭah* or *hamzah* preceded by *alif*. In these two cases, there is no need to add an *alif* before the *tanwīn*. If the final letter in a word is *hamzah* but it is not preceded by an *alif*, then we follow the general rule: add the *alif tanwīn*, then place the *tanwīn fatḥah*.

See the following examples:

	tanwīn fatḥah	Noun
jumlatan	جُـمْـلَةً	جُـمْـلَة
marḥalatan	مَـرْحَـلَةً	مَـرْحَـلَة
muʿjizatan	مُـعْـجِزَةً	مُـعْـجِزَة

Lesson Four

laylatan	لَيْلَةً	لَيْلَة
mā'an	مَاءً	مَاء
samā'an	سَماءً	سَماء
hawā'an	هَواءً	هَواء
juz'an	جُزْءاً	جُزْء

See these greeting words. All appear in a *tanwīn fatḥah* form:

Hi, or hello!	marḥaban	مَرْحَباً
Welcome!	ahlan wa sahlan	أَهْلاً وسَهْلاً
Thanks!	shukran	شُكْراً
You're welcome, or sorry!	ᶜafwan	عَفْواً

It is important to note that *tanwīn* occurs in other cases in Arabic, but these extend beyond the scope of this introductory book. It will suffice to explain here that many proper names and adverbs (see Lesson Eighteen) appear in a *tanwīn* form. See the following Arabic masculine names:

مُحَمَّداً	Muhammad	مُحَمَّد
عَلِيّاً	Ali	عَلِيّ

Vocabulary

Translation	Transliteration	Word
hi, hello	marḥaban	مَرْحَباً
welcome	ahlan wa sahlan	أَهْلاً وسَهْلاً
thanks	shukran	شُكْراً
you're welcome, sorry	ᶜafwan	عَفْواً
for example	mathalan	مَثَلاً
boat	markib	مَركِب
sail	shirāᶜ	شِراع
project	mashrūᶜ	مَشْروع
open	maftūḥ	مَفْتوح
voice	ṣawt	صَوت
night	layl	لَيْل
eye	ᶜayn	عَيْن
fear	khawf	خَوف
fasting	ṣawm	صَوْم
sleeping	nawm	نَوْم
death	mawt	مَوْت
boy	walad	وَلَد
girl	bint	بِنْت
room	ghurfah	غُرْفَة

Lesson Four

Earlier in this lesson, we mentioned many other words as examples for Sun and Moon Letters. For the inquiring minds, here are the translations of all these words. They are provided here without transliteration in order to help you practice pronouncing Arabic without the usual help.

wall	جِدار	hair	شَعْر
beloved	حَبيب	poetry	شِعْر
milk	حَليب	sail	شِراع
lamb	خَروف	dirt, dust	تُراب
horse	فَرَس	alligator	تِمْساح
knight	فارِس	crown	تاج
heart	قَلْب	fox	ثَعْلَب
dog	كَلْب	snow	ثَلْج
words	كلام	serpent	ثُعْبان
rain	مَطَر	bucket	دَلو
woman	مَرْأة	bear	دُبّ
air	هَواء	stairs	دَرَج
day	يَوم	flies	ذُباب
camel	جَمَل	trip	رِحْلَة
king	مَلِك	man	رَجُل
sun	شَمْس	boat	زَورق
moon	قَمَر	age, time	زَمان
book	كِتاب	earthquake	زِلزال

head	رَأس	cross	صَليب
door	بــاب	blind	ضَرير
man	رَجُـــل	road	طَريق
pen	قَـــلَم	envelope	ظَرْف
house, home	بَـيت	meeting	لِقاء
night (m)	لَـيل	light	نور
sentence	جُـملة	brother	أخ
stage	مَرحَلة	sister	أُخت
miracle	مُـعْـجِزة	mother	أُم
night (f)	لَـيلَة	father	أَب
water	مَـاء	humans	بَشَر
a sky, heaven	سَمـاء	door	باب
air	هَوَاء	blessing	بَرَكَة
part (of something)	جُزْء	grandfather	جَدّ

Exercises

Exercise 4.1

Attempt to read the following passage, then underscore each syllable and diphthong in it.

يَومُكُمْ سَعيدٌ. جاري وَلَدٌ صَغيرٌ يُدْعى يوسُفْ. يوسُفْ وَلَدٌ نَشيطٌ. هو يَعيشُ مَعَ أُمِّهِ الأَرْمَلَة الفَقيرَة، يساعِدُها ويُحِبُّها كثيراً.

For inquiring minds, the translation of this passage reads, "Good day to all. My neighbor is a young boy named Joseph. Joseph is an energetic boy. He lives with his poor widowed mother, helps her, and loves her so much."

Exercise 4.2

Circle every *tanwīn* (تَنوين) in the passage above. In addition, locate every definite article and state whether it is followed by a Sun or Moon Letter.

Exercise 4.3

Examine the following passage from the Gospel of John 3:16–17. Attempt to read it as much as you are able, then underscore every *shaddah*, *sukūn*, *tanwīn*, and Sun or Moon Letter.

لِأَنَّهُ هَكَذا أَحَبَّ اللهُ الْعالَمَ حَتَّى بَذَلَ ابْنَهُ الْوَحيدَ لِكَيْ لا يَهْلِكَ كُلُّ مَنْ يُؤْمِنُ بِهِ بَلْ تَكونُ لَهُ الْحَياةُ الْأَبَدِيَّةُ. لِأَنَّهُ لَمْ يُرْسِلِ اللهُ ابْنَهُ إِلَى الْعالَمِ لِيَدينَ الْعالَمَ بَلْ لِيَخْلُصَ بِهِ الْعالَمُ.

Lesson Five
خَمْسَة

Parts of Speech: Words in Arabic

The major categories of Arabic speech are nouns, verbs, and particles. Every word in Arabic must be in one of these three groups.

A noun is called اِسْم (*ism*). It refers to a person, place, thing, or even an idea. A noun serves as a subject of a sentence, object of a preposition, or object of a verb. The plural of اِسْم is أَسْماء. Nouns, unlike verbs, do not depend on time; they do not have a tense. Consider the noun كَلْب. It means "dog." The noun refers to an animal and does not depend on time. There are many useful ways to classify nouns, including gender (masculine or feminine), number (singular, dual, or plural), and definiteness (definite or indefinite). Arabic nouns have many declensions, i.e., they inflect ("decline") to describe a change in definiteness, case, number, or gender.

A verb is called فِعْل (*fiʿl*). It refers to an action performed in a specific time. The plural of فِعْل is أَفْعال. The time factor is essential in the verb form. In Arabic there are past, present, and future tenses, in addition to the imperative verb form. Thus, while nouns indicate meanings unassociated with time, verbs only provide meanings in relation to the three different dimensions of time (past, present, and future). Consider the verb ذَهَبَ. It means "he went." It refers to an action which took place in the past; thus, it is a verb. Now consider a word which refers to time but is not a verb: الْيَوم. It means "today." While this word has an aspect of time, it does not refer to an action done in time. This is a noun. Like nouns, verbs inflect. Inflection of verbs is called conjugation. Verbs conjugate to reflect inflection in tense, person, number, gender, voice (active or passive), and mood (indicative, subjunctive, etc.).

A particle is called حَرْف (*ḥarf*). Its plural form is حُروف. Arabic particles do not convey a meaning on their own. They depend on other words mentioned around them to provide a complete meaning. Arabic particles include prepositions, conjunctions, and other articles. Think of a particle like the preposition عَلَى, which means "on." It cannot be completely understood without other words associated with it, such as "a pen is *on* the table." Particles do not inflect, i.e., they do not change their forms to reflect a grammatical change in case, number, gender, or tense. Consider the previous example of the preposition عَلَى. It appears the same anywhere in a sentence.

Before we study these parts of speech, let us study briefly the two kinds of Arabic sentences.

Arabic Sentences

Arabic sentences are either nominal or verbal.

A nominal sentence is called جُمْلَة اسميّة (*jumlah ismiyyah*), literally, "a sentence of a noun." We identify a sentence as جُمْلَة اسميّة when its first word is a noun (or pronoun).

A verbal sentence is called جُمْلَة فِعْلِيّة (*jumlah fiʿliyyah*), literally, "a sentence of a verb." A sentence is verbal when its first word is a verb.

This does not mean that all Arabic sentences must begin with a noun or verb. Some sentences begin with particles. When this is the case, we examine the word immediately following the particle to see whether it is a noun or a verb. This determines the kind of sentence. Remember, this is a general rule. It is simplistic in order to help you understand, but do not consider it a rule with no exceptions.

Nominal Sentences

The nominal sentence consists of two main components: subject and predicate. We call the subject مُبْتَدَأ (*mubtada'*) and the predicate خَبَر (*khabar*). Linguistically, the word مُبْتَدَأ suggests what "begins" a sentence, while خَبَر refers to what "tells" and provides details about the subject. The مُبْتَدَأ of a nominal sentence is the core topic or subject of this sentence, while the خَبَر is the content or commentary on the subject. The مُبْتَدَأ and the خَبَر always take the nominative case (we will discuss this shortly). The general rule is that the مُبْتَدَأ is definite and always precedes the خَبَر; of course, there are exceptions. In this introductory course we will focus on the general rules. It is important to note, however, that the مُبْتَدَأ is always a noun (or pronoun), while the خَبَر may be a noun, adjective, or verb.

Examine the following nominal sentences, before we discuss important observations:

خَبَر	مُبْتَدَأ	Translation	Nominal Sentence
عَظيمٌ	اللهُ	God is great.	اللهُ عَظيمٌ.
لَطيفٌ	الرَجُلُ	The man is nice.	الرَجُلُ لَطيفٌ.
ضَخمةٌ	الجِبالُ	The mountains are huge.	الجِبالُ ضَخمةٌ.

طالبٌ	إبراهيم	Ibrahim is a student.		إبراهيمُ طالبٌ.
مُهَنْدِسَةٌ	سارةُ	Sarah is an engineer.		سارةُ مُهَنْدِسَةٌ.
طالبٌ	أنتَ	You are a student.		أنتَ طالبٌ.
فَنَانَةٌ	هِيَ	She is an artist.		هِيَ فَنَانَةٌ.
رَجُلٌ	هذا	This is a good man.		هذا رَجُلٌ طَيِّبٌ.
جُمْلَةٌ	هذه	This is a short sentence.		هذه جُمْلَةٌ قَصيرَةٌ.
سَيَّارَةٌ	هذه	This is a car.		هذه سَيَّارَةٌ.
ماهِرَتانِ	المُمَثِّلَتانِ	The (two) actresses are talented.		المُمَثِّلَتانِ ماهِرَتانِ.
نَشيطانِ	العامِلانِ	The workers (md) are energetic.		العامِلانِ نَشيطانِ.
نَشيطَتانِ	العامِلَتانِ	The workers (fd) are energetic.		العامِلَتانِ نَشيطَتانِ.
سَعيداتٌ	العامِلاتُ	The workers (fp) are happy.		العامِلاتُ سَعيداتٌ.
لَطيفٌ	والِدُهم	Their (mp) father is kind.		والِدُهم لَطيفٌ.
مِصْريٌّ	والِدُنا	Our father is Egyptian.		والِدُنا مِصْريٌّ.
يلعبُ	الصَبيُّ	The boy plays.		الصَبيُّ يَلْعَبُ.
يلعبُ الكرةَ	الصَبيُّ	The boy plays soccer.		الصَبيُّ يَلْعَبُ الكُرَةَ.
من أمْريكا	نحنُ	We are from America.		نَحْنُ من أمْريكا.
جميلةٌ	تلك	That lady is beautiful.		تِلْكَ السَّيِّدَةُ جميلةٌ.

From this list of nominal sentences, we can make some important observations:

1. The subject and predicate always take the nominative case. We will study the noun cases shortly, but for now notice how most of the nouns end with a *ḍammah* (or *tanwīn ḍammah*). This is what we call the nominative ending. Note also that, in describing the nominative case, definite nouns take *ḍammah*, while indefinite nouns take *tanwīn ḍammah*.

2. In all these examples, the مُبْتَدَأ is definite, either by the definite article or by using other pronouns (personal or demonstrative), as we will study in Lesson

Lesson Five

Nine. Thus, as a general rule, the subject has to be definite, while the predicate can be definite or indefinite—when indefinite, it takes *tanwīn ḍammah*.

3. The خَبَر can be singular (عَظيمٌ، لطيفٌ، ضخمةٌ), dual (نَشيطَتانِ، نَشيطانِ، ماهِرَتانِ), or plural (سَعيداتٌ). It can also be a verbal phrase (يَلْعَبُ and يَلْعَبُ الكُرَةَ) or a prepositional phrase (مِن أَمْريكا). We will study these aspects later in the course.

4. In translating these nominal sentences into English, we supplied the verb "to be," although the verb itself is not explicitly given in Arabic. Thus, اللهُ عَظيمٌ is translated as "God is great." The Arabic sentence literally reads "God great." As we mentioned earlier, the predicate tells and provides details about the subject; thus, inserting *is* or *are* in our translation is our best choice to communicate the Arabic meaning.

5. A مُبْتَدَأ in a nominal sentence can take multiple predicates. Consider this sentence: أَنتَ مُعَلِّمٌ كاتِبٌ. It means "You are a teacher and author." We have two predicates: مُعَلِّمٌ and كاتِبٌ. We can add more predicates when needed. For instance, the sentence الشَجَرَةُ كَبيرةٌ رائِعَةٌ مُثْمِرَةٌ means "The tree is big, wonderful, and fruitful." It has one مُبْتَدَأ (the definite noun الشَجَرَةُ) and three predicates: كَبيرةٌ رائِعَةٌ مُثْمِرَةٌ. Now, here is an advanced note: In the sentence الشَجَرَةُ كَبيرةٌ رائِعَةٌ مُثْمِرَةٌ, each predicate is foundational and has equal strength in the sentence. This is different from using the particle of conjunction *wāw* (meaning "and") to form الشَجَرَةُ كَبيرةٌ و رائِعَةٌ و مُثْمِرَةٌ, which emphasizes the first word كَبيرةٌ more than what follows it, i.e., رائِعَةٌ و مُثْمِرَةٌ.

6. One final advanced note for the inquiring minds—as stated above, the مُبْتَدَأ of a nominal sentence is usually definite. However, some sentences can have an indefinite مُبْتَدَأ. In this case, the خَبَر should precede the مُبْتَدَأ. We will not expound upon this advanced rule here.

Verbal Sentences

The verbal sentence begins with a verb and consists of two main components: verb and subject. The verb in a verbal sentence is called فِعْل (*fiʿl*), while the subject of this verb is called فاعِل (*fāʿil*). Linguistically, a فِعْل is an action done in a specific time, while the فاعِل is the actor who executes that action. In addition to the فِعْل and the فاعِل, there may be other supplementary items, including direct objects, prepositional phrases (preposition + noun), and adverbs, among others. While a complete verbal sentence consists of فِعْل and فاعِل, sometimes the فاعِل is implied in the verb conjugation; in this case, the فاعِل is not explicitly mentioned.

See the following verbal sentences:

فاعِل	فِعْل	Translation	Verbal Sentence
أُمّي	تَطْبُخُ	My mother cooks at home.	تَطْبُخُ أُمّي في المَنْزِلِ.
أخي	يَعْمَلُ	My brother works at the university.	يَعْمَلُ أخي في الجَامِعَةِ.
الطّالبُ	قَرَأَ	The student (m) read the lesson.	قَرَأَ الطّالبُ الدَّرْسَ.
سارةُ	قَرَأتْ	Sarah read the lesson.	قَرَأتْ سارةُ الدَّرْسَ.
الطفلُ	نامَ	The child slept on the bed.	نامَ الطِّفْلُ عَلى السَّريرِ.
داودُ	سافرَ	Dawood (i.e., David) traveled to Iraq.	سافرَ داودُ إلى العِراقِ.
Implied "I"	أدرُسُ	I study.	أدرُسُ.
Implied "we"	عَمِلْنا	We worked.	عَمِلْنا.

From this list of verbal sentences, we can make some important observations:

1. When translating the verbal sentences into English, the normal English pattern is used: the noun comes first. Note, however, that in Arabic these are still verbal sentences and the verb comes first.

2. Some verbal sentences could be rephrased, rearranged, or restructured as nominal sentences. For instance, we can use أُمّي تَطْبُخُ في المَنْزِلِ instead of تَطْبُخُ أُمّي في المَنْزِلِ. The former is nominal, while the latter is verbal. The difference between the two sentences is mainly the emphasis. What we choose to use first is what is important to us and what we aim to emphasize. Consider the sentence قَرَأتْ سارةُ الدَّرْسَ. If we want to stress the act of reading, we use the verbal sentence. If we desire to emphasize the role of the person, we might use the nominal sentence: سارةُ قَرَأتْ الدَّرْسَ. Similarly, we can use either يَعْمَلُ أخي في الجَامِعَةِ or أخي يَعْمَلُ في الجَامِعَةِ, depending on what we want to emphasize.

Lesson Five

3. In the final two examples from the table above, أَدرُسُ and عَمِلْنا, we have complete verbal sentences, i.e., فِعْل and فاعِل, although each sentence is written in one single word. In these sentences, the فاعِل is not explicitly written and is called فاعِل مُستَتِر (fāʿil mustatir, i.e., implied subject). This فاعِل مُستَتِر is indicated by the conjugation of the فِعْل. Verbal conjugation will be introduced and studied further in Lesson Thirteen. It suffices here to mention that the conjugations are sufficient to help us determine the subject of any given verb. Thus, the suffix ending نا in the past simple tense verb عَمِلْنا refers to first-person plural فاعِل, while the prefix أ in the present simple tense verb أَدرُسُ indicates first-person singular فاعِل.

4. The فاعِل in a verbal sentence always takes a nominative case ending, as we will study shortly. This means that the فاعِل ends with a *ḍammah, tanwīn ḍammah,* or *wāw-nūn.* Therefore, like the case of the مُبْتَدَأ and خَبَر in nominal sentences, the فاعِل in verbal sentences takes a nominative case.

Let us now study how and why some Arabic words inflect (change their forms) and examine the case system in Arabic.

Inflection: Declension and Conjugation

In English the order of words in any given sentence is vital to understand what it conveys. Compare "John visited Sarah" and "Sarah visited John." The two sentences have the exact same words, yet arranged differently. They provide different meanings.

In Arabic words' inflection—not order—is what indicates the various meanings, as well as the function of each word in a sentence. Grammatically, inflection means a change in the form of a word (noun or verb). The change occurs usually (but not always) at the end. The goal of any inflection is to indicate the grammatical function of any given word. It also reflects and explains the change in case, number, person, gender, tense, voice, and mood.

In Arabic the words قَتَلَ، قُتِلَ، قَتْل look similar, but have completely different meanings. The verb قَتَلَ means "he killed," while قُتِلَ means "he was killed." As for قَتْل, it is a noun which means "killing." Similarly, the verbs أَكَلْتُ and أَكَلَتْ mean "I ate" and "she ate," respectively.

More significantly, consider these two sentences: قَتَلَ الرَجُلُ الفَرَسَ and قَتَلَ الرَجُلَ الفَرَسُ. The order of the words is identical in both sentences, but they mean very different things, which is clear in Arabic due to the inflection of the words. The phrase قَتَلَ الرَجُلُ الفَرَسَ means "the man killed the horse," while قَتَلَ الرَجُلَ الفَرَسُ means "the horse killed the man." The noun الرَجُلُ is the subject in the former and the direct object in the latter. This proves that, in Arabic, word inflection—not word order—is the key to understanding the meaning and function of any given word.

Noun inflection is called declension, while verb inflection is called conjugation. Noun declensions express a change in gender (masculine and feminine), number (singular, dual, and plural), or case (nominative, genitive, and accusative), among other things. Verb conjugations describe the change in tense, mood, or voice of an action executed in time. Verbs and verbal conjugation will be introduced and explained in Lessons Thirteen and Fourteen. Now, let us focus on noun cases.

Arabic Case System

In Arabic we use different ending vowels (think of little markings) to determine the function of a word in a sentence. We call these case endings حَرَكات (ḥarakāt).

Consider this sentence: Hana closed the door. In this sentence, "Hana" is a noun. It is the subject of the sentence. It refers to the person who performed the action of the verb. The verb in this sentence is "closed," while "the door" is a noun that we identify as the direct object of the verb, because it identifies what or who receives the action of this verb.

In English you understand the function of each word in the sentence from the context. In Arabic, too, it is the context, and, more importantly, the case endings (حَرَكات) that specify each word's function in a sentence.

To understand grammar correctly we must learn how to use case endings. For each case we use a short vowel above or under the final letter of the word to mark its case.

There are three different cases:

1. The **nominative case** is called مَرْفوع (marfūʿ). A ḍammah is used to describe a nominative case: البَيتُ.

2. The **genitive case** is called مَجْرور (majrūr). A kasrah is used to indicate a genitive case: البَيتِ.

3. The **accusative case** is called مَنْصوب (manṣūb). A fatḥah is used to designate an accusative case: البَيتَ.

Thus, a noun البَيت can receive one of three different case endings, depending on its position in a given sentence. It can appear as البَيتُ, البَيتِ, or البَيتَ to indicate nominative, genitive, or accusative cases, respectively. Note that البَيت is a definite noun and *one* short vowel is used to indicate the case ending. If a noun is indefinite (without the *alif-lām* الـ), the short vowel of the case ending will be doubled (called *tanwīn* تَنوين; see Lesson Four).

For indefinite nominative case, *tanwīn ḍammah* is used: بَيتٌ.

For indefinite genitive case, *tanwīn kasrah* is used: بَيتٍ.

For indefinite accusative case, *tanwīn fatḥā* is used: بَيتًا.

Notice that in the accusative case an *alif* was added before placing the double *fatḥah* to form the *tanwīn*: بَيتًا. This follows the rule explained above in Lesson Four, where nouns ending with any letter other than a *tā' marbūṭah* or *hamzah* (preceded by an *alif*) add an *alif* to carry the *tanwīn fatḥah*.

Note the examples below of an indefinite accusative *tanwīn fatḥah* that ends with a *tā' marbūṭah* or *hamzah* (preceded by an *alif*):

Accusative Form	Translation	Indefinite Noun
فَتاةً	girl	فَتاة
وِعاءً	container	وِعاء
سَخاءً	generosity	سَخاء

Note the examples below of indefinite accusative *tanwīn fatḥah* that end with other letters:

Accusative Form	Translation	Indefinite Noun
صَبِيًّا	boy	صَبِي
ذَكَرًا	male	ذَكَر
مَنْزِلًا	house	مَنْزِل

Now, when do we use nominative, genitive, and accusative?

Nominative Case (مَرْفوع)

We use nominative endings in at least three different kinds of sentences:

1. *Nominal Sentences*

    We discussed nominal sentences, which begin with a noun or a pronoun. We use nominative endings with the subject and predicate of a nominal sentence.

In the sentence المنزلُ كبيرٌ (the house is big), the definite noun المنزلُ is the مُبْتَدَأ (subject), while the indefinite noun كبيرٌ is the خَبَر (predicate). The subject and predicate of a nominal sentence take the nominative case. Remember the general rule which we explained earlier: The subject has to be definite, while the predicate can be definite or indefinite—when indefinite, it takes *tanwīn ḍammah*.

2. *Verbal Sentences*

   We learned that verbal sentences begin with a verb. We use a nominative ending with the subject of a verbal sentence.

   In the verbal sentence ذهبَ الـمُعَلِّمُ إلى الجامعةِ (the teacher went to the university), ذهبَ is the verb and الـمُعَلِّمُ is the subject. The subject of the verb takes the nominative case. Thus, we placed a *ḍammah* at the final letter of الـمُعَلِّمُ.

3. *Vocative Sentences*

   This is a subcategory of nominal sentences. We use vocative sentences when addressing people directly. In speech, the vocative aspect is indicated by intonation, which is usually achieved by the changing of vocal pitch. Grammatically, vocative sentences begin with a vocative particle followed by a noun. The most common Arabic vocative particles are يا (*yā*) and أيُّها (*ayyuhā*), both commonly translated as "O," followed by exclamation mark.

   The vocative sentence يا يَسوعُ means "O Jesus!" It begins with a vocative particle يا, followed by the noun يَسوعُ, which takes a nominative case. Similarly, يا رَبُّ translates as "O Lord!" The noun رَبُّ is in the nominative case. Finally, the famous vocative sentence أيها السَّيِّداتُ والسَّادةُ means "Ladies and gentlemen!" Both السَّيِّداتُ and السَّادةُ are in the nominative case, taking the *ḍammah* at their final letters.

Genitive Case (مَجْرور)

The most common use of the genitive case indicates the object of a preposition. While the following lesson will explain prepositions in more detail, it will suffice here to indicate that the noun that follows a preposition is called the object of the preposition and is always in the genitive case. The genitive noun takes a *kasrah* as its final short vowel. Note that the preposition and its object form a prepositional phrase.

Consider the following examples of the genitive use:

Object of Preposition	Preposition	Translation	Prepositional Phrase
المَسيح	في	in Christ	في المَسيح
الطَّاوِلَةِ	عَلى	on the table	عَلى الطَّاوِلَةِ
المَدينَةِ	مِن	from the city	مِن المَدينَةِ
المَسْجِدِ	إلى	to the mosque	إلى المَسْجِدِ
حَياةٍ	في	in life and death	في حَياةٍ وَمَوتٍ

Note that in each prepositional phrase in the table above, the object of the preposition takes the genitive case (kasrah), with the exception of the last example, in which the object of the preposition is indefinite حَياةٍ. In this case, the tanwīn kasrah is used.

Accusative Case (مَنْصوب)

We encounter the accusative case in many sentences in Arabic. One of the most common uses of the accusative case in a sentence is with the direct object of a verb. It is called مَفْعُوْل بِهِ (mafʿūl bihi, i.e., direct object). The مَفْعُوْل بِهِ refers to the noun (human or nonhuman) that receives the action of the verb. We will elaborate on this when we study Arabic verbs (Lesson Thirteen).

Consider the verbal sentence فَهِمْتُ الدَّرْسَ, which means "I understood the lesson." We have a past simple tense verb فَهِمْتُ, and the subject is implied and understood through the verb conjugation. The noun الدَّرْسَ is the object of the verb. We call this noun مَفْعُوْل بِهِ and always use the accusative case, i.e., its final letter takes a fatḥah. For another example of a verbal sentence, consider رَكِبْنا الحِصانَ. It means "We rode the horse." The noun الحِصانَ is مَفْعُوْل بِهِ and takes an accusative marking.

Declinable and Indeclinable

We conclude this lesson with one final note on Arabic words. All Arabic words fit into one of two categories: declinable and indeclinable. This is to say that some words change their forms to perform different grammatical roles (i.e., declinable), while other words do not change, regardless of their positions in a sentence (i.e., indeclinable). This characteristic is important in Arabic. A declinable word is called مُعْرَب (muʿrab) and an indeclinable word is called مَبْني (mabnī).

All particles are indeclinable. A particle is مَبْنِي because it does not adopt different grammatical roles in a sentence (e.g., object or subject). For instance, the particle إلى always serves as a preposition. It is مَبْنِي and will not change its form. The particle حَتَّى can mean different things, including "until," "while," "to," or "to the extent," but will always look the same, as its grammatical role is unchangeable: preposition. It is always مَبْنِي.

Most verbs are also indeclinable, but a few are declinable. Specifically, any past simple tense verb is مَبْنِي (Lesson Thirteen). Any imperative verb is also مَبْنِي (Lesson Eighteen). Present simple tense forms, however, are complex. Some are مُعْرَب, while others are مَبْنِي (Lesson Sixteen).

Unlike particles and most verbs, nouns are, for the most part, declinable. A noun is مُعْرَب. We should expect each noun to experience different grammatical roles, by changing its form (especially ending). The noun الوَلَدُ (the boy) can appear as الوَلَدُ, الوَلَدَ, الوَلَدِ, depending on its grammatical function in a sentence. A noun is thus مُعْرَب in most cases; however, some nouns are مَبْنِي. For example, separate subject pronouns (أَنَا، أَنْتَ، أَنْتِ، هُمْ، هُمَا) and demonstrative pronouns (هَذا، هَذانِ، هَؤُلاءِ) serve as nouns, although they are always مَبْنِي. The same is true for nouns of interrogation (ماذا، لماذا، كَيْفَ) and several relative pronouns (الَّذي، الَّتي). However, most nouns are مُعْرَب.

Now, in the following lesson, let's focus on various kinds of particles.

Vocabulary

Good morning (greeting)	صَباحُ الخَيْرِ
Good morning (response)	صَباحُ النّورِ
Good evening (greeting)	مَساءُ الخَيْرِ
Good evening (response)	مَساءُ النّورِ
Good evening (literally, evening of flowers)	مَساءُ الوَرْدِ
How is it going?	كَيْفَ الحالُ؟
How are you (for a male)?	كَيْفَ حَالُكَ؟
How are you (for a female)?	كَيْفَ حَالُكِ؟

كَيْفَ حَالُكُمْ؟	How are you (for a mixed group)?
مُمْتاز	Excellent (can be a response to the above question)
أنا تَمام!	I am perfect! (also a response)
نَحْنُ بِخَيْرٍ	We are well (also a response)
أشْكُرُ الله!	I thank God! (another way to respond)
نَشْكُرُ الله!	We thank God! (one more response)
أنا على ما يُرامْ	I am okay (one more response to the question)
الحَمْدُ لله!	Thank God!
أنا أُريدُ	I want
أنا أُريدُ أن ...	I want to …
هوَ يُريدُ أن ...	He wants to …
هيَ تُريدُ أن ...	She wants to …
لَدَيّ	I have …
لَدَيَّ كِتابٌ	I have a book
ليسَ هُنا	not here
ليسَ هُناكَ	not there

Note that some of the words, especially the verbs, will be explained later. Here they are given only for vocabulary matters.

Earlier in the lesson, we translated many nouns, adjectives, and verbs. Here is a list of these words:

she read	قَرَأتْ	God	الله
he slept	نامَ	great	عَظيم
child	طِفْل	nice (m)	لَطيف

bed	سَرير	huge (f)	ضَخْمَة
he traveled	سافَرَ	good, kind (m)	طَيّب
Iraq	العِراقِ	sentence	جُمْلَة
I study	أَدْرُسُ	short (f)	قَصيرَة
we worked	عَمِلْنا	car	سيّارة
girl	فَتاة	clever (m)	ماهِر
container	وِعَاء	energetic (m)	نَشيط
generosity	سَخاء	happy (m)	سَعيد
boy	صَبي	nice, kind (m)	لَطيف
male	ذَكَر	Egyptian (m)	مِصْريّ
house	مَنْزِل	America	أَمْريكا
in Christ	في المَسيحِ	lady	سَيِّدَة
on the table	عَلى الطّاوِلَةِ	she cooks	نَطْبُخ
from the city	مِن المَدينَةِ	mother	أُمّ
to the mosque	إلى المَسْجِدِ	he works	يَعْمَل
in life and death	في حَياةٍ وَ مَوتٍ	he read	قَرَأ

Lesson Five

Exercises

Exercise 5.1

First, attempt to read the following passage out loud, although it might appear difficult at the outset. It is a biblical passage from Genesis 1:26–27 on the creation of man and woman. Second, focus on the case endings and circle every مَرْفوع, underline every مَجْرور, and highlight every مَنْصوب.

وَقَالَ اللهُ: «نَعْمَلُ الانْسَانَ عَلَى صُورَتِنَا كَشَبَهِنَا فَيَتَسَلَّطُونَ عَلَى سَمَكِ الْبَحْرِ وَعَلَى طَيْرِ السَّمَاءِ وَعَلَى الْبَهَائِمِ وَعَلَى كُلِّ الارْضِ وَعَلَى جَمِيعِ الدَّبَابَاتِ الَّتِي تَدِبُّ عَلَى الارْضِ». فَخَلَقَ اللهُ الانْسَانَ عَلَى صُورَتِهِ. عَلَى صُورَةِ اللهِ خَلَقَهُ. ذَكَرا وَانْثَى خَلَقَهُمْ.

With the help of your teacher, identify each noun, verb, and particle in the passage.

Exercise 5.2

The following passage is from the *Biography of Muhammad*.[1] It tells of him seeing the angel Gabriel. Attempt reading the passage and circle every مَرْفوع, underline every مَجْرور, and highlight every مَنْصوب.

فَخَرَجْتُ حَتَّى إِذَا كُنْتُ فِي وَسَطٍ مِنَ الْجَبَلِ سَمِعْتُ صَوْتًا مِنَ السَّمَاءِ يَقُولُ: يَا مُحَمَّدُ، أَنْتَ رَسُولُ اللهِ وَأَنَا جِبْرِيلُ. فَرَفَعْتُ رَأْسِي إِلَى السَّمَاءِ أَنْظُرُ، فَإِذَا جِبْرِيلُ فِي صُورَةِ رَجُلٍ صَافٌّ قَدَمَيْهِ فِي أُفُقِ السَّمَاءِ يَقُولُ: يَا مُحَمَّدُ، أَنْتَ رَسُولُ اللهِ وَأَنَا جِبْرِيلُ.

---

1. ᶜAbd al-Malik Ibn Hishām and Muḥammad Ibn Isḥāq, *al-Sīra al-nabawiyya*, ed. Muṣṭafā al-Saqqā, et al. 2 vols. (Cairo: Maktabat Muṣṭafā al-Ḥalabī, 1375/1955), 1:237.

Lesson Six
سِتَّة

In this lesson the study will go in a bit more depth into the three categories of Arabic speech: particles, nouns, and verbs. We will begin with particles, as they are more straightforward in their treatment than nouns and verbs, perhaps due to their uninflected state.

Particles

The most frequently used set of particles will be studied here: prepositions and particles of conjunction. Both quite often appear in sentences due to their usefulness in constructing important expressions.

Arabic Prepositions (حُروف الـجَرّ)

Arabic prepositions are called حُروف الـجَرّ (ḥurūf al-jarr). They are numerous. The focus here will be on the most frequently used prepositions. Remember, حُروف الـجَرّ do not inflect. They appear the same anywhere in the sentence, unlike nouns and verbs which inflect. One general rule to note—The word which follows the preposition is called the object of the preposition. This object of the preposition always takes the genitive case, which means its final letter takes a *kasrah*, or *tanwīn kasrah* if indefinite.

Below are some examples of prepositions:

Translation	Transliteration	حُروف الـجَرّ
in	fī	في
on	ʿalā	عَلَى
from, of	min	مِن
to, toward, for, into	ilā	إلى
about	ʿan	عَن
with	maʿa	مَعَ

Translation	Transliteration	حُروف الـجَرّ
until	ḥattā	حَتَّى
above	fawqa	فَوْقَ
under	taḥta	تَحْتَ
before	qabla	قَبْلَ
like, as	ka	كَ
by	bi	بِـ
to, in order to	li	لِـ

Below are some examples of prepositional phrases:

in the class	في الصَّفِّ
in a class	في صَفٍّ
in the room	في الغُرْفَةِ
in a room	في غُرْفَةٍ
from the book	مِنْ الكِتابِ
from a book	مِنْ كِتابٍ
from the teacher	مِنْ المُعَلِّمِ
about the professor	عَنْ الأُسْتاذِ
about the Bible	عَنْ الكِتابِ المُقَدَّسِ
about the Quran	عَنْ القُرْآنِ
with the artist	مَعَ الفَنّانِ
with the engineer	مَعَ الـمُهَنْدِّسِ
until the end	حَتَّى النِّهايَةِ
until the beginning	حَتَّى البِدايَةِ
on the table	عَلَى الطّاوِلةِ

Lesson Six

عَلَى المَكْتَبِ	on the desk
تَحْتَ السَرِيرِ	under the bed
تَحْتَ الأريكةِ	under the sofa
قَبْلَ الظُهْرِ	before noon
قَبْلَ السَنَةِ	before the year
كَالِابْنِ	like the son
بِالسَّيَّارةِ	by the car
لِمَدْرَسَةٍ	to school
لِجامِعَةٍ	to university

Note that every noun in this list appears after a preposition. The noun serves as the object of the preposition. These nouns take *kasrah* as their last short vowel, forming the genitive case (مَجْرور). The exception is if the noun is indefinite (without *alif-lām*), in which case it takes *tanwīn kasrah*.

The Particles of Conjunction (حُروف العَطْفِ)

The particles of conjunction are called حُروف العَطْفِ (*ḥurūf al-ʿatf*). They connect two nouns together. A particle of conjunction comes between two nouns and forces the following noun to take the same case as the previous noun. If the particles of prepositions make a following noun genitive, the particles of conjunction force the following noun to take the case of the previous noun.

Before we list the particles of conjunction, consider the following example:

$$\text{في السَّماءِ وَالأرْضِ}$$

The phrase means "in the heaven and the earth." The particle في is a preposition, so the word السَّماءِ takes a genitive case and ends with a *kasrah*. Then, the particle وَ is a particle of conjunction, which means "and." It forces the noun الأرْض to take the same case as السَّماء. Thus, the noun الأرْض takes a genitive case and ends with a *kasrah*. Note that in Arabic there should be no space between the وَ and the noun that follows it. As an exercise, consider a similar sentence: في سَماءٍ وَأرْضٍ. See the minor changes we made.

Lesson Six

Now, examine the list of the particles of conjunction below:

Translation	Transliteration	حُرُوْفُ العَطْفِ
and	wa	وَ
or	aw	أوْ
or	am	أمْ
then (immediately after)	fa	فَـ
then (a while after)	thumma	ثُمَّ
but	lakin	لَكِنْ
even	ḥattā	حَتَّى

The general rule for حُروف العَطْفِ is that the noun that follows any of them takes the same case as the noun that precedes them.

Consider the following examples:

I am at school with the book and the pen.	أنا في المَدْرَسَةِ مَعَ الكِتابِ والقَلَمِ.
Love and hope [are] in my heart.	الحُبُّ والرَّجاءُ في قَلْبي.
I read the book, then (immediately) the newspaper.	قَرَأْتُ الكِتابَ فالجَريدَةَ.
The man entered the church, then (immediately after) the woman.	دَخَلَ الرَّجُلُ فالمَرْأةُ إلى الكَنيسَةِ.
The lad came to the mosque and then (a little while later) the girl.	جاءَ الصَّبيُّ ثُمَّ الفَتاةُ إلى المَسْجِدِ.
The child runs to the mother or the father.	يَرْكُضُ الطِّفْلُ إلى الأمِّ أوْ الأبِ.
Is the trip today to Egypt or Lebanon?	هَلِ الرِّحْلَةُ اليَومَ إلى مِصْرَ أمْ لُبنان؟
Do you study in the morning or at night?	هل تَدْرُسُ صَباحاً أمْ مَساءً؟

Lesson Six

جاءَ الوَلَدُ لا البِنْتُ.	The boy, not the girl, came.
لا أُحِبُّ التُّفَّاحَ لَكِنْ العِنَبَ.	I don't like apples, but (I do like) grapes.
يَجوعُ البَشَرُ حَتَّى الأَقْوِياءُ.	All humans hunger, even the strong ones.

There are some important additional notes:

1. The most commonly used particles of conjunction are و and أو. There are other particles of conjunction, but they are either rarely used or their classification as conjunctions is questionable among Arabists and grammarians. Since this is a basic introduction, we included only the commonly used particles.

2. The particles ثُمَّ and فَـ reflect sequence and a specific order, yet they differ in the speed of this order. The former indicates a longer time or delay, while the latter an immediate succession with short or almost no delay.

3. The particle ثُمَّ often appears in verbal sentences to link consecutive actions. In this section, the study focuses on particles of conjunctions which connect nouns.

4. The particle لَكِنْ is used in negated sentences to confirm one noun and simultaneously deny the opposite.

5. Note that حَتَّى was discussed earlier as a preposition meaning "until," and now it is treated here as a particle of conjunction meaning "even." Both are accurate. This particle is sophisticated and has several uses in Arabic. It will suffice to state now that you must examine the context to discern the meaning. This will enable you to decide whether حَتَّى is a preposition or a conjunction.

6. Finally, the particles of conjunction can be used to link sentences, not only nouns, but this is beyond the scope of this introductory course. The rule you should remember is simply that the noun which follows the particle of conjunction takes the same case as the noun which precedes it.

Lesson Six

Vocabulary

friend	صَديق
beloved	مَحْبوب
fiancé	خَطيب
bridegroom	عَريس
bride	عَروس
messenger	رَسول
prophet	نَبي
angel	مَلاك
devil	شَيْطان
husband	زَوْج
wife	زوجَة
son	ابْن
daughter	ابْنة
mother	أُمّ
father	أَب
father	والِد
mother	والِدة
brother	أخّ
sister	أُخْت
please, come on in, go right away	تَفَضَّل
please, come on in here	تَفَضَّل هُنا
please, have a coffee (for a male)	تَفَضَّل قَهْوَة
please, have the tea (for a female)	تَفَضَّلي الشاي

please, have breakfast (for a group)	تَفَضَّلوا الفُطورَ
lunch	الغَداء
dinner or supper	العشاء
bread	خُبْز
milk	حَليب

Vocabulary explored previously in this lesson:

I read (past tense)	قَرَأتُ	classroom	صَفّ
newspaper	جَريدَة	room	غُرْفَة
he entered	دَخَلَ	teacher (m)	مُعَلِّم
church	كَنيسَة	professor (m)	أُسْتاذ
mosque	مَسجِد	the Bible	الكِتاب المُقَدَّس
boy	صبي	the Quran	القُرْآن
girl	فَتاة	artist (m)	فَنّان
bed	سَرير	engineer (m)	مُهَنْدِّس
trip, journey	رِحْلَة	end	نِهايَة
day	يَوم	beginning	بِدايَة
Egypt	مِصر	table	طاولة
Lebanon	لُبْنان	office, desk	مَكْتَب
child	طِفْل	couch	أَريكة
boy	وَلَد	noon	ظُهْر
girl	بِنْت	year	سَنَة
morning	صَباح	by the car	بالسَّيّارةِ

Lesson Six

evening	مساء	to school	لِمَدْرَسَةٍ
I do not like	لا أُحِبُّ	to a university	لِجامِعَةٍ
I love, like	أُحِبُّ	pen	قَلَم
apples	تُفّاح	love	حُبُّ
grapes	عِنَب	hope	رَجاء
humans	بَشَر	heart	قَلْب
mighty, strong ones	أَقْوِياء	and	وَ
then (a while after)	ثُمَّ	or	أَوْ
but	لَكِنْ	or	أَمْ
even, until	حَتَّى	then (immediately after)	فَ
he came	جاء	he runs	يَرْكُضُ

Exercises

Exercise 6.1

See these two verses from the book of Revelation 1:7–8 and underscore the prepositions, their objects, and the conjunction particles.

لَهُ الْمَجْدُ وَالسُّلْطَانُ إِلَى أَبَدِ الآبِدِينَ.

أَنَا هُوَ الأَلِفُ وَالْيَاءُ.

The translations of the verses are as follows:

> To him be glory and power for ever and ever.

> I am the Alpha and the Omega.

Exercise 6.2

Examine these three verses from the Quran. Highlight the prepositions, their objects, as well as the conjunction particles.

لَن يَدْخُلَ الْجَنَّةَ إِلَّا مَن كَانَ هُودًا أَوْ نَصَارَى.

None will enter paradise except he who is a Jew or a Christian (Q 2:111).

حُرِّمَتْ عَلَيْكُمُ الْمَيْتَةُ وَالدَّمُ وَلَحْمُ الْخِنزِيرِ.

Forbidden to you are dead meat, blood, and the flesh of swine (Q 5:3).

إِنَّا أَنزَلْنَا التَّوْرَاةَ فِيهَا هُدًى وَنُورٌ.

We have revealed the Torah in which was guidance and light (Q 5:44).

Lesson Six

Lesson Seven
سَبْعَة

Nouns (الْأَسْمَاء)

In Arabic a noun is called اسْم. It refers to a person, place, thing, or idea. In addition to proper nouns, this category also includes pronouns, adjectives, and sometimes adverbs, among others. As we begin studying nouns, let us first examine a very important set of pronouns, then study several ways to categorize nouns.

Separate Subject Pronouns (ضَمائِرُ الرَّفْعِ المُنْفَصِلَةُ)

In Arabic, pronouns are called ضَمَائِر. They are definite nouns with no need to add the definite article (ال). They have gender, number, and case.

Consider the following chart:

Translation	Transliteration	Person	Subject Pronoun	Number
I (m/f)	anā	1st	أَنَا	
You (m)	anta	2nd	أَنْتَ	
You (f)	anti	2nd	أَنْتِ	Singular
He	huwa	3rd	هُوَ	
She	hiya	3rd	هِيَ	

We (m/f)	naḥnu	1st	نَحْنُ	
You (m)	antumā	2nd	أَنْتُما	
You (f)	antumā	2nd	أَنْتُما	Dual
They (m)	humā	3rd	هُما	
They (f)	humā	3rd	هُما	
We (m/f)	naḥnu	1st	نَحْنُ	
You (m)	antum	2nd	أَنْتُمْ	
You (f)	antunna	2nd	أَنْتُنَّ	Plural
They (m)	hum	3rd	هُمْ	
They (f)	hunna	3rd	هُنَّ	

A few important observations:

1. The transliteration is meant to help you pronounce the pronouns. In the transliteration the initial *hamzah* has been dropped; thus, you find *anta* instead of *'anta*. In scholarly writings the initial *hamzah* is usually dropped in this way.

2. The first-person dual and the first-person plural are the same *naḥnu*: نَحْنُ, whether masculine or feminine.

3. The second-person dual is the same in masculine and feminine. Both are *antumā* أَنْتُما. The same goes for the third-person dual *humā* هُما; it does not change between masculine and feminine.

4. In Arabic a group of males and females takes a plural masculine pronoun.

Examine the examples below of الضَّمَائِر. All of the sentences are nominal and imply the "to be" verb. Identify the pronouns and attempt to pronounce the words.

Lesson Seven

أنــا في الشّارِعِ وأَنْتَ في البَيـتِ.

I am in the street, and you are at home.

أَنْـتِ امرأةٌ وهُوَ رجلٌ.

You are a woman, and he is a man.

هُوَ أستاذٌ في الجـامِـعَـةِ.

He is a professor at the university.

هِـيَ أُنْـثـى وهُوَ ذَكَرٌ.

She is a female, and he is a male.

نَـحْـنُ في المَـدْرَسَةِ وأَنْـتُـمْ في الشّارِعِ.

We are in the school, and you (mp) are in the street.

أَنْـتُـما مَعَ المُهَـنْـدِسِ في الغُرْفَةِ وهُـمـا مع المُدَرِّسِ في المَـعْـمَـلِ.

You (d) are with the engineer in the room, and they (d) are with the teacher in the laboratory.

أَنْـتُـمْ نـورُ العـالَـمِ.

You (mp) are the light of the world.

نَـحْـنُ شُهودٌ.

We are witnesses.

أَنْـتُـنَّ مَعَ الـفَـنّـانِ في السيّارَةِ.

You (fp) are with the artist in the car.

هُمْ مُـعَـلِّـمـونَ.

They (mp) are teachers.

هُنَّ مُـعَـلِّـماتٌ؟

Are they teachers (fp)?

Gender in Nouns

Arabic nouns are either مُـذَكَّر (*mudhakkar*, masculine) or مؤَنَّث (*mu'annath*, feminine). One of the most common (and easiest) ways to identify feminine nouns is by the *tā' marbūṭah* ending: when a noun ends with *tā' marbūṭah*, it is most likely feminine.

See these nouns:

apartment	shaqqah	شَقَّة
room	ḥujrah	حُجْرَة
courtyard	bāḥah	بَاحَة
rug	sajjādah	سَجَّادَة
table	ṭāwilah	طَاوِلَة
pub	ḥānah	حانَة
tree	shajarah	شَجَرَة

All end with *tā' marbūṭah*. All are feminine.

Now, compare with these masculine nouns:

book	kitāb	كِتاب
chair	kursī	كُرسي
rooster	dīk	ديك
window	shubbāk	شُبَّاك
door	bāb	باب
bed	sarīr	سَرير
pen	qalam	قَلَم

Lesson Seven

Most job nouns are by default masculine and can be made feminine by simply adding a *tā' marbūṭah* suffix. See this list:

Translation	Feminine Noun	Masculine Noun
a Muslim	مُسْلِمة	مُسْلِم
an engineer	مُهَنْدِسة	مُهَنْدِس
a teacher	مُدَرِّسة	مُدَرِّس
a teacher	مُعَلِّمة	مُعَلِّم
a physician	طَبيبة	طَبيب
a professor	أُسْتاذة	أُسْتاذ
a student	طالِبة	طالِب
an artist	فَنّانة	فَنّان
an actor, actress	مُمَثِّلة	مُمَثِّل
a seller, merchant	تاجِرة	تاجِر
a driver	سائِقة	سائِق
a worker	عامِلة	عامِل
a seller	بائِعَة	بائِع
a manager	مُديرَة	مُدير
an accountant	مُحاسِبة	مُحاسِب
an agent, steward	وَكيلة	وَكيل
a writer	كاتِبَة	كاتِب
an expert	خَبيرة	خَبير
a colleague	زَميلة	زَميل

While the *tā' marbūṭah* is the most common indicator of the feminine nouns, it is not the only one. We can also identify feminine nouns—with some exceptions—by the following three endings: ـات، ـاء، ـى. Nouns that end with *alif-tā'*, *alif-hamzah*, or *alif maqṣūrah* are often feminine. Here are examples:

actresses	mumaththilāt	مُمَثِّلات
sky, heaven	samā'	سَماء
female	unthā	أُنْثى

Remember that in our transliteration we drop the initial *hamzah*:

Some nouns are merely feminine due to the way Arabs hear and identify them, although these nouns have no clear feminine indicators. This is true with regard to many human body parts. See the following nouns—all are feminine, although they do not end with a distinctive sign of femininity:

ear	udhun	أُذُن
eye	ᶜayn	عَين
lip	shafah	شَفَة

Number in Nouns

In Arabic there are three kinds of nouns with respect to number: singular, dual, and plural. They are called مُفْرَد (*mufrad*), مُثَنّى (*muthannā*), and جَمْع (*jamᶜ*), respectively. To make a singular noun dual or plural, specific suffixes are added. While there are various rules that dictate how to make a noun dual or plural, the most common and basic rules will be discussed here.

Dual Nouns

"Dual" in Arabic is مُثَنّى (*muthannā*). To make a singular noun dual, add the suffix ان to the singular form of that noun. This applies whether the noun is masculine or feminine. It is important to note that, since the suffix ان is added to both masculine and feminine nouns, we must retain the feminine indicator (usually *tā' marbūṭah*) as it is before adding the suffix. However, because the *tā' marbūṭah* cannot exist in the middle of a word, we will change it into a regular *tā'*, then add the suffix to make a dual feminine noun.

Lesson Seven

See the following examples:

Dual Feminine	Feminine Noun	Dual Masculine	Masculine Noun
أُسْتاذتانِ	أُسْتاذة	أُسْتاذانِ	أُسْتاذ
مُسْلِمتانِ	مُسْلِمة	مُسْلِمانِ	مُسْلِم
مُهَنْدِستانِ	مُهَنْدِسة	مُهَنْدِسانِ	مُهَنْدِس
مُدَرِّستانِ	مُدَرِّسة	مُدَرِّسانِ	مُدَرِّس
مُعَلِّمتانِ	مُعَلِّمة	مُعَلِّمانِ	مُعَلِّم
طَبيبتانِ	طَبيبة	طَبيبانِ	طَبيب
طالِبتانِ	طالِبة	طالِبانِ	طالِب
فَنّانتانِ	فَنّانة	فَنّانانِ	فَنّان
مُمَثِّلتانِ	مُمَثِّلة	مُمَثِّلانِ	مُمَثِّل
تاجِرتانِ	تاجِرة	تاجِرانِ	تاجِر
سائِقتانِ	سائِقة	سائِقانِ	سائِق
عامِلتانِ	عامِلة	عامِلانِ	عامِل
بائِعتانِ	بائِعة	بائِعانِ	بائِع
مُديرتانِ	مُديرة	مُديرانِ	مُدير
مُحاسِبتانِ	مُحاسِبة	مُحاسِبانِ	مُحاسِب
وَكيلتانِ	وَكيلة	وَكيلانِ	وَكيل
كاتِبتانِ	كاتِبة	كاتِبانِ	كاتِب
خَبيرتانِ	خَبيرة	خَبيرانِ	خَبير
زَميلتانِ	زَميلة	زَميلانِ	زَميل

It is important to note that the dual suffix انِ is the nominative case ending. In genitive and accusative grammatical cases, use the suffix ينِ instead of انِ.

Plural Nouns

A plural is called جَمْع (*jamᶜ*). To change a singular noun to plural masculine, add the suffix ونَ to the singular masculine noun—thus, مُهَنْدِس becomes مُهَنْدِسـونَ. This is the general rule for nouns in the nominative case; however, in genitive and accusative grammatical cases the suffix ونَ becomes ينَ.

To make a singular feminine noun plural, add the suffix ات to the singular noun. However, we should first remove the feminine indicator (usually *tā' marbūṭah*), and then add the suffix—thus, مُهَنْدِسة becomes مُهَنْدِسات.

There is one necessary observation to make here. Recall that when a singular feminine noun is made dual, the feminine indicator (usually the *tā' marbūṭah*) is *retained*. Thus, the singular masculine مُهَنْدِس becomes the dual masculine مُهَنْدِسانِ, while the singular feminine مُهَنْدِسة becomes the dual feminine مُهَنْدِستانِ. This is simply because the suffix *alif-nūn* (انِ) is added to the singular noun whether that noun is masculine or feminine. The case is different when a singular noun becomes plural. The masculine plural suffix is different from the feminine plural suffix. Therefore, the feminine marker (usually the *tā' marbūṭah*) does not need to be retained. For example, the singular noun مُهَنْدِس becomes the masculine plural مُهَنْدِسونَ and the feminine plural مُهَنْدِسات.

Consider the following examples of masculine and feminine plural nouns:

Plural Feminine	Feminine Noun	Plural Masculine	Masculine Noun
مُسْلِمات	مُسْلِمة	مُسْلِمونَ	مُسْلِم
مُهَنْدِسات	مُهَنْدِسة	مُهَنْدِسونَ	مُهَنْدِس
مُدَرِّسات	مُدَرِّسة	مُدَرِّسونَ	مُدَرِّس
مُعَلِّمات	مُعَلِّمة	مُعَلِّمونَ	مُعَلِّم
طَبيبات	طَبيبة	*	طَبيب
أُسْتاذات	أُسْتاذة	أُسْتاذونَ*	أُسْتاذ
طالِبات	طالِبة	طالِبونَ*	طالِب
فَنّانات	فَنّانة	فَنّانونَ	فَنّان
مُمَثِّلات	مُمَثِّلة	مُمَثِّلونَ	مُمَثِّل
تاجِرات	تاجِرة	*	تاجِر

Lesson Seven

Plural Feminine	Feminine Noun	Plural Masculine	Masculine Noun
سائِقـات	سائِقـة	سائِقـونَ	سائِق
عامِلات	عامِلة	عامِلـونَ	عامِل
بائِعـات	بائِعَة	بائِعـونَ	بائِع
مُديرات	مُديرَة	مُديرونَ	مُدير
مُحاسِبات	مُحاسِبة	مُحاسِبـونَ	مُحاسِب
وَكيلات	وَكيلة	*	وَكيل
كاتِبات	كاتِبَة	كاتِبـونَ	كاتِب
خَبيرات	خَبيرة	*	خَبير
زَميلات	زَميلة	*	زَميل

Note that for masculine plural nouns the suffix ونَ is in the nominative case. For the genitive and accusative cases the ending changes to ينَ.

The table above highlights two important points. First, most singular nouns follow expected patterns when we make them plural. We call these regular or sound plurals. We form them by adding suffixes to singular nouns. Second, there are several places above where * was added, either after the masculine plural or instead of it. This indicates the second type of plural in Arabic: the broken plural.

The broken plural refers to the type of plural that changes the structure of a singular noun, partially or significantly. In other words, instead of simply adding a suffix, the plural is formed by changing the letters of the singular without following any consistent or systematic pattern. This is in some sense similar to the way we make a noun plural in English: While the standard way is to add an "s" at the end, we still see different forms, such as "men," "women," and "geese."

Some singular nouns can have both sound and broken plurals. See the table above: The nouns أُسْتاذ and طالِب follow the normal pattern of adding the suffix (ونَ) to form the sound plural. However, these two nouns also have broken plural forms. The broken plural of أُسْتاذة is أَساتِذة. The broken plural of طالِب is طُلّاب or طَلَبة; both are valid options. Notice how the broken plural is formed by changing the structure of the singular noun, and how a singular noun can have both sound and broken plurals.

Some nouns in the table above have only broken plural forms, while others have either sound plural forms or sound and broken plural forms. For instance, the following nouns do not have sound plural forms: طَبيب، تاجِر، خَبير، زَميل.

The following table can help you with examples of singular nouns which have both sound and broken plural forms, or only the latter:

Broken Plural	Sound Plural	Singular Noun (Masculine)
أَطِبّاء	–	طَبيب
أَساتِذَة	أُسْتاذونَ	أُسْتاذ
طَلَبة وطُلّاب	طالِبونَ	طالِب
تُجَار وتِجار	–	تاجِر
عُمّال	عامِلونَ	عامِل
باعَة	بائِعونَ	بائِع
مُدَراءُ	مُديرونَ	مُدير
وُكلاءُ	–	وَكيل
كُتّاب وكَتَبة	كاتِبونَ	كاتِب
خُبَراء	–	خَبير
زُمَلاء	–	زَميل

There are two final observations in this regard.

1. We studied the three different noun cases (nominative, genitive, and accusative). It is necessary to state that, when forming a sound plural masculine, we add the suffix ونَ to the singular masculine noun if the noun is in the nominative case, and we add the suffix ينَ if the noun is in the genitive or accusative case. As for forming a sound plural feminine, the suffix ات is used for all noun cases. However, this suffix will take a different final short vowel depending on the noun case: in the nominative case, we use اتُ, and in the genitive and accusative cases اتِ. This is the case when the plural feminine is definite, i.e., with *alif-lām*. If the sound plural feminine noun is indefinite, we use *tanwīn* forms: in the nominative case اتٌ, and in genitive and accusative اتٍ.

Lesson Seven

2. Broken plurals should be memorized. There are various attempts to establish regular patterns for broken plurals, but they extend beyond the scope of this introductory course.

Vocabulary

witnesses	شُهُود	world	عَالَم
car	سَيَّارَة	laboratory	مَعْمَل
lip	شَفَة	laboratory	مُخْتَبَر
you (md/fd)	أَنْتُما	I	أَنا
they (md/fd)	هُما	you (ms)	أَنْتَ
you (mp)	أَنْتُمْ	you (fs)	أَنْتِ
you (fp)	أَنْتُنَّ	he	هُوَ
they (mp)	هُمْ	she	هِيَ
they (fp)	هُنَّ	we	نَحْنُ
apartment	شَقَّة	a Muslim	مُسْلِم
room	حُجْرَة	an engineer	مُهَنْدِس
courtyard	بَاحَة	a teacher	مُدَرِّس
rug	سَجَّادَة	a teacher	مُعَلِّم
table	طَاوِلَة	a physician	طَبِيب
pub	حَانَة	a professor	أُسْتاذ
tree	شَجَرَة	a student	طَالِب
book	كِتاب	an artist	فَنَّان
chair	كُرْسِيّ	an actor/actress	مُمَثِّل
rooster	دِيك	a seller, merchant	تاجِر
window	شُبَّاك	a driver	سائِق
door	باب	a worker	عامِل

bed	سَرير	a seller	بائِع
pen	قَلَم	a manager	مُدير
singular	مُفْرَد	an accountant	مُحاسِب
dual	مُثَنّى	an agent, steward	وَكيل
plural	جَمْع	a writer	كاتِب
a colleague	زَميل	an expert	خَبير
actresses	مُمَثِّلات	pronouns	ضَمائِر
sky, heaven	سَماء	ear	أُذُن
female	أُنْثى	eye	عَين

Lesson Seven

Exercises

Exercise 7.1

See the following verses from the Quran. Identify the pronouns and attempt to pronounce the words.

1. أَنتُمَا وَمَنِ اتَّبَعَكُمَا الْغَالِبُونَ.

2. وَأَنتُمْ ظَالِمُونَ.

3. أَنتَ الْعَلِيمُ الْحَكِيمُ.

4. فَهَلْ أَنتُمْ شَاكِرُونَ؟

5. يَا آدَمُ اسْكُنْ أَنتَ وَزَوْجُكَ الْجَنَّةَ.

6. فَهَلْ أَنتُم مُّسْلِمُونَ؟

7. قَالَ الْحَوَارِيُّونَ نَحْنُ أَنصَارُ اللَّهِ آمَنَّا بِاللَّهِ.

8. وَقَالَتِ الْيَهُودُ وَالنَّصَارَىٰ نَحْنُ أَبْنَاءُ اللَّهِ.

Exercise 7.2

Translate these words into English.

1. كِتابان

2. طالِبتان

3. كَلْبان

4. قَلَمَين

5. خَبيرين

Exercise 7.3

Examine these nouns. Read them out loud. Make each of them dual masculine.

1. صَديق
2. مُدَرِّسَة
3. مُمَثِّل
4. طالِبات
5. صَبِيُّ
6. رَسول
7. بَيت
8. مَعبد
9. صَف

Exercise 7.4

First, identify each of the nouns below as either masculine or feminine. Second, make each noun dual.

1. الغُرْفَة
2. نور
3. مُعَلِّمات
4. الجامِعَة
5. السَّيَّارَة
6. باحَة
7. حانة

Lesson Seven

8. كِتاب

9. شَقَّة

10. حُجْرَة

11. طاوِلَة

12. ديك

13. شُبَّاك

14. سَرير

15. سَجّادَة

16. شَجَرَة

17. كُرسيّ

18. الزَّوج

19. المَسْرَح

20. الأُسْتاذ

21. الكَنيسَة

22. باب

23. قَلَم

Lesson Eight
ثَمَانِيَة

Adjectives (الصِفات)

In Arabic adjectives are called صِفات (singular, صِفة). They are nouns of description and explain or designate aspects of other nouns. We call the adjective صِفة and the noun it modifies مَوصوف. When a noun is definite, adjectives *explain* its features; when indefinite, adjectives *designate* and *identify* aspects about it. In Arabic, adjectives come *after* nouns to highlight aspects about them. In English one says, "The clean shirt," where the adjective "clean" precedes the noun "shirt" and modifies it. In Arabic the phrase becomes القَميصُ النَّظيفُ, where the adjective النَّظيفُ comes after the noun القَميصُ. Grammatically, adjectives fall within a category called "the followers," because they are "followers" in at least two ways: (1) they always come after the word (usually a noun) they modify, and (2) they agree with that word in case, definiteness, number, and gender.

In any given sentence, adjectives can appear in two different ways: (1) as a single noun or several consecutive nouns separated by *wāw*s, or (2) as a sentence or semi-sentence. Our focus will be on the former.

See the following pairs of adjectives:

fast	سَريع	good	جَيِّد
slow	بَطيء	bad	رَديء
smart	ذَكي	large, old	كَبير
stupid	غَبي	small, young	صَغير
beautiful	جَميل	rich	غَني
ugly	قَبيح	poor	فَقير
easy	سَهْل	clean	نَظيف
hard	صَعْب	dirty	قَذِر (وَسِخ)

hot	ساخِن	heavy	ثَقيل
cold	بارِد	light	خَفيف
near	قَريب	short	قَصير
remote	بَعيد	tall, long	طَويل
sick	مَريض	old	قَديم
fine (not sick)	سَليم	new	جَديد
energetic (active)	نَشيط	happy	سَعيد
lazy	كَسول	sad	حَزين
honest	صادِق	expensive	غالي
liar	كاذِب	inexpensive	رَخيص
wide	واسِع	delicious	لَذيذ
narrow	ضَيِّق	unpleasant	بَغيض

Here are some adjectives (attributes) describing God:

merciful	رَحيم
marvelous, wondrous	عَجيب
great	عَظيم
holy	قُدّوس
wise	حَكيم
just	عادِل

See the following phrases, and notice how the adjective must follow the noun it modifies. Adjectives also agree with the noun in definiteness (ال), gender, case (final vowel), and number. Note how indefinite nouns take *tanwīn*, while definite nouns take only a single short vowel.

Adjective(s)	Translation	Phrase
وَسِخ	a dirty dress	ثَوْبٌ وَسِخٌ
النَظيف	the clean shirt	القَميصُ النَظيفُ
السَعيد والجَميل	the happy and beautiful world	العالَمُ السَعيد والجَميل
كَبير وكَريم	a big and generous heart	قَلبٌ كَبيرٌ وكَريمٌ
كَبيرة	in a large map	في خَريطَةٍ كَبيرةٍ
الغَنيّ	the rich friend	الصَديقُ الغَنيُّ
سَريع	a fast train	قِطارٌ سَريعٌ
البَطيء	the slow donkey	الحِمار البَطيء
البَطيئة	the slow cow	البَقَرَةُ البَطيئةُ
سَهل	an easy test	اخْتِبارٌ سَهلٌ
الصَعب	the hard examination	الامْتِحانُ الصَعبُ
لَذيذ	a delicious food	طَعامٌ لَذيذٌ
الـلُبنانيّات	the Lebanese artists (fp)	الفَنّاناتُ الـلُبنانيّاتُ
صَغيرة	a small town	مَدينةٌ صَغيرةٌ
الصَغير	the small house	البيتُ الصَغيرُ
القَديم	the old book	الكِتابُ القَديمُ
جَديد	a new pen	قَلَمٌ جَديدٌ
جَديد	with a new pen	مع قَلَمٍ جَديدٍ
الجَديد	with the new pen	مع القَلَمِ الجَديدِ
الذَكيّ	the smart student is in class	الطالبُ الذَكيُّ في الفَصلِ

Lesson Eight

الحَكيم	with the wise teacher	مع المُعلِّم الحَكيمِ
عَظيمة ونَظيفة	Cairo is a great and clean city.	القاهرةُ مدينةٌ عظيمةٌ ونَظيفةٌ.

From this table, we can make several remarks.

First, to explain an aspect of a noun, we can use a chain of adjectives linked by *wāw*s, such as عظيمةٌ ونَظيفةٌ and السَعيد والجَميل. Second, unlike in English, Arabic adjectives come *after* the noun they modify. In our translation to English, however, we use what makes sense in English, thus reversing the order. Third, since Arabic adjectives are followers, they agree with the noun they modify in several ways. When the noun changes its case, number, or gender, the adjective changes accordingly.

For instance, see how the adjective صَغير changes between مَدينةٌ صَغيرةٌ and البيتُ الصغيرُ. In مَدينةٌ صَغيرةٌ, the noun مَدينةٌ is indefinite, singular, and feminine; therefore, the adjective صَغيرةٌ follows the same pattern. The noun and the adjective, moreover, receive a *tanwīn ḍammah* instead of a simple *ḍammah*, because they are indefinite. Similarly, in the phrase البيتُ الصغيرُ, the noun البيتُ is definite, singular, and masculine. The adjective الصغيرُ follows the pattern of the noun it modifies.

Finally, let's examine these advanced phrases, as well:

Adjective(s)	Translation	Phrase
نَشيطةٌ	Samiya (fs) is an energetic engineer.	سامية مُهنْدِسةٌ نَشيطةٌ.
كَسولانِ	They (md) are lazy engineers.	هُما مُهنْدِسانِ كَسولانِ.
نَشيطتانِ	Samar and Suad (fd) are energetic engineers.	سَمَر وسُعاد مُهنْدِستانِ نَشيطتانِ.

Arabic Cardinal Numbers (الأَرْقَام)

We use cardinal numbers to count. Numbers are أَرْقَام (arqām), and the singular is رَقْم (raqam). In Arabic we have masculine and feminine forms of these numbers. See the table:

	In digits	Feminine مُؤَنَّث	Masculine مُذَكَّر
	\multicolumn{3}{c}{Arabic Cardinal Numbers}	
1	١	واحِدة	واحِد
2	٢	اثْنَتان	اثْنان
3	٣	ثَلاثة	ثَلاث
4	٤	أَرْبَعة	أَرْبَع
5	٥	خَمْسة	خَمْس
6	٦	سِتّة	سِتّ
7	٧	سَبْعة	سَبْع
8	٨	ثَمانية	ثَمانٍ
9	٩	تِسْعة	تِسْع
10	١٠	عَشْرة	عَشْر

You notice that the feminine number is formed by adding a *tā' marbūṭah* to the masculine form, except in the case of ثَمانٍ we add *yā'* before placing the *tā' marbūṭah*. The number zero is صِفْر (ṣifr). It is gender neutral. Moreover, note that اثْنان and اثْنَتان are in the nominative case; when genitive or accusative, they become اثْنَي and اثْنَتين, respectively.

Arabic numbers serve as adjectives. Would they then use the same rules as adjectives?

Lesson Eight

The answer is not straightforward. It is actually yes/no. Numbers one and two will come after the noun they modify and agree in case and gender. As for numbers three through ten, they disagree in gender and precede the noun they modify.

See the following examples:

one day (m)	يَومٌ واحِدٌ
one room (f)	حُجرَةٌ واحِدَةٌ
one teacher (m)	مُعَلِّمٌ واحِدٌ
one teacher (f)	مُعَلِّمَةٌ واحِدَةٌ
two teachers (m)	مُعَلِّمانِ اثْنانِ
two teachers (f)	مُعَلِّمتانِ اثْنَتانِ
three teachers (f)	ثَلاثُ مُدَرِّساتٍ
seven teachers (m)	سَبْعَةُ مُدَرِّسينَ
four ladies	أَرْبَعُ سيداتٍ
four students (m)	أَرْبَعَةُ طُلّابٍ
nine cars (f)	تِسْعُ سَيّاراتٍ
ten engineers (m)	عَشْرَةُ مُهَنْدِسينَ

You notice that numbers three through ten disagree in gender with the noun they modify. The numbers come before the noun they modify, and the noun is always in the genitive case. This structure is called *iḍāfah* construct and we will study it in Lesson Eleven. For now, these examples should suffice in introducing you to Arabic cardinal numbers.

Vocabulary

Here are the new (and old) important words to memorize for this lesson:

fast	سَريع	good	جَيِّد
slow	بَطيء	bad	رَديء
smart	ذَكي	large, old	كَبير

stupid	غَبي	small, young	صَغير
beautiful	جَميل	rich	غَنيّ
ugly	قَبيح	poor	فَقير
easy	سَهْل	clean	نَظيف
hard	صَعْب	dirty	قَذِر (وَسِخ)
hot	ساخِن	heavy	ثَقيل
cold	بارِد	light	خَفيف
near	قَريب	short	قَصير
remote	بَعيد	tall, long	طَويل
sick	مَريض	old	قَديم
fine (not sick)	سَليم	new	جَديد
energetic (active)	نَشيط	happy	سَعيد
lazy	كَسول	sad	حَزين
honest	صادِق	expensive	غالي
liar	كاذِب	inexpensive	رَخيص
wide	واسِع	delicious	لَذيذ
narrow	ضَيّق	unpleasant	بَغيض
one	واحِد	merciful	رَحيم
two	اثْنان	marvelous	عَجيب
three	ثَلاثة	great	عَظيم
four	أرْبَعة	holy	قُدّوس
five	خَمْسة	wise	حَكيم
six	سِتّة	just	عادِل
seven	سَبْعة	dress	ثَوْب

Lesson Eight

eight	ثَمانية	shirt	قَميص
nine	تِسْعة	food	طَعام
ten	عَشْرة	generous	كَريم
delicious	لَذيذ	map	خَريطَة
town	مَدينَة	friend	صَديق
city	مَدينَة	train	قِطار
Lebanon	لُبْنان	donkey	الحِمار
number	رَقْم	cow	بَقَرة
examination	امْتِحان	test	اخْتِبار
one room	حُجْرَةٌ واحِدَةٌ	one	واحِد
four ladies	أرْبَعُ سيداتٍ	one teacher (m)	مُعَلِّمٌ واحِدٌ
four students (m)	أرْبَعَةُ طُلّابٍ	one teacher (f)	مُعَلِّمةٌ واحِدَةٌ
nine cars (f)	تِسْعُ سَيّاراتٍ	two teachers (m)	مُعَلِّمانِ اثْنانِ
ten engineers (m)	عَشْرةُ مُهَنْدِسينَ	two teachers (f)	مُعَلِّمتان اثْنَتان
Jesus Christ	يَسوعُ المَسيح	world	عالَم
Muhammad	مُحَمَّد	heart	قَلب
a god	إله	Cairo	القاهِرَة
church	كَنيسَة	Alexandria	الإسْكَنْدَرِيَّة
mosque	مَسْجِد / جامِع	Damascus	دِمَشْق
synagogue	مَعْبَد	Aleppo	حَلَب
reverend	قَسّ	Beirut	بيروت
priest	كاهِن	Oman	عَمَان
imam	إمام	Khartoum	الخُرْطوم

I want	أَنا أُريدُ	Jerusalem	أُورْشَليم (القُدْس)
he wants	هُوَ يُريدُ	Nazareth	النّاصِرَة
she wants	هِيَ تُريدُ	I went	أَنَا ذَهَبْتُ
we want	نَحْنُ نُريدُ	he went	هُوَ ذَهَبَ
I studied	أَنَا دَرَسْتُ	she went	هِيَ ذَهَبَتْ
he studied	هُوَ دَرَسَ	we went	نَحْنُ ذَهَبْنَا
she studied	هِيَ دَرَسَتْ	gospel	إنجيل
we studied	نَحْنُ دَرَسْنا	cross	صَليب

Lesson Eight

Exercises

Exercise 8.1

State whether the phrase is correct or wrong. Correct the mistakes.

1. الطّالِبُ الطَويلة
2. مُعَلِّمَةٌ الجَميلَة
3. ثَلاثُ فَنَاناتٍ
4. مُعَلِمانِ اثْنَتانِ
5. غُرْفَةٌ كَبيرةٌ
6. حُجْرَةٌ واحِدةٌ
7. رَجُلٌ قَصيرةٌ
8. كُرسيّ الرَخيصٌ
9. مُعَلِمٌ واحِدٌ
10. عَشْرةُ مُهَنْدِسينَ
11. طالِبٌ ذَكِيٌّ
12. الحِمارُ السَريعٌ
13. يَومٌ واحِدةٌ
14. مُعَلِّمةٌ واحِدةٌ
15. مُعَلِّمَتانِ اثْنَتانِ
16. سِتَّةُ سَيّاراتٍ
17. تِسْعُ مُدَرِّسينَ

18. أَرْبَعَةُ طُلَّابٍ

19. أَرْبَعُ سيداتٍ

Exercise 8.2

Translate the following phrases into Arabic.

1. A clean dress

2. The clean heart

3. In a large map

4. The rich engineer

5. A new book

6. With a new book

7. With the new book

8. A small church and big mosque

9. A lazy student (feminine)

10. The fast car

11. Alexandria is beautiful

12. The beautiful Alexandria

Lesson Eight

Lesson Nine
تِسْعَة

Demonstratives (أَسْمَاء الإشَارَة)

The demonstratives are pointers and determiners. In English we have a few determiners which we use to point to people (rational beings) or objects, either far from or near to us in proximity: this, that, these, and those. We call them demonstratives: "This table is sturdy," "these men are tall," and "those cars are new."

In Arabic we have similar demonstratives but with far more sophisticated options. Demonstratives are basically nouns functioning as nouns of pointing. We call them أَسْمَاء الإشَارَة (asmā' al-ishārah), as أَسْمَاء refers to them as nouns, while إِشَارَة highlights their pointing function. Like proper nouns and personal pronouns, demonstratives are always definite. They do not need definite articles for definiteness. Some are rarely used; you would only encounter them in Classical Arabic texts. Our focus here will be on the most commonly used demonstratives.

We divide them into two groups: near and distant. They are also categorized by gender and number. Here are the most commonly occurring demonstratives:

Feminine	Masculine	Feminine	Masculine	
Distant بَعِيد		Near قَرِيب		
تِلْكَ that	ذَلِكَ that	هَذِهِ this	هَذَا this	Singular مُفْرَد
تَانِكَ those	ذَانِكَ those	هَاتَانِ these	هَذَانِ these	Dual مُثَنَّى
أُولَائِكَ those		هَؤُلَاءِ these		Plural جَمْع

Since we are trying to learn how to read and pronounce Arabic, we will not use transliteration from now on, except in rare cases for clarification. This is to help you expend adequate effort to read and pronounce Arabic. You should also familiarize yourself with the following words: مُفرَد, مُثنَّى, and جَمْع, as well as مُذَكَّر and مُؤَنَّثُ; singular, dual, plural, masculine, and feminine, respectively.

There are three important remarks to make at the beginning:

First, the distant dual masculine/feminine is rarely used, although we included them here.

Second, the dual forms given in the table above are for the nominative noun case. If the noun is genitive or accusative, we use the following forms (replacing *alif* with *yā'*):

هَذَيْنِ

هَاتَيْنِ

ذَيْنِكَ

تَيْنِكَ

Third, in some Arabic writing you may find slightly modified forms, أُولَئِكَ، هَتَانِ، هَتَيْنِ, instead of هَاتَيْنِ، هَاتَانِ، أُولَائِكَ. The explanation behind placing the *alif* or suppressing it is complex and goes beyond the scope of this introductory material. Use the forms in the table above, and do not confuse yourself with the modified forms.

Grammatically, Arabic demonstratives can function in two major ways: as adjectives or as pronouns. Consider the following two sentences:

هَذا الرَجُلُ طَويلٌ.	This man is tall.
هَذا رَجُلٌ طَويلٌ.	This is a tall man.

These sentences represent the two major uses of demonstratives. Let's discuss them.

Demonstratives as Adjectives

In the sentence هَذا الرَجُلُ طَويلٌ, the word هَذا is a demonstrative pronoun and serves as مُبْتَدأ, the subject of the sentence. The word الرَجُلُ is in apposition to هَذا. Apposition places two words in a relationship of exchange—they are side by side and can represent each other, either completely or partially. In this case, الرَجُلُ is in apposition to the subject of the sentence هَذا, because the two words refer to the same

Lesson Nine

person. The literal translation of هذا الرَجُلُ is "this person, the man," but it suffices to render it "this man." As for طَويلٌ, it serves as خَبَر (a predicate) to the subject هَذا.

You notice here that the combination of the demonstrative and the apposition هَذا الرَجُلُ does not form a complete sentence. We call the phrase هَذا الرَجُلُ, a basic demonstrative phrase. It includes a demonstrative pronoun followed by a definite noun. Here are some examples of adjectival demonstrative phrases and their translations:

Translation	Demonstrative Phrase
this student (ms)	هَذَا الطَّالِب
this day (ms)	هَذَا اليَوْم
this car (fs)	هَذِهِ السَّيَّارَة
this carpet (fs)	هَذِهِ السَّجَّادَة
that champion (ms)	ذَلِكَ البَطَل
that mountain (ms)	ذَلِكَ الجَبَل
that plateau (fs)	تِلْكَ الهَضَبَة
that physician (fs)	تِلْكَ الطَبيبَة
these phones (md)	هَذَانِ الهَاتِفَان
these desks (md)	هَذَانِ المَكْتَبان
these sentences (fd)	هَاتَانِ الجُمْلَتَان
these actresses (fd)	هَاتَانِ المُمَثِّلَتان
these men (mp)	هَؤُلَاءِ الرِّجال
these girls (fp)	هَؤُلَاءِ البَنات
those artists (mp)	أُولَائِكَ الفَنَّانون
those artists (fp)	أُولَائِكَ الفَنَّانات

Note that these adjectival demonstrative phrases do not make complete sentences. They must be combined with other parts of speech—including nouns, adjectives, verbs, or others—in order to make a complete sentence. In other words, a demonstrative pronoun points to someone or something that is elaborated upon or somewhat identified in other parts of the phrase.

Now consider the plural demonstratives. Both هَؤُلاءِ and أُولائِكَ are not gender sensitive. They are used with masculine and feminine nouns. Most importantly, they are only used with human beings and cannot be used with objects or things (nonhuman). In referring to nonhuman objects, use the feminine singular demonstrative: هَذِهِ السَّيّارات (these cars) and تِلكَ المَكْتَبات (those bookstores/libraries).

Here are more examples of demonstratives with nonhuman plurals:

Translation	Demonstrative Phrase
these books	هَذِهِ الكُتُب
these roses	هَذِهِ الوُرود
these fish	هَذِهِ الأسْماك
those keys	تِلكَ المَفاتيح
those homes/houses	تِلكَ البُيوت / المَنازِل
those gates	تِلكَ البَوّابات
those doors	تِلكَ الأبْواب
those dishes	تِلكَ الصُّحون

This structure (demonstrative + definite noun) is called the adjectival use of demonstratives. The definiteness of the noun is crucial, as it distinguishes this case from the abovementioned sentence هَذا رَجُلٌ طَويلٌ, in which رَجُلٌ is indefinite. In this case, رَجُلٌ becomes the predicate of هَذا and طَويلٌ an adjective. This is another use of demonstratives, where they serve as pronouns. Let's discuss it.

Demonstratives as Pronouns

In the sentence هَذا رَجُلٌ طَويلٌ, the structure is demonstrative + indefinite noun + adjective. The demonstrative هَذا serves as a pronoun. It is the subject of the sentence. The indefinite noun رَجُلٌ is the predicate of هَذا. The word طَويل is an adjective.

Lesson Nine

Consider the following nominal sentences:

Translation	Nominal Phrases
This [is] a student (ms).	هَذَا طَالِبٌ.
This [is] a day (ms).	هَذَا يَوْمٌ.
This [is] a car (fs).	هَذِهِ سَيَّارَةٌ.
This [is] a carpet (fs).	هَذِهِ سَجَّادَةٌ.
That [is] a champion (ms).	ذَلِكَ بَطَلٌ.
That [is] a mountain (ms).	ذَلِكَ جَبَلٌ.
That [is] a plateau (fs).	تِلْكَ هَضَبَةٌ.
That [is] a physician (fs).	تِلْكَ طَبِيبَةٌ.
These [are] phones (md).	هَذَانِ هَاتِفَانِ.
These [are] desks (md).	هَذَانِ مَكْتَبَانِ.
These [are] sentences (fd).	هَاتَانِ جُمْلَتَانِ.
These [are] actresses (fd).	هَاتَانِ مُمَثِّلَتَانِ.
These [are] men (mp).	هَؤُلَاءِ رِجَالٌ.
These [are] girls (fp).	هَؤُلَاءِ بَنَاتٌ.
Those [are] artists (mp).	أُولَائِكَ فَنَّانُونَ.
Those [are] artists (fp).	أُولَائِكَ فَنَّانَاتٌ.

In these sentences, there are four major observations.

1. Each demonstrative is followed by an indefinite noun.

2. The phrases (demonstrative + indefinite noun) convey somewhat complete sentences with their two parts; however, there is usually an adjective following the noun to qualify it.

3. The demonstrative pronoun serves as the مُبْتَدَأ (subject) of the sentence, while the indefinite noun is its خَبَر (predicate).

4. As discussed in previous lessons, the تَنْوِين (tanwīn) is a mark of indefiniteness, i.e., unspecified nouns. In the table above, we see tanwīn ḍammah at the end of indefinite nouns where there are no suffixes added for dual or plural. We should note, however, that we use tanwīn ḍammah because the type of tanwīn depends on the grammatical case of the noun. In the examples above, tanwīn ḍammah is used because the nouns are predicates.

Although we will study verbs later, it is important to reiterate that in Arabic there is no verb "to be" in the present tense. This is the reason that verb "to be" is placed in brackets.

There is one final important note. In Arabic there are two more words used as pointers. The word هُنَا means "here," while هناك means "there." The former points to a nearby object, while the latter points to a distant one. Sometimes the modified form هُنَالِكَ is used instead of هناك, although both have the same meaning.

Vocabulary

homes	بُيُوت	demonstratives	أَسْمَاء الإِشَارَة
that (ms)	ذَلِكَ	feminine	مُؤَنَّثُ
that (fs)	تِلْكَ	masculine	مُذَكَّرُ
those (md)	ذَانِكَ	this (fs)	هَذِهِ
those (fd)	تَانِكَ	this (ms)	هَذَا
those (m/f, p)	أُولَائِكَ	these (md)	هَذَانِ
these (m/f, p)	هَؤُلَاءِ	these (fd)	هَاتَانِ
student	طَالِب	books	كُتُب
day	يَوْم	cars	سَيَّارات
car	سَيَّارَة	roses	وُرود
carpet	سَجَّادَة	fish (p)	أَسْماك
champion (ms)	بَطَل	keys	مَفاتيح
mountain (ms)	جَبَل	houses	مَنازِل
plateau (fs)	هَضَبَة	gates	بَوَّابات

physician (fs)	طَبِيبَة	doors	أبْواب
phones (md)	هاتِفَان	dishes	صُحون
desks (md)	مَكْتَبان	men (mp)	رِجال
sentences (fd)	جُمْلَتان	girls (fp)	بَنات
actresses (fd)	مُمَثِّلَتان	artists (mp)	فَنّانون
student (ms)	طالِب	artists (fp)	فَنّانات
white (f/m)	بَيْضاء / أَبْيَض	green (f/m)	خَضْراء / أَخْضَر
black (f/m)	سَوْداء / أَسْوَد	blue (f/m)	زَرْقاء / أَزْرَق
red (f/m)	حَمْراء / أَحْمَر	yellow (f/m)	صَفْراء / أَصْفَر

Exercises

Exercise 9.1

1. Translate into English. Be sensitive to gender and number.

1. هَذِه فَتاةٌ

2. هَذِه الفَتاةُ

3. هَذَا قَلَمٌ

4. ذَلِكَ الطَّالِبُ

5. هَاتَانِ المُمَثِّلَتانِ ماهِرتانِ

6. هَذَانِ الطَّبيبانِ

7. ذَلِكَ كِتابٌ

8. ذَلِكَ الكِتابُ

9. هَاتَانِ طبيبتانِ جَيِّدَتانِ

Exercise 9.2

Use the correct demonstrative to fill in the blank.

_____ بَناتٌ

_____ طَبيبَةٌ

_____ السَيّارات

_____ سَجَّادَةٌ جَميلَةٌ

_____ هَاتِفَانِ و _____ جُمْلَتانِ

_____ رِجالٌ و _____ فَنَّاناتٌ

_____ مَكْتَبان و _____ مُمَثِّلَتان

_____ الكُتُبُ كثيرةٌ

Exercise 9.3

Determine whether each statement is correct or wrong.

1. هَذا سَجَّادَةٌ كَبيرةٌ.

2. هَذِهِ بَناتٌ.

3. هَؤُلاءِ السَيّاراتِ.

4. تِلْكَ الطَبيبُ.

5. هَذانِ مُهَنْدِسين.

6. هَاتانِ جُمْلَتين.

7. هَذِهِ رِجالٌ.

8. أُولائِكَ فَنّانانِ.

9. هَذانِ مَكْتَبانِ وهَاتانِ مُمَثِّلَتانِ.

10. هَؤُلاءِ كُتُبٌ.

Lesson Ten
عَشَرَة

The *Nisbah* Adjective (النِّسْبَة)

The نِسْبَة (*nisbah*) is the relative adjective. It is derived from a noun to form a relationship. The term *nisbah* literally means "the referring to" adjective. It indicates an adjective "in reference to" a noun, in relation to something or somebody. For instance, if the noun is مِصْر (Egypt), its relative adjective, the *nisbah*, is مِصْرِيّ (Egyptian). In other words, from the noun مِصْر (*miṣr*), we form the *nisbah* adjective مِصْرِيّ (*miṣriyy*). Learning the *nisbah* is important, as it is used quite often in Arabic to coin unique terms and establish relationships with common nouns.

The *nisbah* is formed by adding a suffix *yā'* with a *shaddah* (يّ) to the noun, thus transforming it into a relative adjective.

There are two important remarks at the outset. First, by adding the suffix يّ to a noun, the noun's last letter is forced to take a كَسْرَة. Notice the كَسْرَة underneath the *rā'* (رِ) in *miṣriyy* (مِصْرِيّ). Second, the addition of the شَدّة on suffix *yā'* (يّ) is extremely important. You should not neglect this شَدّة, because without it the noun will be considered possessive—the term مِصْرِي means "my Egypt," while مِصْرِيّ means "Egyptian"—as we will explain in the next lesson.

Consider the following words:

Translation (ms)	Nisbah (ms)	Translation	Noun
Egyptian	مِصْرِيّ	Egypt	مِصْر
Lebanese	لُبْنانِيّ	Lebanon	لُبْنان
Israeli	إِسْرائيليّ	Israel	إِسْرائيل
Palestinian	فَلَسْطينيّ	Palestine	فَلَسْطين
Tunisian	تونِسيّ	Tunisia	تونِس
northern	شَماليّ	north	شَمال

Translation	Nisbah	Noun (English)	Noun
southern	جَنوبيّ	south	جَنوب
eastern	شَرْقيّ	east	شَرْق
western	غَربيّ	west	غَرب
relating to white	أَبْيَضيّ	white (ms)	أَبْيَض
relating to red	أَحْمَريّ	red (ms)	أَحْمَر

As you may have noticed, the table provides only the masculine singular forms of the *nisbah*. What if we want the feminine forms? Simply add the *tā' marbūṭah* (ة) *after* the *yā'* (يّ), but make sure to keep the *shaddah* above the *yā'*. See the feminine forms here:

Translation	Nisbah (fs)	Nisbah (ms)	Noun
Egyptian	مِصْريَّة	مِصْريّ	مِصْر
Lebanese	لُبْنانيَّة	لُبْنانيّ	لُبْنان
Israeli	إسْرائيليَّة	إسْرائيليّ	إسْرائيل
Palestinian	فَلَسْطينيَّة	فَلَسْطينيّ	فَلَسْطين
Tunisian	تونسيَّة	تونسيّ	تونس
northern	شَماليَّة	شَماليّ	شَمال
southern	جَنوبيَّة	جَنوبيّ	جَنوب
eastern	شَرْقيَّة	شَرْقيّ	شَرْق
western	غَربيَّة	غَربيّ	غَرب

If the Arabic noun begins with *alif-lām*, we remove it when we add the *yā' shaddah* (يّ) to form the *nisbah*. Here are some examples:

Nisbah (fs)	Nisbah (ms)	Translation	Noun
أَنْدَلُسيَّة	أَنْدَلُسيّ	Andalusia	الأَنْدَلُس
مَغْربيَّة	مَغْربيّ	Morocco	المَغْرِب
جَزائِريَّة	جَزائِريّ	Algeria	الجَزائِر

Nisbah (fs)	Nisbah (ms)	Translation	Noun
سودانيّة	سودانيّ	Sudan	السودان
أُرْدُنيّة	أُرْدُنيّ	Jordan	الأُرْدُن
عِراقيّة	عِراقيّ	Iraq	العِراق
سَنِغاليّة	سَنِغاليّ	Senegal	السَّنِغال
سَويديّة	سَويديّ	Sweden	السَّويد
بُرتُغاليّة	بُرتُغاليّ	Portugal	البُرتُغال
يونانيّة	يونانيّ	Greece	اليونان
دِنْماركيّة	دِنْماركيّ	Denmark	الدِّنْمارْك
يابانيّة	يابانيّ	Japan	اليابان
صينيّة	صينيّ	China	الصين

You notice that we dropped the *alif-lām* to form the *nisbah*. We say هو مَغْرِبيّ, meaning "he is Moroccan," and هي جَزائِريّة, meaning "she is Algerian."

However, if we want to refer to someone in particular, for example, "the Moroccan," we can still use the *alif-lām* to identify the person. We can say هو المَغْرِبيّ وهي العِراقيّة, meaning "he is the Moroccan, and she is the Iraqi."

Here are some more *nisbah* examples:

Nisbah (fs)	Nisbah (ms)	Translation	Noun
دِمَشْقيّة	دِمَشْقيّ	Damascus	دِمَشْق
بَغْداديّة	بَغْداديّ	Baghdad	بَغْداد
عِلْميّة	عِلْميّ	science	عِلْم

Nouns Ending with *Alif* or *Tā' Marbūṭah*

To form the *nisbah* from nouns that end with *alif* or *tā' marbūṭah*, take off the *alif* or the *tā' marbūṭah*, then add the *yā' shaddah* (يّ). Note, however, that in some cases after you drop off the ending *alif*, the final letter is a *yā'*. In this case, simply add the شَدَّة above this *yā'* to form the *nisbah*. See these examples:

Nisbah (fs)	Nisbah (ms)	Translation	Noun
أَمْريكِيَّة	أَمْريكِيّ	America	أَمْريكا
فَرَنْسِيَّة	فَرَنْسِيّ	France	فَرَنْسا
سوريَّة	سوريّ	Syria	سوريا
تُرْكِيَّة	تُرْكِيّ	Turkey	تُرْكيا
بريطانيَّة	بريطانيّ	Britain	بريطانيا
أُستراليَّة	أُستراليّ	Australia	أُستراليا
قاهِرِيَّة	قاهِرِيّ	Cairo	القاهِرة
مَدْرَسِيَّة	مَدْرَسِيّ	school	مَدْرَسة
جامِعِيَّة	جامِعِيّ	university	جامِعة
سُنِّيَّة	سُنِّيّ	Sunna	سُنَّة
شيعِيَّة	شيعِيّ	Shiite	شيعَة
فاطِمِيَّة	فاطِمِيّ	Fatima	فاطِمَة

You notice in the previous table that we formed the *nisbah* from nouns of places and persons, not only countries. From the noun القاهِرة, the *nisbah* قاهِريّ (from Cairo) is formed, as one may say أنا قاهِريّ, meaning "I am from Cairo," or "I am Cairene." Similarly, by using the *nisbah* of جامِعة, one can form مُدَرِّس جامِعيّ (university teacher) or هو مُدَرِّس جامِعيّ (he is a university teacher).

Furthermore, notice the connection between the Muslim noun Sunna سُنَّة and the relative adjective Sunni سُنِّيّ. The noun refers to the Sunna of Muhammad (his example or way of life), while the *nisbah* سُنِّيّ refers to a Muslim who adheres or belongs to the practice of Muhammad's Sunna. Also, the word شيعَة refers to the group of Imam Ali's supporters, or his faction and company, while the *nisbah* شيعيّ (Shiite) is the person who belongs to such a group.

Nouns Ending with *Alif-Hamzah*

Like the nouns ending with *alif* or *tā' marbūṭah*, those ending with *alif-hamzah* are unique. They are relatively more complex when we create their *nisbah*. You may recall from an earlier lesson that the ending *alif-hamzah* often refers to feminine nouns. In general, you can simply turn the *hamzah* into a *wāw* and add the *yā' shaddah* (ّي) to form the *nisbah*. However, there is more to this rule than this simple generalization. This explanation is as follows: The *hamzah* in the *alif-hamzah* combination can be either for feminization or part of the noun root. If the *hamzah* is for feminization, then we change it into a *wāw* and add the *yā' shaddah* (ّي) to form the *nisbah*. This is by far the most common case. However, if the *hamzah* in the *alif-hamzah* combination is part of the word and not simply for feminization, there are two options: (1) the preferred one is to keep the *hamzah* and add the *yā' shaddah*, or (2) simply change the *hamzah* into *wāw* (similar to the previous case of feminine nouns) and add the *yā' shaddah* to form the *nisbah*. See the following two tables.

Feminine words ending with *alif-hamzah* are below:

Nisbah	Translation	Feminine Noun
بَيْضاويّ	white	بَيْضاء
سَوْداويّ	black	سَوْداء
حَمْراويّ	red	حَمْراء
خَضْراويّ	green	خَضْراء
زَرْقاويّ	blue	زَرْقاء
صَفْراويّ	yellow	صَفْراء
صَحَراويّ	desert	صَحَراء
عَذْراويّ	virgin	عَذْراء

Words ending with *alif-hamzah* where the *hamzah* is part of the root are below:

Nisbah Option 2	*Nisbah* Option 1	Translation	Noun
فَضاويّ	فَضائيّ	space	فَضاء
سَماويّ	سَمائيّ	sky, heaven	سَماء
كِساويّ	كِسائيّ	robe, clothes	كِساء
هَواويّ	هَوائيّ	air	هَواء
رِداويّ	رِدائيّ	gown, dress	رِداء

Lesson Ten

Arabic-speaking people typically prefer Option 1 in forming their *nisbah* when the *hamzah* is part of the root.

Dual and Plural Forms with the *Nisbah* Adjectives

In order to make a *nisbah* dual or plural, form the *nisbah* first, then add the suffixes of dual and plural nouns as explained in Lesson Seven. For the most part, most *nisbah* plurals are sound, not broken.

Study the following examples of the dual forms of the *nisbah*:

Nisbah (fd)	*Nisbah* (fs)	*Nisbah* (md)	*Nisbah* (ms)
مِصْرِيَتان	مِصْرِيَة	مِصْرِيّان	مِصْرِيّ
لُبْنانِيَتان	لُبْنانِيَة	لُبْنانِيّان	لُبْنانِيّ
تُونُسِيَتان	تُونُسِيَّ	تُونُسِيّان	تُونُسِيّ
مَغْرِبِيَتان	مَغْرِبِيَة	مَغْرِبِيّان	مَغْرِبِيّ
صينِيَتان	صينِيَة	صينِيّان	صينِيّ
فَرَنْسِيَتان	فَرَنْسِيَة	فَرَنْسِيّان	فَرَنْسِيّ
بريطانِيَتان	بريطانِيَة	بريطانِيّان	بريطانِيّ

Remember two important rules: (1) retain the *tā'* in the feminine dual forms, and (2) add ان to form a nominative dual nouns and ين for genitive or accusative ones.

Now, consider these examples for the plural forms of the *nisbah*:

Nisbah (fp)	*Nisbah* (mp)	*Nisbah* (ms)
إسْرائيلِيَّات	إسْرائيلِيّون	إسْرائيلِيّ
فَلَسْطينِيَّات	فَلَسْطينِيّون	فَلَسْطينِيّ
شَمالِيَّات	شَمالِيّون	شَمالِيّ
يابانِيَّات	يابانِيّون	يابانِيّ
قاهِرِيَّات	قاهِرِيّون	قاهِرِيّ
دِمَشْقِيَّات	دِمَشْقِيّون	دِمَشْقِيّ
بَغْدادِيَّات	بَغْدادِيّون	بَغْدادِيّ

Vocabulary

Portugal	البُرتُغال	Egypt	مِصْر
Greece	اليونان	Lebanon	لُبْنان
Denmark	الدِّنْمارْك	Israel	إسْرائيل
Japan	اليابان	Palestine	فَلَسْطين
China	الصين	Tunisia	تونِس
America	أمْريكا	Andalusia	الأنْدَلُس
France	فَرَنْسا	Morocco	المَغْرِب
Syria	سوريا	Algeria	الجَزائِر
Turkey	تُرْكيا	Sudan	السودان
Britain	بريطانيا	Jordan	الأُرْدُن
Australia	أُستِراليا	Senegal	السِّنِغال
Iraq	العِراق	Sweden	السَّويد
north	شَمال	Cairo	القاهِرة
south	جَنوب	school	مَدْرَسَة
east	شَرْق	university	جامِعَة
west	غَرب	Sunna	سُنَّة
white (ms)	أبْيَض	Shiite	شيعَة
red (ms)	أحْمَر	red (fs)	حَمْراء
green (fs)	خَضْراء	Fatima	فاطِمَة
blue (fs)	زَرْقاء	white	بَيْضاء
yellow (fs)	صَفْراء	black	سَوْداء
desert	صَحَراء	gown, dress	رِداء
virgin	عَذْراء	space	فَضاء
air	هَواء	sky, heaven	سَماء
		robe, clothes	كِساء

Lesson Ten

Exercises

Exercise 10.1

The following are Arabic famous names. Create the *nisbah* of each name (both ms and fs).

1. فاطِمَة
2. خَالِد
3. إِبْراهيم
4. عائِشَة
5. مُحَمَّد
6. يَسوع
7. المَسيح
8. مَرْيَم
9. عُمَر
10. داود
11. سَعْد
12. حُسين

Exercise 10.2

Translate into English. Make sure you clarify the gender and number of the *nisbah* adjectives.

1. نَحْنُ فَرَنْسِيّان وهو إِسْرائيليّ.
2. أنا في المَنْزِلِ مع العِراقيّة والمَغْرِبيّ.

3. هو أُرْدُنِيّ وهُما سوريّتان.

4. هذا لُبْنانيّ وهَؤُلاء أميركيّون.

Exercise 10.3

Translate into Arabic.

1. This (m) is Egyptian.

2. He is Egyptian, and she is Syrian.

3. These are (fd) good teachers.

4. She is white American, and her husband is Lebanese.

5. You (fd) are Tunisians.

6. They (fp) are Israelis.

Lesson Eleven
أَحَدَ عَشَرَ

Possessive Pronouns (ضَمائِرُ المُلْكِيّة)

Arabic-speaking people indicate possession in various ways, one of which is by attaching suffixes to nouns. These suffixes are called ضَمائِرُ المُلْكِيّة. They are ضَمائِر (pronouns), indicating مُلْكِيّة (possession).

In English we say "my pen" to state that a pen belongs to me. In Arabic, we can accomplish this by adding the suffix ي to the noun قَلَمٌ. The result is قَلَمـي, meaning "my pen." Notice that the noun قَلَمٌ by itself is indefinite, which is the reason it has *tanwīn*. However, when we add the possessive pronoun suffix ـي, the resulting noun قَلَمـي becomes definite. Thus, adding possessive pronouns to nouns is one more way to indicate noun definiteness.

Here is the complete list of ضَمائِرُ المُلْكِيّة, using the noun قَلَم:

Examples	Translation of Pronoun	Possessive Pronoun Suffix	
قَلَمـي	my	ـي	مُفرَد Singular
قَلَمُـكَ	your (m)	ـكَ	
قَلَمُـكِ	your (f)	ـكِ	
قَلَمُـهُ	his	ـهُ	
قَلَمُـها	her	ـها	
قَلَمُـنا	our (m/f)	ـنا	مُثَنّى Dual
قَلَمُـكُما	your (m/f)	ـكُما	
قَلَمُـهُما	their (m/f)	ـهُما	

	نا	our (m/f)	قَلَمُنا
	كُم	your (m)	قَلَمُكُم
جَمع Plural	كُنَّ	your (f)	قَلَمُكُنَّ
	هُم	their (m)	قَلَمُهُم
	هُنَّ	their (f)	قَلَمُهُنَّ

The attached suffixes indicate who possesses the noun.

When a noun ends with a *tā' marbūṭah* (ة or ـة), we change it to regular *tā'* (ت) before we add the possessive pronoun suffix. See these examples:

Translation	Possessive Noun	Translation	Singular Noun
her (fs) ship	سَفينَتُها	a ship	سَفينَة
our sentence	جُمْلَتُنا	a sentence	جُمْلَة
your (d) gift	هَديَّتُكُما	a gift	هَديَّة
their (fp) rose	وَرْدَتُهُنَّ	a rose	وَرْدَة
your (mp) flower	زَهْرَتُكُم	a flower	زَهْرَة

Note that in this table all possessive nouns are treated as if they were in the nominative case, i.e., the noun ends with a *ḍammah* before adding the possessive pronoun suffix.

Here are some more examples:

Translation	Possessive Noun	Translation	Singular Noun
my child	طِفْلي	child	طِفْل
your (fs) children	أَطْفالُكِ	children	أَطْفال
my bed	سَريري	bed	سَرير
his book	كِتابُهُ	book	كِتاب

Lesson Eleven

Translation	Possessive Noun	Translation	Singular Noun
her books	كُتُبُها	books	كُتُب
their (fp) boat	قارِبُهُنَّ	boat	قارِب
his uncle	خالُهُ	uncle (mother's side)	خال
our uncle	عَمُّنا	uncle (father's side)	عَم
your (sm) mother	أُمُّكَ	mother	أُم
my love	حُبِّي	love	حُب
your (fs) kindness	لُطْفُكِ	kindness	لُطْف
his desk	مَكْتَبُهُ	desk	مَكْتَب
your (ms) article	مَقالَتُكَ	article	مَقالة
your (d) window	نافِذتُكُما	window	نافِذة
our window	شُبّاكُنا	window	شُبّاك
your (mp) windows	شَبابيكُكُم	windows	شَبابيك
your (fp) newspaper	جَريدَتُكُنَّ	newspaper	جَريدة
your (fs) car	سَيّارَتُكِ	car	سَيّارة
their (mp) bicycle	دَرّاجَتُهُم	bicycle	دَرّاجة
my earphone	سَمّاعَتي	earphone	سَمّاعة
our sign	إشارَتُنا	sign	إشارة
your (fs) signal	إشارَتُكِ	signal	إشارة

There are a few matters to note regarding this list.

First, every possessive pronoun suffix begins with a consonant (ـكَ، ـكِ، هُ، ها، نـا، كُما، هُما، نـا، كُم، كُنَّ، هُم، هُنَّ), except the first one (ي-), which is a long vowel.

Second, when you add a possessive pronoun suffix to a noun, the noun will inflect. However, the first possessive pronoun suffix in the list ي- prevents this, because the long vowel is strong and will force the last letter in the noun to receive a *kasrah*. Do not confuse the possessive suffix ي- with the *nisbah* ending, which must include a *shaddah* ـيّ.

Third, the suffixes هُ، هُما، هُم، هُنَّ all begin with a *hā'-ḍammah*. When these suffixes connect to a noun ending with a ي- (*yā'*) or *kasrah* (due to the genitive case), the *ḍammah* changes into a *kasrah*.

For instance, consider the noun سَيّارَةٌ. The *tanwīn* indicates it is indefinite. To say "his car," you write سَيّارَتُهُ, which is now definite. The form سَيّارَتُهُ is in the nominative case, such as the one used as the subject of a nominal sentence: سَيّارَتُهُ جَدِيدَة (his car [is] new). Notice the possessive suffix kept its form ـهُ, i.e., the *ḍammah* does not change. However, when we want to use the same possessive noun سَيّارَتُهُ in a sentence like "he [is] in his car," we write هو في سَيّارَتِهِ. The possessive noun "his car" is in the genitive case due to the preposition في. Here, the possessive suffix, which is normally ـهُ, must undergo a change. We change the *ḍammah* into a *kasrah*, because the noun itself ends with a *kasrah*. Thus سَيّارَتُهُ becomes سَيّارَتِهِ.

Study the following examples to distinguish how the case of a noun can change the form of a possessive suffix:

هذه إِشارَتُـنـا

مع إِشارَتِـنـا

قارِبُـهُنَّ كَبيرٌ

على قارِبِـهِنَّ

دَرّاجَتُـهُم سَريعَةٌ

في دَرّاجَتِـهِم

كُتُبُـها كَثيرَةٌ

مِن كُتُبِـها

Fourth, indefinite nouns become definite once they receive the possessive suffixes. Thus, while بَيتٌ is indefinite, بَيتُها and بَيتُهُ are definite. This becomes very important when we use modifying adjectives with possessive nouns. Since adjectives follow the noun they modify in definiteness, adjectives modifying بَيتٌ should be indefinite, while those modifying بَيتُها and بَيتُهُ must be definite. Study these examples:

an old house	بيتٌ قديمٌ
his old house	بيتُهُ القديمُ
a fast donkey	حمارٌ سريعٌ
her fast donkey	حمارُها السريعُ
a smart student	طالبٌ ذكيٌّ
our smart student	طالبُنا الذكيُ
a new school	مَدْرَسَةٌ جديدةٌ
your (ms) new school	مَدْرَسَتُكَ الجديدةُ
a new teacher (f)	مُدَرِّسَةٌ جديدةٌ
your (ms) new teacher (f)	مُدَرِّسَتُكَ الجديدةُ
an excellent teacher (m)	مُدَرِّسٌ مُمْتازٌ
your (fs) excellent teacher (m)	مُدَرِّسُكِ المُمْتازُ

You will notice in the table that adjectives modifying a definite noun are definite, too. We make adjectives definite by using the definite article.

Consider the last example in the table: مُدَرِّسُكِ المُمْتازُ, which translates as "Your (fs) excellent teacher (m)." The word المُمْتازُ is an adjective. Now, consider a slightly different phrase مُدَرِّسُكِ مُمْتازٌ. The translation becomes "Your (fs) teacher (m) is excellent." In this case مُمْتازٌ is the predicate, while مُدَرِّسُكِ is the subject of a nominal sentence.

It is important to remember the difference between الـمَـنْـزِلُ الكَبيرُ and الـمَـنْـزِلُ كَبيرٌ. The phrase الـمَـنْـزِلُ كَبيرٌ is translated as "the house is big," while الـمَـنْـزِلُ الكَبيرُ is translated as "the big house." Also, remember the difference between هَذا الرَجُلُ طَويلٌ (this man is tall) and هَذا رَجُلٌ طَويلٌ (this is a tall man). The noun الرَجُلُ is in apposition to هَذا in the first sentence, while رَجُلٌ is the predicate of هَذا in the second.

Examine some more examples with possessive nouns:

a new teacher	مُعَلِّمٌ جَديدٌ
your (ms) new teacher (m)	مُعَلِّمُكَ الجَديدُ
your (ms) teacher (m) is new	مُعَلِّمُكَ جَديدٌ
an old street	شارِعٌ قَديمٌ
our old street	شارِعُنا القَديمُ
our street is old	شارِعُنا قَديمٌ
a short shirt	قَميصٌ قَصيرٌ
his short shirt	قَميصُهُ القَصيرُ
his shirt is short	قَميصُهُ قَصيرٌ
a beautiful face	وَجْهٌ جَميلٌ
her beautiful face	وَجْهُها الجَميلُ
her face is beautiful	وَجْهُها جَميلٌ
a clean desk (or office)	مَكْتَبٌ نَظيفٌ
your (d) clean desk	مَكْتَبُكُما النَظيفُ
your (d) desk is clean	مَكْتَبُكُما نَظيفٌ
a dirty room	غُرْفَةٌ قَذِرَةٌ

Lesson Eleven

their (mp) dirty room	غُرْفَتُهُمُ القَذِرَةُ
their (mp) room is dirty	غُرْفَتُهُمْ قَذِرَةٌ
a good dog	كَلْبٌ طَيِّبٌ
their (fp) good dog (m)	كَلْبُهُنَّ الطَّيِّبُ
their (fp) dog (m) is good	كَلْبُهُنَّ طَيِّبٌ
a hard test (or trial, or exam)	امْتِحانٌ صَعْبٌ
their (d) hard test	امْتِحانُهُما الصَّعْبُ
their (d) test is hard	امْتِحانُهُما صَعْبٌ

The *Iḍāfah* Construct

In Lesson Five we explained that the basic elements of Arabic speech are nouns, verbs, and particles. We also studied the two major types of sentences: nominal and verbal. The nominal sentence consists mainly of a subject and predicate, while the verbal includes a verb and its subject. Subjects, predicates, and verbs are the primary parts of any given sentence. In addition to these primary parts, sentences also include secondary elements which clarify, confirm, and describe.

One of these secondary elements is known as the مُضاف إليه (*muḍāf ilayhi*), which is part of an important Arabic structure called the إضافة (*iḍāfah*) construct. Like possessive pronouns, the إضافة is another way to describe possession in Arabic.

Consider the following English phrases: David's car, Sarah's book, and Jack's phone. In Arabic we use the إضافة (*iḍāfah*) construct to render these phrases.

The إضافة construct consists of two consecutive parts: مُضاف (*muḍāf*) and مُضاف إليه (*muḍāf ilayhi*). Both must be nouns. The مُضاف is a governing word, and the مُضاف إليه is a governed word. The two words (مُضاف and مُضاف إليه) must be consecutive with no separation between them in order for the إضافة construct to be valid.

In the إضافة construct the first part (the مُضاف) can be in any case, while the second part (the مُضاف إليه) is always مَجْرور (genitive).

The إضافة construct is often used to create human names. These names consist of two words: the first is a nominative subject governing the second, which is in the genitive. For example, a male name is Abdullah. His name is written as عَبْدُ اللهِ. This name means "the servant of God." The word عَبْدُ is the مُضاف and in the nominative, while اللهِ is the genitive مُضاف إليه. Similarly, a woman is called أُمُّ قِرْفَةِ. The name means "the mother of *qirfah*," where أُمُّ is the nominative مُضاف and قِرْفَةِ is the genitive مُضاف إليه. Moreover, أَبُو الهَوْلِ means "the father of *al-hawl* (fear, terror)," which is the Sphinx, where أَبُو is the مُضاف and الهَوْلِ is the مُضاف إليه. Arabic-speakers use أُمُّ and أَبُو to refer to parents, connecting them with their children, especially their firstborns. In Arabic, Adam is named as أَبُو البَشَرِ (the father of humans).

In addition to names, the إضافة construct is used to describe ownership and possession. This appears in the following examples:

مُضاف إليه	مُضاف	Translation	*Iḍāfah* Construct
الممثلِ	بيتُ	the actor's house (the house of the actor)	بيتُ المُمَثِّلِ
ممثلٍ	بيتُ	actor's house	بيتُ مُمَثِّلٍ
المُهَندِسِ	سَيّارةُ	the engineer's car	سَيّارةُ المُهَندِسِ
الطَبيبِ	سَماعةُ	the doctor's stethoscope	سَماعةُ الطَبيبِ
الجامِعةِ	أستاذُ	professor of the university	أستاذُ الجامِعةِ
جامعةٍ	أستاذُ	professor of a university	أستاذُ جامعةٍ
المَدرَسةِ	مُدَرِّسةُ	teacher (f) of the school	مُدَرِّسةُ المَدرَسةِ
الشُرْطَةِ	رَجُلُ	man of the police (policeman)	رَجُلُ الشُرْطَةِ
المَسْجِدِ	إمامُ	imam of the mosque	إمامُ المَسْجِدِ
الكَنيسةِ	خادِمُ	minister of the church	خادِمُ الكَنيسةِ
الكَنيسةِ	كاهِنُ	priest of the church	كاهِنُ الكَنيسةِ

There are important observations to make regarding this table.

First, in all these examples the first noun (the مُضاف) is nominative, while the second (the مُضاف إليه) is genitive. However, you should note that while the مُضاف إليه is always genitive, the مُضاف can be in any case, depending on its role in the sentence. Consider the first example in the table above: بيتُ المُمَثِّلِ.

Lesson Eleven

Let's use this construct in two sentences to show the difference:

The actor's house is beautiful.	بيتُ المُمَثِّلِ جَميلٌ.
I am now at the actor's house.	أنا الآن في بيتِ المُمَثِّلِ.

While the noun بيت serves in both phrases as the مُضاف, it is inflected differently. It is بيتُ in the first example and بيتِ in the second. This is because in the first example it is in the nominative case as the subject of the phrase, while in the second it is the object of preposition في and thus in the genitive.

Second, the إضافة construct is a secondary part in a nominal or verbal sentence. In all previous examples the إضافة construct consisted of two nouns, but in some cases it can have more than two. Consider the إضافة construct: سَيّارَةُ مُدَرِّسِ الجامِعَةِ. This phrase means "the car of the teacher of the university." This إضافة construct includes three parts. In this case, all terms other than the first term are in the genitive case. In other words, in the إضافة construct the first noun (the مُضاف) can be in any case depending on its role as a noun in the sentence, while all other terms (forming the مُضاف إليه) must be in the genitive case.

Third, in the إضافة construct the first noun (the مُضاف) never receives an *alif-lām* (except in very advanced cases). As a general rule, although the construct will be definite, the first term (the مُضاف) does not take the definite article. Thus, one way to spot the إضافة construct is to locate two (or more) consecutive nouns in a sentence, with the first having no definite article.

Fourth, in the إضافة construct the مُضاف إليه receives *tanwīn kasrah* if indefinite. Compare أستاذُ الجامِعَةِ to أستاذُ جامعةٍ. This leads us to state three important roles regarding the إضافة construct in its relation to *tanwīn*: (1) the first term of the construct (the مُضاف) cannot be in *tanwīn* at all; (2) the second term of the construct (the مُضاف إليه) takes *tanwīn kasrah* if it is indefinite; (3) if the مُضاف إليه consists of more than one noun, the *tanwīn* goes only with the last noun if—and only if—it is indefinite.

Fifth, the إضافة construct is concerned only with nouns, not verbs or particles. This means verbs and particles cannot be مُضاف or مُضاف إليه.

Sixth, in all previous examples singular nouns have served as مُضاف إليه, and they were genitive. A singular مُضاف إليه only receives a *kasrah* (or *tanwīn kasrah*) to indicate it is مَجْرور (genitive). However, a dual noun or a masculine plural noun becomes مَجْرور by using a *yā'* to create the genitive case: مُعَلِّمون becomes مُعَلِّمين, while كَلْبان becomes كَلْبين.

Finally, you recall that in Lesson Eight we explained Arabic cardinal numbers. Remember that numbers three through ten disagree in gender with the noun they modify. These numbers come *before* the noun they modify, and the modified noun is always in the genitive case. This is another case of the إضافة construct, where the cardinal number is مُضاف and the noun is مُضاف إليه.

See the following examples:

ثَلاثُ مُدَرِّساتٍ

أَرْبَعُ سيداتٍ

أَرْبَعَةُ طُلّابٍ

تِسْعُ سَيّاراتٍ

سَبْعَةُ مُدَرِّسينَ

عَشْرَةُ مُهَنْدِسينَ

These phrases are إضافة constructs. Each one consists of a cardinal number (anywhere from three through ten) followed by a noun. The number modifies the noun, and they disagree in gender. In these phrases, the cardinal numbers serve as مُضاف, while the nouns serve as مُضاف إليه. The numbers are all in the nominative case, while the nouns are in the genitive. For the genitive case, feminine and broken plural use *tanwīn kasrah*, while masculine plural take ينَ.

Interrogative Particles (حُروفُ الاسْتِفْهام)

Arabic has many interrogative particles. They are called حُروفُ الاسْتِفْهام (*ḥurūf al-istifhām*). All of them are indeclinable—they do not change their ending.

Here are the most common particles and their meanings:

Interrogative Particles	حُروفُ الاسْتِفْهام
when	مَتَى
where	أَيْنَ
how	كَيْفَ
what	مَا / مَاذا

Lesson Eleven

why, for what	لِمَاذا
who	مَنْ
do, is (questions)	هَلْ
how many/much	كَمْ
which of	أَيّ

Consider these examples of how to use the interrogative particles:

Translation	Interrogative Phrase
When did the husband come?	مَتى جاءَ الزَّوجُ؟
When do you (ms) go to the theater?	مَتى تَذْهَبُ إلى المَسْرَحِ؟
Where is my father?	أَيْنَ والِدي؟
Where is the professor (m)?	أَيْنَ الأُسْتاذُ؟
How are you (m)?	كَيْفَ حالُكَ؟
How do you (m) go to church?	كَيْفَ تَذْهَبُ إلى الكَنيسَةِ؟
What is your (m) name?	ما اسْمُكَ؟
What is your (f) name?	ما اسْمُكِ؟
What do you (ms) like/love?	ماذا تُحِبُّ؟
What do you (ms) prefer?	ماذا تُفَضِّلُ؟
Why do you (ms) go to the market?	لِمَاذا تَذْهَبُ إلى المَتْجَرِ؟
Why do you (ms) go to church?	لِمَاذا تَذْهَبُ إلى الكَنيسَةِ؟
Who is your (ms) teacher?	مَنْ مُعَلِّمُكَ؟
Who is your (ms) sister?	مَنْ أُخْتُكَ؟
Who is your (fs) husband?	مَنْ زَوجُكِ؟
Who is your (ms) wife?	مَنْ زَوجَتُكَ؟
Are you Ibrahim?	هَلْ أَنْتَ إبراهيمُ؟

Are you Sarah?	هَلْ أَنْتِ سارَةُ؟
Do you like bananas?	هَلْ تُحِبُّ المَوْزِ؟
What is your (ms) age (i.e., how old are you)?	كَمْ عُمْرُكَ؟
How old is she?	كَمْ عُمْرُها؟
Which meal do you (ms) like?	أَيَّ وَجْبَةٍ تُحِبُّ؟
Which pen do you (ms) prefer?	أَيَّ قَلَمٍ تُفَضِّلُ؟

It should be noted that مَنْ always asks about humans, and ما and ماذا asks about things. The particle أيّ asks about the noun immediately following it.

Vocabulary

This vocabulary list includes new nouns, in addition to some basic verbs. These verbs are introduced here so that students can familiarize themselves with their basic forms in preparation for the forthcoming lessons.

pen	قَلَم	ship	سَفينَة
the doctor's stethoscope	سَماعَةُ الطَبيبِ	sentence	جُمْلَة
man of the police (policeman)	رَجُلُ الشُرْطَةِ	gift	هَدِيَّة
imam of the mosque	إمامُ المَسْجِدِ	rose	وَرْدَة
minister of the church	خادِمُ الكَنيسَةِ	flower	زَهْرَة
priest of the church	كاهِنُ الكَنيسَةِ	child	طِفْل
when	مَتَى	children	أَطْفال
where	أَيْنَ	bed	سَرير
how	كَيْفَ	book	كِتاب
what	ماذا	books	كُتُب

Lesson Eleven

why, for what	لِما / لِمَاذا	boat	قارِب
who	مَنْ	uncle (mother's side)	خال
do, is (questions)	هَلْ	uncle (father's side)	عَمّ
how many/much	كَمْ	mother	أُمّ
which of	أيّ	love	حُبّ
he created	خَلَقَ	kindness	لُطْف
he wrote	كَتَبَ	desk, office	مَكْتَب
he sat, sat down	جَلَسَ	article	مَقالَة
he exited	خَرَجَ	window	نافِذة
he entered	دَخَلَ	window	شُبّاك
he opened	فَتَحَ	windows	شَبابيك
he closed	غَلَقَ	newspaper	جَريدة
he hit	ضَرَبَ	car	سَيّارَة
he made	صَنَعَ	bicycle	دَرّاجَة
he bowed	سَجَدَ	earphone	سَمّاعَة
he kneeled	رَكَعَ	sign	إشارَة
he worshiped	عَبَدَ	signal	إشارَة
he succeeded	نَجَحَ	story	قِصّة
he washed	غَسَلَ	problem	مُشْكِلَة
he thanked	شَكَرَ	bathroom	حَمّام
theater	مَسْرَح	library	مَكْتَبَة
bananas	مَوْز	a sheet of paper	وَرَقَة
your name (m/f)	اسمُكَ/اسمُكِ	a page	صَفْحَة
your (m) sister	أُخْتُكَ	an hour, a clock	ساعَة

your (m) age	عُمْرُكَ	question	سُؤال
her age	عُمْرُها	radio	راديو
I have…	أنا عِنْدي	light	نور
I am thirsty	أنا عَطْشان	darkness	ظَلام / ظُلْمَة
I am hungry	أنا جَوعان	I am happy	أنا سَعيد

Exercises

Exercise 11.1

Write the following in Arabic.

1. my flower

2. her rose

3. an old pen

4. his old pen

5. his pen is old

6. a beautiful shirt

7. her beautiful shirt

8. her shirt is beautiful

9. a clean office

10. the clean office

11. your (md) office is clean

12. seven engineers (m) and four artists (f) are in her house

Exercise 11.2

Translate the following into English.

1. رَجُلٌ طَيِّبٌ.

2. رَجُلُهَا الطَّيِّبُ...

3. رَجُلُهَا طَيِّبٌ.

4. امْتِحَانُهُما الصَّعْبُ...

5. امْتِحَانٌ صَعْبٌ في المَدْرَسَةِ.

6. امْتِحَانُهُما صَعْبٌ مع أرْبَعِ مُدَرِّساتٍ.

Exercise 11.3

In the following, each phrase is inaccurate. Locate the mistake(s) and fix it.

1. بيتٌ المُمَثِّلِ جَميلٌ.

2. بيتُ المُمَثِّلٍ جَميلٌ.

3. أنا الآن في بيتُ المُمَثِّلِ.

4. أنا مع المُدَرِّسِ في سَيّارةِ المُهَندِسُ.

5. سَمّاعَةُ الطبيبِ.

6. هو أُستاذُ الجامِعَةِ.

7. مع أُستاذِ جامعةِ.

8. هذا رَجُلُ الشُرطَةِ.

9. هذا إمامُ المَسْجِدِ مع خادِمُ الكَنيسَةِ.

10. كاهِنُ الكَنيسَةِ في سَفينتِهِ.

11. أنا مع ثَلاثُ مُدَرِّساتٍ وأرْبَعةِ طُلّابٍ.

12. هنا أرْبَعةُ سيداتٍ.

13. تِسْعَةُ سَيّاراتٍ.

14. في الفَصْلِ، سَبْعُ مُدَرِّسينَ وعَشرُ مُهَندِسينَ.

*A bonus exercise for advanced students: After you fix the phrases, translate them.

Lesson Eleven

Exercise 11.4

Translate the following sentences into Arabic.

1. Where is your (d) house?

2. Where is your (ms) teacher (m)?

3. How are you (fd)?

4. What is your (ms) name?

5. What is your (fs) name?

6. Who is your (ms) mother?

7. Who is your (fs) sister?

8. Are you Fatima? I am Ibrahim.

9. Who [is] in your (mp) ship?

10. Which sentence do you (ms) prefer? And why?

Lesson Twelve
اِثْنَا عَشَرَ

Introduction to Arabic Verbs (الأفعال)

As previously explained in Lesson Four, a verb is called فِعْل. It refers to an action performed in a specific time. Here we will spend adequate time and effort to study the Arabic verb system, which is the heart of the language. We will begin with the heart of any verb: its root.

Verb Roots

Every verb has a root. The root refers to the most basic letters which appear in most of the verb's inflections (conjugations) or forms. These basic letters—usually called radicals—form the verb's most indeclinable form.

A root is called جَذْر in Arabic. We speak of جَذْرُ الشَّجَرَةِ (the root of the tree), which is the source of all branches. In verbs, the root of the verb is called جَذْرُ الفِعْلِ. The concept of جَذْرُ الفِعْلِ in Arabic is different than its English equivalent. However, consider an example in English to familiarize yourself with the concept of جَذْرُ الفِعْلِ.

Think of these words: "walk," "walked," and "walking." Notice that there are letters which appear in all three words. In English the verb root refers to its base form, which is the form listed in the dictionary. It is the form which does not include any ending, such as the infinitive form without the "to" before it.

Now consider these Arabic words: ذَهَبَ، أَذْهَبُ، سَأَذهَبُ. These are different words, but there are letters which appear in all of them: ذ.هـ.ب. These letters form جَذْرُ الفِعْلِ (the verb root). The three radical letters of these words are ذ.هـ.ب.

Now, consider the following table as we focus on the meaning of these different words, and others:

Translation	Verb
he went	ذَهَبَ
I go	أَذْهَبُ
I will go	سَأَذهَبُ

خَلَقَ	he created
خَلَقْنا	we created
خَلَقْتُما	you (d) created
خَلَقْتُم	you (mp) created
دَرَسَ	he studied
تَدْرُسُ	you (ms) study
تَدْرُسينَ	you (fs) study

Examine these words, compare each group of words, and attempt to pronounce them. There are several important points to notice in this table.

First, the words ذَهَبَ، أَذْهَبُ، سَأَذْهَبُ not only share the basic letters ذ.هـ.ب in this *very* sequence, but their meanings also relate to the act of "going" or verb "to go." We say that these three words share the verb root ذ.هـ.ب. This جَذْرُ carries the notion of "going." Similarly, the four words خَلَقَ، خَلَقْنا، خَلَقْتُما، خَلَقْتُم all share the same root خ.ل.ق. This جَذْرُ carries the notion of the act of creating, from which stems all the different forms of the verb "to create." Thus, we say that خ.ل.ق is the جَذْرُ of these four words, which means that خ.ل.ق is the source of these words and it establishes the various forms of the verb "to create." While the four words are past tense, we should expect that present and future tense forms will also include the same letters خ.ل.ق in addition to prefixes or suffixes.

The same goes for the verbs of the last group in the table. The verbs دَرَسَ، تَدْرُسُ، تَدْرُسينَ share similar basic letters د.ر.س. This is the جَذْرُ of the three verbs (conjugations). It is also the جَذْرُ of all other verb forms that convey the meaning "to study." Notice that the first word دَرَسَ is past tense while the last two تَدْرُسُ and تَدْرُسينَ are present. The prefixes and suffixes are added to indicate a change of person, but all of the verbs convey an act of "studying." We say that the root د.ر.س illustrates the notion of studying.

Second, the sequence of letters in the جَذْرُ is very important. The root د.ر.س is completely different from س.ر.د. While they include the same letters, their sequence is not the same, and thus the meanings are different. The verb دَرَسَ means "he studied," while سَرَدَ means "he narrated." The same is true for the verbs حَلَفَ and لَفَحَ. They use the same letters, but their roots are different. The former means "he swore," while the second means "he hit." The جَذْرُ of the former is ح.ل.ف, while that of the latter is ح.ف.ل. This highlights that we should be very careful because the sequence of any given جَذْرُ is crucial.

Third, the conjugation of a verb indicates its subject. In other words, the subject is implied from the way the verb is formed. This will be explained shortly when we examine the verb paradigms. For now, it is sufficient to say that we do not need to see a فاعِل (subject) of the following verbs خَلَقَ، خَلَقْنا، خَلَقْتُما، خَلَقْتُم in order to discern each of their subjects. The conjugation خَلَقَ—as we will discuss in the next lesson—is for third person, singular, and masculine in the past simple tense. The conjugation خَلَقْتُما tells the reader that the subject is "you," second person, dual, masculine or feminine, and the verb is also past simple tense.

Fourth, the number of root letters in the previous examples can be misleading: It may give you the impression that all Arabic verbs derive from a three-letter root, which is incorrect. Arabic verbs can have more than three root letters (or three radical letters). Indeed, the most common are triliterals (three root letters), although quadriliterals (four root letters) do exist. We call a triliteral verb الفِعْلُ الثُلاثي and a quadriliteral الفِعْلُ الرُباعي. In this introductory book, we will focus only on verbs which have a three-letter (triliteral) root, i.e., three radical letters.

Fifth, each root serves as the foundation of various verb forms or patterns, which are created by adding, dropping, or changing letters, including suffixes or prefixes. While we will study verb forms in the next lesson, for now it suffices to mention just one example. The root د.ر.س can form all of the following verbs (and more):

دَرَسَ

دَرَّسَ

اندرسَ

استَدْرَسَ

أَسْتَدْرِسُ

اِسْتَدْرِسُنَّ

تُسْتَدْرَسِي

أَدْرُسْ

دُرِسَ

Each of the above verbs has a distinct meaning. While the root of these verbs is the same, the forms and meanings differ, although all of the meanings relate to the act of "studying," which is what the جَذْرُ denotes. The different forms are created by adding letters, including doubling consonants as in the case of adding a شَدَّة. The forms we established carry additional, deeper, and advanced meanings related to studying. Thus, the جَذْرُ carries the main, basic, and core indication of a verb, while the forms advance various modifications of this initial indication.

Sixth, not only verbs but also nouns have roots. In this case, we are talking about declinable nouns. While pronouns are basically nouns, they are indeclinable and do not have roots in the way we are discussing here. Each declinable noun has a جَذْرُ. For example, consider the root د.ر.س. It can form many nouns, including دارِس، مُدَرِّس، دِراسَة. All of these nouns relate to "studying," which is what this جَذْرُ conveys. The point here is not about memorizing words but rather recognizing their different patterns and shared root.

A final stylistic remark is this: Arabic speakers call the root جَذْر or جِذْر. We prefer جَذْرُ and will use it throughout. The plural of جَذْرُ is جُذُور.

Al-Awzān (الأَوْزان)

Before we begin our study of the verb tenses and paradigms, there is a unique Arabic feature which will help tremendously when we proceed with verb forms and tenses. It is called الأَوْزان (*al-awzān*).

At the outset, this lesson is not about the meaning of Arabic words but about discerning patterns and distinguishing between forms. Do not occupy yourself with a word's meaning but rather with its form and shape. In the next lesson, we will study the meanings and conjugations of verbs.

The word أَوْزان (*awzān*) literally means "weights." Its singular form is وَزْن (*wazn*). In Arabic every word has a وَزْن (weight). This means that a word can be weighed against another fixed pattern.

We have many fixed Arabic أَوْزان. To understand أَوْزان, think of the old-fashioned scales where you place metal weights on one side and fruits or vegetables on the other to weigh your groceries. These metal weights are the أَوْزان—they are the standard weights used on a scale to weigh Arabic words. These أَوْزان are fixed templates, which we use to weigh—measure or compare—all verbs and declinable nouns.

Theoretically, every word consists of a جَذْر plus additional letters. Classical Arabs created and memorized standard أَوْزان to weigh every word against these fixed patterns. These أَوْزان serve in identifying the root and additional letters of a given word.

For instance, when encountering a new word you have never seen before, you should try to compare it (or weigh it) against the standard أَوْزان. This will enable you to identify the root and the additional letters, and you will be able to determine its forms and possible changes.

So, how do these standard أَوْزان operate? What is the وَزْن of any Arabic word?

As mentioned earlier, a word in Arabic may have a جَذْر of three or four letters (or, in some rare cases, more). However, the three-letter جَذْر is the most common. Realizing this fact, Arab linguists established the أَوْزان based on the three-letter جَذْر form. Specifically, they used the root letters ف.ع.ل as the basic letters against which every word should be weighed. Thus, the letters ف.ع.ل are the standard letters for the وَزْن of every word. But why?

These letters correspond to the verb فَعَلَ, which means "he did." In Arabic, the most basic verb form—as we will study shortly—is that of the past simple tense of the third-person singular masculine (هو). This basic form has only the جَذْر plus short vowels. In Arabic there is not an infinitive form of the verb, but instead the third-person masculine singular—in the past tense—is used as the most basic conjugation. For instance, consider the verb "to write" in Arabic. Unlike in English, the basic form in Arabic is not the infinitive but the past simple tense of the form associated with هوَ. The جَذْرُ of "to write" is triliteral ك.ت.ب. When we say هوَ كَتَبَ, which means "he wrote," we are using the most basic form of the verb كَتَبَ, which is basically the جَذْر plus three short vowels. The same is true for هوَ دَرَسَ, which means "he studied," and هوَ فَعَلَ, meaning "he did." In these three examples, we are using the most basic form of the verbs.

Consider also the fact that the Arabic word for an act or action is فِعْل, while the verb "to do" is فَعَلَ (i.e., "he did"). In comparing these two words, Arab linguists realized that their core is the three letters ف.ع.ل. Thus, they used these as the base letters of the أَوْزان of Arabic words. Each Arabic word is referenced in one way or another to these three letters. These letters serve as the scale upon which we weigh all words. They are the standard letters. Some examples will clarify.

We say that دَرَسَ (he studied) is "on the scale of" فَعَلَ, while شَرِبَ (he drank) is "on the scale of" فَعِلَ. The phrase "on the scale of" in Arabic is عَلَى وَزْن (ᶜalā wazn). Therefore, we compared both verbs دَرَسَ and شَرِبَ to the letters ف.ع.ل and used the same vowels of each verb to form its *wazn*. Of course, the *wazn* of فَعَلَ is different from فَعِلَ.

Lesson Twelve

Consider another example: We say that the word دَرَّس is ᶜalā wazn فَعَّل, and the word دارَس is ᶜalā wazn فاعِل. Notice that when we added the *shaddah*, it was added on the وَزْن, and when we added a letter, it was also added to the *wazn*. Similarly, we say that the word مَشْروب is ᶜalā wazn مَفْعول, while the word شارِب is ᶜalā wazn فاعِل.

The significance of this discussion lies in the fact that, once we figure out the وَزْن of a word, we can then determine not only its جَذْر but also its other possible forms, thus expanding the number of words stemming from the same جَذْر and creating more meanings. The جَذْر provides the basic meaning, but the various forms which rely on it advance more notions and depth.

For instance, once we encounter words like مَشْروب and شارِب and pronounce them, we—by practicing—can say that they are ᶜalā wazn مَفْعول and فاعِل, respectively. We can also determine the root of these two words by identifying the corresponding letters ف ع ل, which indicate the root. By comparison, we can state that the ف corresponds to ش, the ع to ر, and the ل to ب. Thus, the root of the words مَشْروب and شارِب is ش.ر.ب. Arabic speakers usually seek to determine الفاء والعَين واللّام, i.e., the ف ع ل of a word in order to discern its forms, conjugations, or declinations.

As mentioned earlier, in this lesson you should not be concerned with determining the meaning of every word (this will be done in the following chapters), but instead with patterns and shapes. Here we will focus on deducing the core letters and the additional letters.

The core letters are those of the جَذْر. The additional letters are letters added to the جَذْر to create more meanings. Principally, any additional letter must fall into one of the following ten letters:

س أ ل ت م و ن ي ه ا

Arab linguists combined the letters into a word to make it easy to remember: سألتمونيها. This means that, for instance, letters such as ق ف غ ع ظ ط ض ر ز ط د, among others, cannot be additional—they are always original. They are always from the root. We will revisit this in the next lesson, but for now, let us examine a few words in order to learn how to discern the *awzān*. This table will help you determine the *wazn* of various words, their جَذْر, thus identifying the original letters and the additional ones:

الكلمة	عَلى وَزْن	الجَذْر
زَرَعَ	فَعَلَ	ز.ر.ع
قَتَلَ	فَعَلَ	ق.ت.ل

س.ب.ح	فَعَلَ	سَبَحَ
س.ب.ح	إفْعال	إسْباح
س.ب.ح	فَعَّلَ	سَبَّحَ
س.ب.ح	تَفْعيلَة	تَسْبيحَة
ق.ط.ع	إفْعال	إقْطاع
ع.ل.م	فَعِلَ	عَلِمَ
م.د.د	فَعَلَ	مَدَّ
ش.د.د	فَعَلَ	شَدَّ
ع.د.د	فَعَلَ	عَدَّ
س.ب.ح	تَفاعيلُ	تَسابيحُ
ع.م.ل	فاعِل	عامِل
س.م.ع	فاعِل	سامِع
س.ج.د	فاعِل	ساجِد
ز.ر.ع	مَفْعول	مَزْروع
ح.ر.ث	مَفْعول	مَحْروث
س.م.ح	مَفْعول	مَسْموح

Vocabulary

In addition to the vocabulary list, we present here some common Arabic phrases related to the use of the name of God in daily expressions.

by Allah (oath)	واللهِ	root	جَذْر
God willing	إن شاءَ اللهُ	the tree root	جَذْرُ الشَّجَرَةِ
O my God!	ما شاءَ اللهُ	the verb root	جَذْرُ الفِعْلِ
I seek refuge in God!	أعوذُ باللهِ	he went	ذَهَبَ

Lesson Twelve

God forbid!	حاشا لله	I go	أَذْهَبُ
Thank God!	الحَمْدُ لله!	I will go	سَأَذْهَبُ
he studied	دَرَسَ	he created	خَلَقَ
you (ms) study	تَدْرُسُ	we created	خَلَقْنا
you (fs) study	تَدْرُسينَ	you (md/fd) created	خَلَقْتُما
		you (mp) created	خَلَقْتُمْ

Here is a short list of masculine and feminine human names. Be familiar with them.

Female names		Male names	
Maha	مَها	Khalid	خالِد
Nisrin	نِسرين	Umar	عُمَر
Hind	هِنْد	Bakr	بَكْر
Souad	سُعاد	Mustafa	مُصْطَفى
Nahid	ناهِد	Mahmoud	مَحْمود
Aisha	عائِشَة	Ali	عَلي
Fatima	فاطِمَة	Ahmad	أَحْمَد
Majida	ماجِدة	Yusuf	يوسُف
Nour	نور	Amir	أَمير
Zahra	زَهْرَة	Jamal	جَمال

Exercises

Exercise 12.1

This exercise aims to help students deducing the وَزْن ("the scale" or *wazn*) of certain Arabic words, thus determining the root's radicals and the additional letters.

1. If the verb زَرَعَ is on the *wazn* فَعَلَ, what is the *wazn* وَزْن of each of the following words?

    1. زَرَعَتْ

    2. أَزْرَعُ

    3. تَزْرَعَانِ

    4. تُزْرَعَا

2. If the noun إِقْطَاع is on the *wazn* إِفْعَال, what is the وَزْن of each of the following words?

    1. قَطَعَ

    2. تَقْطَعُ

    3. أَقْطَعْ

    4. يُقْطَعَ

3. If the participle مَسْموح is on the pattern مَفْعول, what is the root of the triliteral verb upon which this participle is built? Also, what is the وَزْن of each of the following words?

    1. تَسْمَحِينَ

    2. سَمَحْتُمَا

    3. يَسْمَحُونَ

Lesson Twelve

Exercise 12.2

Identify the root of each of the following words.

1. أشْراف

2. فِراشَة

3. تَشَرّفْنا

4. شَرِبَ

5. سَعيد

6. المَفْعول

7. كِتاب

8. خالِق

9. مَفهوم

Exercise 12.3

Here you are given three sets of words. In each set circle the word that does not have the same root.

قَتَلَ، قَتيل، قاتِل، قُلْتُ

أَعْسَمْ، سَمِعَ، أَسْمَعُ، سميع

ضَرَبا، رَبَضوا، ضُرِبْنَ، أَضْرَبَ

Lesson Thirteen
ثَلاثَةَ عَشَرَ

Arabic Verbs: Categories

In Arabic verbs are called أفْعال. There are several ways to categorize verbs. In terms of the verb tense, which is called زَمَنُ الفِعْل, there are three: الماضي (past), المُضارِع (present), and المُسْتَقْبَل (future). There is also the imperative, which is called الأمْر. Each verb has a mood: indicative or subjunctive for the past tense, and indicative, subjunctive, or jussive for the present and future tenses. A third categorization is a verb's voice, which can be active or passive.

We will begin by studying الفِعْلُ الماضي (the past tense).

The Past Tense (الفِعْل الماضي)

The past tense refers to an action that already occurred. A tense is called زَمَن in Arabic. This is why الفِعْل الماضي is called perfective. One important reason to begin the examination of Arabic verbs with studying الماضي is that it links the root system with verb conjugations, because the conjugation of the third-person masculine singular is typically reflective of both the verb root and the core form of all other conjugations. The conjugations of الماضي only include suffixes added to the root (while the other tenses use prefixes and suffixes).

Once you learn one paradigm chart, you can apply it to many other verbs. Examine the verb "to do" فَعَلَ:

	الضَّمائِر	الفِعْل الماضي	Translation
مُفْرَد Singular	أنَا	فَعَلْتُ	I did
	أنْتَ	فَعَلْتَ	you (m) did
	أنْتِ	فَعَلْتِ	you (f) did
	هُوَ	فَعَلَ	he did
	هِيَ	فَعَلَتْ	she did

we (d) did	فَعَلْـنَا	نَحْنُ	مُثَنّى Dual
you (m) did	فَعَلْـتُمَا	أَنْتُما (مُذَكَّر)	
you (f) did	فَعَلْـتُمَا	أَنْتُما (مؤَنَّث)	
they (m) did	فَعَـلَا	هُما (مُذَكَّر)	
they (f) did	فَعَلَـتَا	هُما (مؤَنَّث)	
we did	فَعَلْـنَا	نَحْنُ	جَمْع Plural
you (m) did	فَعَلْـتُم	أَنْتُمْ	
You (f) did	فَعَلْـتُنَّ	أَنْتُنَّ	
They (m) did	فَعَلُـوا	هُمْ	
They (f) did	فَعَلْـنَ	هُنَّ	

From this table, you notice that the only form which does not have any additional letters is فَعَلَ, with the pronoun هُوَ. Every other form has فَعَلـ in addition to a suffix. You also see how the pronoun نَحْنُ takes the same verb conjugation in its dual or plural forms, despite the gender. Remember that most verbs are indeclinable, especially الفِعْل الماضي. Indeclinable is called مَبْني in Arabic. This means that the forms in this table do not change to indicate a change in grammatical role—they always appear as in the table. In other words, these suffixes—exactly as you see them here—will appear in every Arabic verb in the past tense. Note that the core form فَعَلـ is always followed by one of the following: فَتْحَة، ضَمَّة، سُكون, not, for instance, شَدَّة or كَسْرَة.

One final important remark on these conjugations is this: In sentences a separate pronoun does not necessarily appear before a verb, because the conjugation of the verb indicates the subject clearly. When one says فَعَلْـتُ, the pronoun أَنَا is not needed for us to understand that this person is talking about himself or herself. However, whenever pronouns are used, the speaker is likely emphasizing the subject (actor) of the verb.

Based on the conjugations of this verb, we can conjugate almost every other triliteral verb. Consider another example—the verb دَرَسَ, meaning "to study":

Translation	الفِعْل الماضي	الضَمائِر	
I studied	دَرَسْتُ	أَنَا	مُفْرَد
you (m) studied	دَرَسْتَ	أَنْتَ	
you (f) studied	دَرَسْتِ	أَنْتِ	
he studied	دَرَسَ	هُوَ	
she studied	دَرَسَتْ	هِيَ	
we studied	دَرَسْنا	نَحْنُ	مُثَنَّى
you (m) studied	دَرَسْتُما	أَنْتُما (مُذَكَّر)	
you (f) studied	دَرَسْتُما	أَنْتُما (مُؤَنَّث)	
they (m) studied	دَرَسَا	هُما (مُذَكَّر)	
they (f) studied	دَرَسَتَا	هُما (مُؤَنَّث)	
we studied	دَرَسْنا	نَحْنُ	جَمْع
you (m) studied	دَرَسْتُم	أَنْتُم	
you (f) studied	دَرَسْتُنَّ	أَنْتُنَّ	
they (m) studied	دَرَسوا	هُم	
they (f) studied	دَرَسْنَ	هُنَّ	

Consider one last example of a triliteral verb: the verb ذَهَبَ (to go). Attempt to conjugate the verb before you look at the following table:

Lesson Thirteen

	Translation	الفِعْل الماضي	الضَمائر	
	I went	ذَهَبْتُ	أَنَا	
	you (m) went	ذَهَبْتَ	أَنْتَ	
	you (f) went	ذَهَبْتِ	أَنْتِ	مُفْرَد
	he went	ذَهَبَ	هُوَ	
	she went	ذَهَبَتْ	هِيَ	
	we went	ذَهَبْنَا	نَحْنُ	
	you (m) went	ذَهَبْتُما	أَنْتُما (مُذَكَّر)	
	you (f) went	ذَهَبْتُما	أَنْتُما (مؤنَّث)	مُثَنَّى
	they (m) went	ذَهَبَا	هُما (مُذَكَّر)	
	they (f) went	ذَهَبَتَا	هُما (مؤنَّث)	
	we went	ذَهَبْنَا	نَحْنُ	
	you (m) went	ذَهَبْتُم	أَنْتُم	
	you (f) went	ذَهَبْتُنَّ	أَنْتُنَّ	جَمْع
	they (m) went	ذَهَبُوا	هُم	
	they (f) went	ذَهَبْنَ	هُنَّ	

Here are some more triliteral verbs for you to conjugate, and their meaning in English. You should memorize them:

he sat/sat down	جَلَسَ
he created	خَلَقَ
he hit	ضَرَبَ
he stole	سَرَقَ

Lesson Thirteen

he made	صَنَعَ
he shaved	حَلَقَ
he won, overcame, conquered	غَلَبَ
he kneeled	رَكَعَ
he bowed, prostrated	سَجَدَ
he served	خَدَمَ
he withdrew	سَحَبَ
he wrote	كَتَبَ
he supported, made victorious	نَصَرَ
he worshiped, adored	عَبَدَ
he entered	دَخَلَ
he exited	خَرَجَ
he went up, appeared	طَلَعَ
he went down	نَزَلَ
he planted (a tree)	زَرَعَ
he killed	قَتَلَ
he crossed over	عَبَرَ
he allowed	سَمَحَ
he spent (money)	صَرَفَ
he left (something)	تَرَكَ
he cut	قَطَعَ
he appeared	ظَهَرَ
he outran, preceded	سَبَقَ
he cooked	طَبَخَ

Lesson Thirteen

he washed	غَسَلَ
he thanked	شَكَرَ
he looked	نَظَرَ
he searched, explored, discussed	بَحَثَ
he succeeded	نَجَحَ
it happened, occurred	حَدَثَ
he carried	حَمَلَ
he lived, resided, settled	سَكَنَ
he paid, pushed	دَفَعَ
he opened	فَتَحَ
he closed	غَلَقَ
he knew	عَرَفَ
he danced	رَقَصَ
he mentioned, recalled	ذَكَرَ

Now, let's study these verbs in sentences. We will use various subjects to make use of the different verb conjugations. Attempt to translate the following sentences before you look at the translation:

1. Ahmad and Nadia sat at home.

   أَحْمَدُ ونادِيَة جَلَسا في المَنْزِلِ.

2. God created the heaven and the earth.

   اللهُ خَلَقَ السَّماءَ والأَرْضَ (أو خلق الله السَّماءَ والأَرْضَ).

3. Mark and Sarah hit the table.

   مارك وسارة ضَرَبا المِنْضَدَةَ (أو الطاوِلَةَ).

4. The school's student (m) stole the pen.

   طالبُ المدرسةِ سَرَقَ القلمَ.

5. Khadija, Mona, and Souad made a new chair.

خَديجَةُ ومُنَى وسُعادُ صَنَعْنَ كُرْسِيّاً جديداً.

6. The American (m) and the Syrian (m) entered the hotel.

الأمريكيّ والسوريّ دَخَلا إلى الفندق.

7. The policeman shaved his head.

رَجُلُ الشُرْطَةِ حَلَقَ رَأْسَهُ (أو الشُرْطِيُّ حَلَقَ رأسَهُ).

8. Jesus Christ conquered sin and death.

يَسوعُ المَسيح غَلَبَ الخَطيئَةَ والمَوْتَ.

9. Majidah and her husband kneeled at church.

ماجِدَةُ وزوجُها رَكَعا في الكَنيسَةِ.

10. The men withdrew the money from the bank.

الرِّجالُ سَحَبوا المالَ من البَنْكِ.

11. You (d) wrote the long article.

أَنْتُما كَتَبْتُما المَقالَةَ الطَويلَةَ.

12. God supported the believers.

اللهُ نَصَرَ المُؤمنينَ.

13. Hana and George worshiped at church.

هَناء وجورج عَبَدا في الكَنيسَةِ.

14. Fatima and Muhammad exited (came out) from the mosque.

فاطمةُ ومُحَمَّدُ خَرَجا من المَسْجِدِ.

15. Ali went up the mountain.

عَلِي صَعَدَ إلى الجَبَلِ (أو صَعَدَ علي إلى الجَبَلِ).

16. The moon appeared in the sky.

القَمَرُ طَلَعَ في السَّماءِ.

17. The company's engineer went down from the ladder.

مُهَنْدِسُ الشَرِكَةِ نَزَلَ من السُلَّمِ (نَزَلَ مُهَنْدِسُ الشَّرِكَةِ من السُلَّمِ).

Lesson Thirteen

18. Hasan planted a short tree.

حَسَنُ زَرَعَ شجرةً قصيرةً (أو زَرَعَ حَسَنُ شجرةً قصيرةً).

19. The solider killed his enemy.

الجُنْدِيُ قَتَلَ عدوَّهُ.

20. Sami and Samia crossed the road.

سامي وسامية عَبَرا الطَّريقَ.

21. Muhammad and Karimah spent the money.

مُحَمَّد وكَريمَةُ صَرَفا المالَ.

22. The students left the school.

الطُّلابُ تَرَكوا المَدْرَسَةَ.

23. Nisrin and Nahid cut the bread.

نِسرين وناهِدُ قَطَعَتا الخُبْزَ.

24. The sun (f) appeared behind the big cloud.

الشَّمْسُ ظَهَرَتْ خَلْفَ السَّحابَةِ الكَبيرَةِ.

25. The boy outran everyone.

الصَّبِيُ سَبَقَ الكُلَّ (أو الصَّبِيُ سَبَقَ الجميعَ).

26. His mother cooked a great meal.

والِدَتُهُ (أو أُمُّهُ) طَبَخَتْ وَجْبَةٌ رائِعَةً (أو طَبَخَتْ أُمُّهُ وَجْبَةً رائِعَةً).

27. Majidah washed her face with water.

ماجدة غَسَلَتْ وَجْهَها بالماءِ (أو غَسَلَتْ ماجدة وَجْهَها بالماءِ).

28. Ahmad thanked Amjad.

أحمدُ شَكَرَ أمجدَ.

29. He looked at her beauty.

نَظَرَ إلى جَمالِها.

30. She and her son searched for the book.

هي وابنُها بَحَثا عن الكِتابِ.

31. The student succeeded in her exam.

الطَّالِبَةُ نَجَحَتْ في الامتحانِ (أو الاختبارِ).

32. It occurred on this same day (in history).

حَدَثَ في مِثْلِ هذا اليومِ (أو حَدَثَ في نَفَسِ هذا اليومِ).

33. The man carried the lamb on his shoulder.

الرَّجُلُ حَمَلَ الخَروفَ على كَتِفِهِ (حَمَلَ الرَّجُلُ الخَروفَ على كَتِفِهِ).

34. The husband and his wife lived in a big and new house.

الرَّجُلُ وزوجَتُهُ سَكَنا في مَنْزِلٍ كبيرٍ وجديدٍ.

35. The horse pushed the cart.

الحِصانُ دَفَعَ العَرَبَةَ (أو دَفَعَ الحِصانُ العَرَبَةَ).

36. The lady paid a bill.

السَّيِّدَةُ دَفَعَتْ فاتورَةً.

37. The imam of the mosque opened the gate.

إمامُ المَسْجِدِ فَتَحَ البَوّابَةَ.

38. The priest of the church closed the room.

كاهِنُ الكَنيسَةِ غَلَقَ الغُرْفَةَ.

39. The artist danced with his wife at the party.

الفَنّانُ رَقَصَ مع زوجَتِهِ في الحَفْلَةِ.

40. The teacher (f) mentioned a story.

المُعَلِّمَةُ ذَكَرَتْ قِصَّةً.

These examples should provide a good starting point for understanding verb conjugations. However, notice that all the verbs used above are ᶜalā wazn فَـعَـلَ. This can be misleading if it gives you the impression that all triliteral verbs follow this particular pattern, which is not the case.

There are three different أَوْزان (patterns) for triliteral verbs in the past tense:

فَـعَـلَ

فَـعِـلَ

فَـعُـلَ

Lesson Thirteen

All Arabic past simple tense verbs should follow one of the three patterns. Notice that the three forms share the first and final short vowels and differ only in the middle vowel.

Here are some examples of verbs using the pattern فَـعِـلَ:

he understood	فَهِمَ
he heard	سَمِعَ
he got tired	تَعِبَ
he rejoiced	فَرِحَ
he got angry	غَضِبَ
he played	لَعِبَ
he rode	رَكِبَ
he failed	فَشِلَ
he got sick	مَرِضَ
he wore	لَبِسَ
he accepted	قَبِلَ
he praised	حَمِدَ
he counted	حَسِبَ
he realized, knew	عَلِمَ
he made	عَمِلَ
he drank	شَرِبَ
he laughed	ضَحِكَ

Also, here are some verbs following the pattern فَـعُـلَ:

he became generous	كَرُمَ
it became small	صَغُرَ

Lesson Thirteen

كَبُرَ	it became big
سَهُلَ	it became easy
صَعُبَ	it became hard

The conjugations of verbs on the patterns فَعِلَ or فَعُلَ are straightforward in the past tense. They follow exactly the conjugations given above for verbs *ʿalā wazn* فَعَلَ, yet they maintain the vowel of the second radical as it is.

For instance, any verb *ʿalā wazn* فَعِلَ will be conjugated exactly as with فَعَلَ, with the exception of keeping the كَسْرَة of the second root letter as it is. Similarly, for verbs *ʿalā wazn* فَعُلَ, the second vowel will remain always a ضَمَّة.

Consider the verb فَهِمَ as an example:

I understood	فَهِمْتُ	أَنَا	
you (m) understood	فَهِمْتَ	أَنْتَ	
you (f) understood	فَهِمْتِ	أَنْتِ	مُفْرَد
he understood	فَهِمَ	هُوَ	
she understood	فَهِمَتْ	هِيَ	
we understood	فَهِمْنَا	نَحْنُ	
you (m) understood	فَهِمْتُمَا	أَنْتُما (مُذَكَّر)	
you (f) understood	فَهِمْتُمَا	أَنْتُما (مُؤَنَّث)	مُثَنَّى
they (m) understood	فَهِمَا	هُما (مُذَكَّر)	
they (f) understood	فَهِمَتَا	هُما (مُؤَنَّث)	

Lesson Thirteen

	نَحْنُ	فَهِمْنَا	we understood
	أَنْتُمْ	فَهِمْتُمْ	you (m) understood
جَمْع	أَنْتُنَّ	فَهِمْتُنَّ	you (f) understood
	هُمْ	فَهِمُوا	they (m) understood
	هُنَّ	فَهِمْنَ	they (f) understood

In conjugating فَهِمَ, we followed the same patterns in the conjugations of verbs ᶜalā wazn فَعَلَ, yet only used the كَسْرَة for the second vowel instead of the فَتْحَة. As an exercise, conjugate the full paradigm of the other verbs:

سَمِعَ، لَعِبَ، فَرِحَ، رَكِبَ، فَشِلَ، غَضِبَ، مَرِضَ، لَبِسَ، قَبِلَ، حَمِدَ، حَسِبَ، تَعِبَ

Now examine this example of a verb ᶜalā wazn فَعُلَ:

	أَنَا	سَهُلْتُ	I became easy
	أَنْتَ	سَهُلْتَ	you (m) became easy
مُفْرَد	أَنْتِ	سَهُلْتِ	you (f) became easy
	هُوَ	سَهُلَ	it (or he) became easy
	هِيَ	سَهُلَتْ	she became easy
	نَحْنُ	سَهُلْنَا	we became easy
	أَنْتُما (مُذَكَّر)	سَهُلْتُما	you (m) became easy
مُثَنَّى	أَنْتُما (مؤَنَّث)	سَهُلْتُما	you (f) became easy
	هُما (مُذَكَّر)	سَهُلَا	they (m) became easy
	هُما (مؤَنَّث)	سَهُلَتَا	they (f) became easy

	نَحْنُ	سَهُلْنَا	we became easy
	أَنْتُمْ	سَهُلْتُمْ	you (m) became easy
جَمْع	أَنْتُنَّ	سَهُلْتُنَّ	you (f) became easy
	هُمْ	سَهُلُوا	they (m) became easy
	هُنَّ	سَهُلْنَ	they (f) became easy

In conjugating سَهُلَ, we simply followed the same forms of the verbs ʿalā wazn فَعَلَ, yet we used a ضَمَّة for the second vowel instead of a فَتْحَة. It is understood that in English "becoming easy" does not make sense with pronouns like "I." The verb in the table above is rare, and is usually used in the context of "something," "matters," or "situations" became easy. In this case, we use the pronoun "it" or "they."

Attempt to conjugate the full paradigm of the other verbs: كَرُمَ، صَغُرَ، كَبُرَ، صَعُبَ.

One final remark is important regarding the three forms فَعَلَ, فَعِلَ, and فَعُلَ. Mostly, verbs which follow the pattern فَعَلَ indicate force, strength, and action executed by the subject within a specific timeframe. These verbs are usually dynamic and energetic, such as "to create," "to eat," "to ask," "to make," and "to go." As for the verbs following the pattern فَعِلَ, they can, first, indicate dynamic and strong actions, or, second, describe the state or the being of a subject. In the فَعِلَ pattern, verbs such as "to drink," "to make," and "to laugh" indicate dynamic actions, while verbs "to understand," "to realize," and "to become weary" reflect the state of the subject. Finally, verbs following the pattern فَعُلَ are clearly stative. They explain how the subject is becoming or being something: becoming young, being old, becoming difficult, or being easy.

In concluding this section, study these two solved assignments: sentence examples and parsing examples.

First, examine the following sentences. They use verbs following the patterns فَعِلَ and فَعُلَ. Attempt to read and translate these sentences before checking the answers:

1. That boy understood the lesson.

   ذَلِكَ الوَلَدُ (أو الفَتَى) فَهِمَ الدَرْسَ.

2. These (fd) girls heard the song.

   هاتانِ البِنْتانِ سَمِعَتا الأُغْنِيَّةَ.

Lesson Thirteen

3. These (mp) men got tired after the long journey.

هَؤُلاءِ الرِّجالُ تَعِبوا بعد الرِحْلَة الطَويلَة.

4. The students (mp) rejoiced after the exam.

الطُّلّابُ فَرِحوا بعد الامتحان.

5. The teachers (md) played the game.

المُعَلِّمانِ لَعِبا اللُّعْبَةَ.

6. The artists (fp) rode the bus.

الفَنّانات رَكِبْنَ الحافِلَةَ (أو الأُتوبيس، أو الباص).

7. The man and his wife failed the test.

الرَّجُلُ وزَوجَتُهُ فَشِلا في الاخْتِبارِ.

8. The teacher (f) of the school got sick.

مُدَرِّسَةُ المَدْرَسَةِ مَرِضَتْ.

9. The professor (f) of the university wore her dress.

أُسْتاذَةُ الجامِعَةِ لَبِسَتْ ثَوبَها.

10. The women accepted the invitation from the university.

النِّساءُ قَبِلْنَ الدعوةَ من الجامِعَةِ.

11. Paul counted the loss.

بولُس حَسِبَ الخَسارَةَ.

12. You (mp) drank water.

أَنْتُمْ شَرِبْتُمْ ماءً.

13. The ladies laughed at him.

السَّيِّدات ضَحِكْنَ عَلَيهِ.

14. Daniel became generous in his tithes.

دانيالُ كَرُمَ في عُشورِهِ.

15. The trip became easy.

الرِّحْلَةُ سَهُلَتْ.

16. The work (m) became hard.

العَمَلُ صَعُبَ.

Second, let's study examples of verb parsing. Parsing is very important in Arabic, especially, as we know from earlier lessons, considering the presence of declinable and indeclinable words. In Arabic parsing is called إِعْرَاب. It seeks to analyze a word in terms of its role in a sentence. When we parse a verb, we state its tense (past, present, or future), person (first, second, or third), gender (masculine or feminine), number (singular, dual, or plural), root, and translation. This sequence of parsing will be used throughout this book.

الإِعْرَاب	الكَلِمَة
Past, 3ms, ح.م.ل, he carried	حَمَلَ
Past, 3fs, د.ف.ع, she paid	دَفَعَتْ
Past, 2md/2fd, ف.ه.م, you understood	فَهِمْتُمَا
Past, 2fp, س.ه.ل, you became easy	سَهُلْتُنَّ
Past, 3ms, ك.ب.ر, it became big	كَبُرَ

We will practice parsing more in the exercise section. Now let's turn our focus to examining the relationship between a verb and its subject, as there are important matters to learn.

The Verb and Its Subject (الفِعْلُ والفاعِلُ)

This section examines the relationship between a فِعْل (verb) and its فاعِل (subject). The فِعْل describes an action executed in a specific time. The فاعِل is a noun which usually follows the فِعْل, in order to indicate who did the action. There are important points to examine regarding the case ending of the subject and its relationship to the verb.

First, the فاعِل is مَرْفوع (nominative) in most cases, especially when it comes after an active verb (other cases are advanced and extend beyond the scope of this introductory book). If the فاعِل is singular, it always takes a ضَمّة as its ending vowel. See these sentences:

كَتَبَ الرَّجُلُ المَقالةَ.

سَمِعَتْ فاطِمةُ الدَّرْسَ.

ذَهَبَ الوَلَدُ إلى المَدْرَسةِ.

The nouns الرَّجُلُ, فاطِمةُ, and الوَلَدُ serve as subjects. All of them are nominative. They receive a ضَمّة at the end. In this case, we parse the فاعِل as مَرْفوع بِالضَمّة, which

Lesson Thirteen

literally means "nominative by the *ḍammah*." This is also the case with broken plurals, such as الطُّلَّابُ (students) or الأطْفالُ (children).

The matter is different when the فاعِل is dual. In this case, we use the ending ان to designate the nominative case, and we parse the فاعِل as مَرْفوع بالألف, which literally translates as, "nominative by the *alif*." In this case, the فاعِل appears as الرَّجُلانِ، المُهَنْدِسانِ، البِنْتانِ.

For regular masculine plural nouns, we use the ending ون to designate the nominative case and we parse the فاعِل as مَرْفوع بالواو, which literally states, "nominative by the *wāw*," as in the plural nouns المُهَنْدِسونَ، المُؤْمِنونَ.

Second, the relationship between a verb and its subject regarding gender and plurality is very important.

Concerning the gender, the gender of the two must match. Here are some examples:

الفاعِل	الفِعْل	Translation	
اللهُ	خَلَقَ	God created the world.	خَلَقَ اللهُ العالَمَ.
السَّيِّدةُ	عَمِلَتْ	Souad made the food.	عَمِلَتْ سُعادُ الطَّعامَ.
المُهَنْدِسُ	صَنَعَ	The engineer made the car.	صَنَعَ المُهَنْدِسُ السَّيَّارةَ.
الوَلَدُ	كَسَرَ	The boy broke the plate.	كَسَرَ الوَلَدُ الطَّبَقَ.

In these four examples notice that الفِعْل and الفاعِل agree in gender. In the phrases خَلَقَ اللهُ, صَنَعَ المُهَنْدِسُ, and كَسَرَ الوَلَدُ, the فِعْلُ and the فاعِلُ are masculine. In عَمِلَتْ سُعادُ, both الفِعْلُ and الفاعِلُ are feminine. As a rule, the verb's gender must agree with its subject's gender.

Concerning the verb's number, the matter is more complex—and, in some sense, unexpected—for non-Arabic speakers. The rule is as follows: the verb remains *singular* if الفاعِل is dual or plural.

Consider these examples. In Arabic it is correct to say the following:

دَرَسَ الطّالِبُ.
دَرَسَ الطّالِبان.
دَرَسَ الطُّلَّابُ.

It is *not* correct to say the following:

دَرَسا الطّالِبانِ.

دَرَسوا الطُّلّابُ.

Similarly, it is correct in Arabic to write كَتَبَ الْكَاتِبُ, كَتَبَ الْكَاتِبَانِ, and كَتَبَ الْكَاتِبُونَ. However, it is incorrect to say كَتَبَا الْكَاتِبَانِ or كَتَبُوا الْكَاتِبُونَ.

But what if we are talking about a feminine noun as the verb's subject, i.e., الطّالِبات and الكَاتِبات؟

As mentioned earlier, the gender of the verb must agree with the gender of the subject. Thus, the gender must be feminine and the number singular. So, it is correct to write the following:

دَرَسَتْ نِسرينُ الدرسَ.

دَرَسَتْ نِسرينُ وماجِدة الدرسَ.

دَرَسَتْ نِسرينُ وماجِدة ومَها الدرسَ.

كَتَبَتْ زَهْرَةُ المَقالَةَ.

كَتَبَتْ زَهْرَة وعائِشَةُ المَقالَةَ.

It is wrong to write the following:

دَرَسْنَ نِسرينُ و ماجِدة و مَها الدرسَ.

كَتَبَتا زَهْرَة وعائِشَةُ المَقالَةَ.

Finally, it is crucial to note that these rules apply *only* when the subject *follows* the verb, i.e., when we are dealing with a verbal sentence — when a verb begins the sentence. If the subject precedes the verb, then it is a nominal sentence — where the subject is usually a pronoun and the predicate is a verb — and the verb follows the number of the pronoun.

As a concluding exercise, study the following examples. All of them are correct. Focus particularly on the difference between a nominal sentence and a verbal one, especially regarding the number and gender of the verb and its subject:

الكَاتِبُ كَتَبَ.

الكَاتِبَةُ كَتَبَتْ.

الكَاتِبَاتُ كَتَبْنَ.

الكَاتِبُونَ كَتَبُوا.

Lesson Thirteen

الكُتّابُ كَتَبُوا.

الكَاتِبَانِ كَتَبَا.

الكَاتِبَتَانِ كَتَبَتَا.

أَنْتُما كَتَبْتُمَا.

نَحْنُ كَتَبْنَا.

كَتَبَ الْكَاتِبُ.

كَتَبَ الْكَاتِبَانِ.

كَتَبَ الكَاتِبُونَ.

كَتَبَتْ هِنْدُ وسُعاد.

عَمِلَ المُهَنْدِسونَ.

عَمِلَتْ مُهَنْدِساتُ المَدْرَسَةِ.

المُهَنْدِسات عَمِلْنَ.

ذَهَبَ أَحمَدُ.

ذَهَبَ أَحمَدُ وناديةُ.

أحمَدُ وناديةُ ذَهَبَا.

سُعادُ وناديةُ ذَهَبَتا.

ذَهَبَتْ ناديةُ.

To conclude, it is important to summarize the rules of the verb-subject relationship regarding gender and plurality. First, concerning the gender of a verb, it is straightforward: the verb's gender agrees with the subject's gender. Second, the verb's number is a bit more complex. If the subject of the verb is explicitly mentioned *after* the verb (e.g., in a verbal sentence), the verb will be singular. If a pronoun subject precedes a verb (e.g., in a nominal sentence), the verb will agree with the number of the pronoun.

Vocabulary

You should learn and memorize the many new triliteral verbs and their meanings. In addition, there are some new nouns we learned in the translated sentences. Here is your list.

present	مُضارِع	past	ماضي
imperative	أَمْر	future	مُسْتَقْبَل
tense, or time	زَمَن	day, today	يَوْم
he crossed over	عَبَرَ	he did	فَعَلَ
he allowed	سَمَحَ	he studied	دَرَسَ
he spent (money)	صَرَفَ	he went	ذَهَبَ
he left (something)	تَرَكَ	he sat	جَلَسَ
he cut	قَطَعَ	he created	خَلَقَ
he appeared	ظَهَرَ	he hit	ضَرَبَ
he outran, preceded	سَبَقَ	he stole	سَرَقَ
he cooked	طَبَخَ	he made	صَنَعَ
he washed	غَسَلَ	he shaved	حَلَقَ
he thanked	شَكَرَ	he won, overcame	غَلَبَ
he looked	نَظَرَ	he kneeled	رَكَعَ
he searched, discussed	بَحَثَ	he bowed, prostrated	سَجَدَ
he succeeded	نَجَحَ	he served	خَدَمَ
it happened, occurred	حَدَثَ	he withdrew	سَحَبَ
he carried	حَمَلَ	he wrote	كَتَبَ
he lived, resided, settled	سَكَنَ	he supported, made victorious	نَصَرَ

Lesson Thirteen

he paid, pushed	دَفَعَ	he worshiped, adored	عَبَدَ
he opened	فَتَحَ	he entered	دَخَلَ
he closed	غَلَقَ	he exited	خَرَجَ
he danced	رَقَصَ	he went up, appeared	طَلَعَ
he mentioned, recalled	ذَكَرَ	he went down	نَزَلَ
he understood	فَهِمَ	he planted (a tree)	زَرَعَ
he heard	سَمِعَ	he killed	قَتَلَ
he got tired	تَعِبَ	he wore	لَبِسَ
he rejoiced	فَرِحَ	he accepted	قَبِلَ
he got angry	غَضِبَ	he praised	حَمِدَ
he played	لَعِبَ	he counted	حَسِبَ
he rode	رَكِبَ	he knew	عَرَفَ
he failed	فَشِلَ	he realized, knew	عَلِمَ
he got sick	مَرِضَ	he made, worked	عَمِلَ
he became generous	كَرُمَ	he drank	شَرِبَ
it became small	صَغُرَ	he laughed	ضَحِكَ
it became big	كَبُرَ	it became easy	سَهُلَ
lamb	خَروف	it became hard, difficult	صَعُبَ
shoulder	كَتِف	table	مِنْضَدَة / طاوِلَة
cart, trolley	عَرَبَة	hotel	فندق
bill	فاتورَة	sin	خَطيئَة
gate	بَوّابَة	death	مَوت

room	غُرْفَة	bank	بَنْك
party	حَفْلَة	article	مَقالَة
story	قِصَّة	believer	مُؤْمِن
lesson	دَرْس	enemy	عَدوّ
song	أُغْنِيّة	road, path	طريق
game	لُعْبَة	money	مال
work	عَمَل	bread	خُبز
dress	ثَوب	behind	خَلف
invitation	دَعْوَة	cloud	سَحابَة
loss	خَسارَة	meal	وَجْبَة
decision	قَرار	face	وَجْه
tithes	عُشور	water	ماء
trip, journey	رِحْلَة	beauty	جَمال
bus	حافِلَة / أُتوبيس	exam, test	امتحان / اختبار

Lesson Thirteen

Exercises

Exercise 13.1

Determine which of the following sentences is correct. Then correct those which are incorrect.

1. الطَّالِبَانِ نَجَحَتا.

2. نَجَحَتا الطَّالِبَتانِ.

3. ذَهَبَا مُحَمَّدٌ وخَدِيجَةُ.

4. كَتَبْنَ المُدَرِّسات.

5. المُدَرِّسات كَتَبوا.

6. دَرَسا الطَّالِبان.

7. نَجَحَوا الطُّلابُ.

8. المُهَنْدِسات عَمِلَتْ.

Exercise 13.2

Parse the following verbs (follow the sequence we used in the lesson).

1. رَقَصْتُ

2. فَتَحْتُمَا

3. نَجَحْتُنَّ

4. رَكِبْنَ

5. حَمِدُوا

6. ضَحِكْنَا

7. غَضِبْتُمَا

8. حَمِدْتُنَّ

9. ضَحِكْتُم

10. كَرُمَ

11. صَعُبْنَا

Exercise 13.3

Translate the following into English.

1. طالبُ المدرسةِ جَلَسَ على الأرضِ.

2. خَديجَةُ وسارة سَرَقَتا المِنْضَدَةَ.

3. الأمريكيّ والسوريّ صَنَعا كُرْسِيّاً.

4. ماجِدَةُ وزَوجُها دَخَلا إلى البيتِ.

5. هَناء وجورج سَجَدا في الكَنيسَةِ.

6. خَلَقَ اللهُ السَّماءَ والأرْضَ.

7. مُهَنْدِسُ الشَرِكَةِ خَرَجَ من المَسْجِدِ.

8. نِسرينُ نَجَحَتْ في الامتحانِ.

9. كاهِنُ الكَنيسَةِ دَفَعَ الفاتورَةَ.

10. الرَّجُلُ وزَوجَتُهُ طَبَخَا وَجْبَةٌ رائِعَةً.

Exercise 13.4

Translate the following into Arabic.

1. The school's student (m) hit the table.

2. Mark thanked Sarah.

3. Khadija, Mona, and Souad sat at home.

4. The policeman killed his enemy.

5. You (d) wrote the short lesson.

6. Hana and George kneeled at church.

7. God created the moon and the sun.

8. Khadija planted a short tree.

9. Muhammad and Samia crossed the road.

10. Nisrin washed her face with water.

Lesson Fourteen
أَرْبَعَةَ عَشَرَ

Verbs and Their Accusative Direct Objects

In this lesson the goal is to examine the direct object of a verb and the passive forms of the past simple tense.

In previous lessons, we explored the various noun cases: مَرْفوع (nominative), مَجْرور (genitive), and مَنْصوب (accusative). Nouns are in the مَرْفوع case when they are مُبْتَدَأ (subject) or خَبَر (predicate) in a nominal sentence, or the فاعِل (subject) of a verb in a verbal sentence. The مَجْرور case appears when a noun is the object of preposition, while the مَنْصوب case is used if a noun is the direct object of a verb. This case of the direct object is our focus in this section.

In Arabic a direct object is called مَفْعول بِهِ (mafʿūl bihi). Arabic verbs can be categorized into two groups in terms of whether they require a direct object. A transitive verb requires a direct object, while an intransitive verb does not. We call the transitive verb المُتَعَدي and the intransitive اللازِم. While all verbs have subjects (فاعِل), whether explicit or implicit, some verbs do not have direct objects.

Examine the following examples of verbal sentences with intransitive verbs:

The man slept.	نامَ الرَّجُلُ.
The teacher left.	ذَهَبَ المُعَلِّمُ.
Souad went (came) down.	نَزَلَتْ سُعادُ.
The child became satisfied.	شَبِعَ الطِّفْلُ.

From this table, it is obvious that the sentences are complete without direct objects. The verbs نامَ، ذَهَبَ، نَزَلَ، شَبِعَ are intransitive and do not require مَفْعول بِهِ (a direct object).

Consider the following examples of transitive verbs:

مَفْعول بِهِ	فاعِل	فِعْل		
طَعاماً	الرَّجُلُ	أَكَلَ	The man ate food.	أَكَلَ الرَّجُلُ طَعاماً.
قَهْوَةً	المُعَلِّمُ	شَرِبَ	The teacher drank coffee.	شَرِبَ المُعَلِّمُ قَهْوَةً.
كِتاباً	هِنْدُ	قَرَأَتْ	Hind read a book.	قَرَأَتْ هِنْدُ كِتاباً.
قَميصاً	الطِّفْلُ	لَبِسَ	The child wore a shirt.	لَبِسَ الطِّفْلُ قَميصاً.

From this table, أَكَلَ، شَرِبَ، قَرَأَ، لَبِسَ are transitive verbs, as all of them require مَفْعول بِهِ. Notice that the فاعِل is always مَرْفوع, while the مَفْعول بِهِ is مَنْصوب. Thus, the singular مَفْعول بِهِ should end with a فَتْحَة—but because all four words used above are indefinite, we must use تَنْوين فَتْحَة. Also, it is important to remember to add an *alif* before inserting the تَنْوين فَتْحَة, unless the last letter of the noun is *tā' marbūṭah* or *hamzah* preceded by *alif* (see Lesson Four).

In Arabic there is no specific way to distinguish transitive from intransitive verbs. Arabic-speaking people simply discern this by listening and practicing. The main point in this section is to highlight that a transitive verb requires مَفْعول بِهِ. This مَفْعول بِهِ takes the accusative case (مَنْصوب).

Now study the following examples regarding the direct object.

Consider the sentence خَلَقْتُ الأَرْضَ.

It means "I created the earth." The فِعْل (verb) is خَلَقْتُ. The فاعِل (subject) of the verb is not explicit, but implicit. We can identify the فاعِل by comparing the verb ending with the past tense paradigm. The ending تُ exists only with the pronoun أَنا. Personal pronouns—such as أَنا—are usually implicit and not explicit, unless the speaker is seeking to emphasize the actor (or subject) of the verb (e.g., one can still say, أَنا خَلَقْتُ الأَرْضَ). Finally, notice that the noun الأَرْضَ is مَفْعول بِهِ (the direct object) of the verb خَلَقْتُ. The مَفْعول بِهِ is always مَنْصوب (accusative). Here the accusative case is evident in the use of the فَتْحَة as the final vowel. Note that, since الأَرْضَ is definite, we did not need to use تَنْوين فَتْحَة, as in a previous example.

As an exercise, identify the فِعْل, فاعِل, and مَفْعول بِهِ in the following verbal sentences. As a sample, the مَفْعول بِهِ is given:

مَفْعول بِهِ	Translation	جُمْلَة فِعْلِيّة
الطِّفْلُ	I heard the lesson.	سَمِعْتُ الدَّرْسَ.
الكِتابَ	You (mp) studied the book.	دَرَسْتُم الكِتابَ.
القَهْوَةَ	We drank the coffee.	شَرِبْنا القَهْوَةَ.
القِصَّةَ	You (fp) read the story.	قَرَأْتُنَّ القِصَّةَ.
القَميصَ	He wore the shirt.	لَبِسَ القَميصَ.
سَلاماً	He sought (asked for) peace.	طَلَبَ سَلاماً.
مَقالاً	He wrote an article.	كَتَبَ مَقالاً.
قِصَّةً	He heard a story.	سَمِعَ قِصَّةً.
صورَةً	She drew a picture.	رَسَمَتْ صورَةً.
عَشاءً	He ate dinner.	أَكَلَ عَشاءً.

One final remark—some verbs can receive more than one direct object, but this extends beyond the scope of this introductory book. Now we turn to creating the passive voice of past simple tense verbs.

Past Passive (الماضي المَجْهول)

As in English, Arabic verbs can be divided into two groups in relation to voice: active and passive. We call the active voice مَعْلوم (maʿlūm) and the passive مَجْهول (majhūl). Recall that in Lesson Four we studied the مُعْرَب (declinable) and مَبْني (indeclinable) parts of speech, where we stated that most verbs are مَبْني and do not experience a change in form while indicating grammatical inflections. Since the past tense is always مَبْني, we call the active voice مَبْني لِلمَعْلوم and the passive voice مَبْني لِلمَجْهول.

All the verbs we have studied so far have been in the active voice. When a فِعْل is in the active voice, we can identify its فاعِل and sometimes its مَفْعول بِهِ. In the passive voice, however, the مَفْعول بِهِ replaces the فاعِل.

For example, الرَّجُلُ كَسَرَ الطَّبَقَ (the man broke the plate) becomes كُسِرَ الطَّبَقُ (the plate was broken). The verb كَسَرَ is active, while كُسِرَ is passive. Notice that we create the passive verb by changing the short vowels of the original active verb. We then assign the مَفْعول بِهِ the role of the فاعِل in the new (passive) sentence.

Similarly, the active sentence خَلَقَ اللهُ الإِنْسانَ (God created man) becomes the passive الإِنْسانُ خُلِقَ (man was created). The verb خَلَقَ is active, while خُلِقَ is passive. If we compare the two forms, we see that to render the passive خُلِـقَ from خَلَـقَ we kept the letters as they were and only changed some vowels: we altered the first vowel from فَتْحَة to ضَمَّة, then we changed the second vowel from فَتْحَة to كَسْرَة, and, finally, we did not change the third vowel. This resulted in the passive verb خُلِـقَ. Finally, to form the passive sentence, you place the direct object (of the active sentence) as the subject of the passive verb: الإِنْسانُ خُلِقَ.

As an example, here is the full paradigm of the passive verb خُلِـقَ:

Translation	Past Passive	الضَّمائِر	
I was created	خُلِقْتُ	أَنَا	مُفْرَد
you (m) were created	خُلِقْتَ	أَنْتَ	
you (f) were created	خُلِقْتِ	أَنْتِ	
he was created	خُلِقَ	هُوَ	
she was created	خُلِقَتْ	هِيَ	
we were created	خُلِقْنَا	نَحْنُ	مُثَنَّى
you (m) were created	خُلِقْتُمَا	أَنْتُما (مُذَكَّر)	
you (f) were created	خُلِقْتُمَا	أَنْتُما (مؤَنَّث)	
they (m) were created	خُلِقَا	هُما (مُذَكَّر)	
they (f) were created	خُلِقَتَا	هُما (مؤَنَّث)	

	نَحْنُ	خُلِقْنَا	we were created
	أَنْتُمْ	خُلِقْتُم	you (m) were created
جَمْع	أَنْتُنَّ	خُلِقْتُنَّ	you (f) were created
	هُمْ	خُلِقُوا	they (m) were created
	هُنَّ	خُلِقْنَ	they (f) were created

Note that the suffixes are the same as those in the active verb paradigm. The only change is in short vowels.

After you form the passive verb and place the direct object as its new subject, you should pay attention to one final matter: Ensure that the conjugation of the passive verb matches the new subject. In the previous example, we formed the passive sentence الإِنْسانُ خُلِقَ. The new subject الإِنْسانُ is third-person masculine singular, so there was no need to adjust the conjugation of the passive verb خُلِقَ. In some cases, the conjugation of the passive verb (mainly its suffixes) should be adjusted. To clarify, consider the following example.

In the active sentence هُوَ خَلَقَ الأَرْضَ, the active verb is خَلَقَ. Its explicit subject is هُوَ, which is third-person masculine singular. The direct object is الأَرْضَ, and it is third-person feminine singular. In order to make this sentence passive, change the short vowels of خَلَقَ to create خُلِقَ, and place الأرض as the subject of the passive verb. Since الأرض is now the new subject, it should be nominative الأرضُ. The result is الأَرْضُ خُلِقَ. But الأرضُ is feminine, while خُلِقَ is masculine. The passive verb should match the new subject. An adjustment is needed: from خُلِقَ to خُلِقَتْ. Thus, the correct passive sentence becomes الأرضُ خُلِقَتْ. The rule is that the conjugation of the passive verb must match the new subject.

For more examples examine the past tense passive of two verbs: فَعَلَ and دَرَسَ:

Past Passive of دَرَسَ	Past Passive of فَعَلَ	الضَّمائِر	
دُرِسْتُ	فُعِلْتُ	أَنَا	مُفْرَد
دُرِسْتَ	فُعِلْتَ	أَنْتَ	
دُرِسْتِ	فُعِلْتِ	أَنْتِ	
دُرِسَ	فُعِلَ	هُوَ	
دُرِسَتْ	فُعِلَتْ	هِيَ	
دُرِسْنَا	فُعِلْنَا	نَحْنُ	مُثَنَّى
دُرِسْتُمَا	فُعِلْتُمَا	أَنْتُما (مُذَكَّر)	
دُرِسْتُمَا	فُعِلْتُمَا	أَنْتُما (مؤنَّث)	
دُرِسَا	فُعِلَا	هُما (مُذَكَّر)	
دُرِسَتَا	فُعِلَتَا	هُما (مؤَنَّث)	
دُرِسْنَا	فُعِلْنَا	نَحْنُ	جَمْع
دُرِسْتُم	فُعِلْتُم	أَنْتُم	
دُرِسْتُنَّ	فُعِلْتُنَّ	أَنْتُنَّ	
دُرِسُوا	فُعِلُوا	هُمْ	
دُرِسْنَ	فُعِلْنَ	هُنَّ	

To conclude the study of the past passive, one final comment is necessary.

In the examples discussed above, one form of the active verb is examined, namely, the pattern فَعَلَ. However, remember there are three different patterns for triliteral past verbs: فَعَلَ، فَعِلَ، فَعُلَ. What should be done with the other two patterns فَعُلَ and فَعِلَ when we create their passive forms?

The straightforward answer is to follow the same rules given above: change the first vowel to ضَمَّة, the second to كَسْرَة, and keep the third as it is.

Consider the active verb فَهِمَ (to understand). It is on the pattern فَــعِــلَ. Here is the table for فَهِمَ, with active next to passive for comparison:

	الضَمائِر	Past Active of فَهِمَ (الماضي المعلوم)	Past Passive of فَهِمَ (الماضي المجهول)
مُفْرَد	أَنَا	فَهِمْتُ	فُهِمْتُ
	أَنْتَ	فَهِمْتَ	فُهِمْتَ
	أَنْتِ	فَهِمْتِ	فُهِمْتِ
	هُوَ	فَهِمَ	فُهِمَ
	هِيَ	فَهِمَتْ	فُهِمَتْ
مُثَنَّى	نَحْنُ	فَهِمْنَا	فُهِمْنَا
	أَنْتُما (مُذَكَّر)	فَهِمْتُمَا	فُهِمْتُمَا
	أَنْتُما (مُؤَنَّث)	فَهِمْتُمَا	فُهِمْتُمَا
	هُما (مُذَكَّر)	فَهِمَا	فُهِمَا
	هُما (مُؤَنَّث)	فَهِمَتَا	فُهِمَتَا
جَمْع	نَحْنُ	فَهِمْنَا	فُهِمْنَا
	أَنْتُمْ	فَهِمْتُم	فُهِمْتُم
	أَنْتُنَّ	فَهِمْتُنَّ	فُهِمْتُنَّ
	هُمْ	فَهِمُوا	فُهِمُوا
	هُنَّ	فَهِمْنَ	فُهِمْنَ

Notice an interesting feature in the table: in the case of the verbs ᶜalā wazn فَــعِــلَ, when we apply the rules to create a passive from the active form, we merely change the first vowel to a ضَمَّة, which creates the passive (since the second vowel is a كَسْرَة already).

As an exercise, form the passive chart for the verb سَمِعَ before checking the answers below:

	الضّمائر	Past Active of سَمِعَ (الماضي المعلوم)	Past Passive of سَمِعَ (الماضي المجهول)
مُفْرَد	أَنَا	سَمِعْتُ	سُمِعْتُ
	أَنْتَ	سَمِعْتَ	سُمِعْتَ
	أَنْتِ	سَمِعْتِ	سُمِعْتِ
	هُوَ	سَمِعَ	سُمِعَ
	هِيَ	سَمِعَتْ	سُمِعَتْ
مُثَنَّى	نَحْنُ	سَمِعْنَا	سُمِعْنَا
	أَنْتُما (مُذَكَّر)	سَمِعْتُمَا	سُمِعْتُمَا
	أَنْتُما (مُؤَنَّث)	سَمِعْتُمَا	سُمِعْتُمَا
	هُما (مُذَكَّر)	سَمِعَا	سُمِعَا
	هُما (مؤَنَّث)	سَمِعَتَا	سُمِعَتَا
جَمْع	نَحْنُ	سَمِعْنَا	سُمِعْنَا
	أَنْتُمْ	سَمِعْتُمْ	سُمِعْتُمْ
	أَنْتُنَّ	سَمِعْتُنَّ	سُمِعْتُنَّ
	هُمْ	سَمِعُوا	سُمِعُوا
	هُنَّ	سَمِعْنَ	سُمِعْنَ

Finally, let's study passive forms of a verb on the pattern فَعُلَ. Consider the active verb سَهُلَ (to become easy). Attempt to form the passive paradigm before reviewing the table below:

	Past Passive of سَهُلَ (الماضي المجهول)	Past Active of سَهُلَ (الماضي المعلوم)	الضَّمائِر	
	سُهِلْتُ	سَهُلْتُ	أَنَا	مُفْرَد
	سُهِلْتَ	سَهُلْتَ	أَنْتَ	
	سُهِلْتِ	سَهُلْتِ	أَنْتِ	
	سُهِلَ	سَهُلَ	هُوَ	
	سُهِلَتْ	سَهُلَتْ	هِيَ	
	سُهِلْنَا	سَهُلْنَا	نَحْنُ	مُثَنَّى
	سُهِلْتُمَا	سَهُلْتُمَا	أَنْتُما (مُذَكَّر)	
	سُهِلْتُمَا	سَهُلْتُمَا	أَنْتُما (مؤنَّث)	
	سُهِلَا	سَهُلَا	هُما (مُذَكَّر)	
	سُهِلَتَا	سَهُلَتَا	هُما (مؤنَّث)	
	سُهِلْنَا	سَهُلْنَا	نَحْنُ	جَمْع
	سُهِلْتُم	سَهُلْتُم	أَنْتُمْ	
	سُهِلْتُنَّ	سَهُلْتُنَّ	أَنْتُنَّ	
	سُهِلُوا	سَهُلُوا	هُمْ	
	سُهِلْنَ	سَهُلْنَ	هُنَّ	

Note that we are only using this table as an exercise, as the passive of verbs on the pattern فَعُلَ is very rare.

Lesson Fourteen

Vocabulary

Please! (said to a male)	مِن فَضْلِكَ!
Please! (spoken to a female)	مِن فَضْلِكِ!
Congratulations!	مَبْروك!
chance, opportunity	فُرْصَة
Nice to meet you! (Literally, happy chance!)	فُرْصَة سعيدة!
I think that…	أنا أَظُنُّ أن …
I think that…	أنا أَعْتَقِدُ أن …
he needs…	هو يَحْتاجُ…
she needs…	هي تَحْتاجُ…
government	حُكومَة
court	مَحْكَمَة
lecture	مُحاضَرَة
sport	رِياضَة
message/messages	رِسالَة / رَسائِل
photo/photos	صورَة / صُوَر
district/districts	مِنْطَقَة / مَناطِق
fellow/fellows (also, classmate/classmates)	زَميل / زُملاء
science/sciences	عِلْم / عُلوم
weather	جَوّ
hot/cold	حار / بارد

Exercises

Exercise 14.1

Attempt to create the مَفْعُول بِهِ for the nouns in the table below. Pay attention to the definiteness and the ending of each noun in order to choose the correct accusative case.

الشمس	حُجْرَة	الماء	السِّلْعَة
قَمَر	مُمَثِّلَة	الماس	مَنْزِل
السَّماء	شُبّاك	عَين	بَلَد
مَقالَة	جُمْلَة	شَقَّة	شَرِكَة

Exercise 14.2

These are active verbs. Make them passive.

1. طَلَعَ
2. طَبَخَ
3. دَرَسَ
4. دَرَسْتُمَا
5. دَرَسَا
6. ذَهَبَ
7. ذَهَبَا
8. شَكَرَ
9. نَجَحَ
10. غَضِبَ

11. رَكِبَ

12. كَبُرَ

13. صَعُبَ

Exercise 14.3

Make these sentences passive.

1. المُعَلِّمُ كَتَبَ المَقالَ.

2. اللهُ خَلَقَ السَّماءَ.

3. الوَلَدُ ضَرَبَ الكُرَةَ.

4. الأُمُّ طَبَخَتْ الطَّعامَ.

5. الطَّالِبُ سَمِعَ الدَّرْسَ.

6. أحمدُ شَكَرَ الرَجُلَ.

7. مها وسماحُ فَتَحَتا البابَ.

8. القِسُّ حَمِدَ اللهَ.

9. مُصْطَفَى ومَحْمود رَكِبا السيارةَ.

10. سَمِعْنا العِظةَ.

Note that المَقالَ, الطَّعامَ, and البابَ are masculine, while السَّماءَ is feminine. Remember that the gender of a noun can be generally determined from its ending.

Lesson Fifteen
خَمْسَةَ عَشَرَ

Past Tense Verbs: Negation and Other Forms

In this lesson the focus is final matters related to past simple tense, before we examine present tense in the following lesson.

Past Tense with the Particle قَدْ

Past tense verbs are often preceded by the particle قَدْ (*qad*). This particle reflects one important feature of a perfect tense: the act of the verb is completed at the moment of speaking or immediately prior to the present time. When you read قَدْ دَرَسَ or قَدْ سَمِعَ, it is conveyed that these actions of دَرَسَ and سَمِعَ have just been accomplished at that moment.

The usage of the particle قَدْ also affirms the action of the verb. Some teachers prefer to compare this usage to the English present perfect tense (e.g., I have read the book), but there is no such tense in Arabic. It is also noteworthy to mention that قَدْ does not change anything in the conjugation of the verb. It can also precede both active and passive past verbs but can never be separated from the verb it precedes (except in very rare cases).

In translating perfective verbs preceded by قَدْ, consider, for instance, قَدْ دَرَسْتُ. It can be rendered as "I have just studied." As for قَدْ نَجَحَ الرَّجُلُ, it reads "the man has just succeeded."

Negating Past Tense

There are two major ways to negate الفِعْلُ الماضي. We will study the first here and the second after we study the present simple tense because they are connected.

To negate الفِعْلُ الماضي, we simply precede it with the particle ما. This particle is مَبْني (indeclinable)—it always appears the same way regardless of its position in a sentence. A negated verb is called مَنْفي (*manfi*). So, the negated past tense verb is الفِعْل الماضي المَنْفي.

As an example, here is the مَنْفي chart for the active verb دَرَسَ:

Translation	الفِعْل الماضي المَنْفي	الضَّمائِر	
I didn't study	ما دَرَسْتُ	أَنَا	مُفْرَد
you (m) didn't study	ما دَرَسْتَ	أَنْتَ	
you (f) didn't study	ما دَرَسْتِ	أَنْتِ	
he didn't study	ما دَرَسَ	هُوَ	
she didn't study	ما دَرَسَتْ	هِيَ	
we didn't study	ما دَرَسْنا	نَحْنُ	مُثَنَّى
you (m) didn't study	ما دَرَسْتُما	أَنْتُما (مُذَكَّر)	
you (f) didn't study	ما دَرَسْتُما	أَنْتُما (مؤَنَّث)	
they (m) didn't study	ما دَرَسَا	هُما (مُذَكَّر)	
they (f) didn't study	ما دَرَسَتَا	هُما (مؤَنَّث)	
We didn't study	ما دَرَسْنا	نَحْنُ	جَمْع
you (m) didn't study	ما دَرَسْتُم	أَنْتُم	
you (f) didn't study	ما دَرَسْتُنَّ	أَنْتُنَّ	
they (m) didn't study	ما دَرَسوا	هُمْ	
they (f) didn't study	ما دَرَسْنَ	هُنَّ	

What if we want to negate a passive perfect verb? The answer is straightforward: use ما in the same way as you do in the active perfect tense.

As an exercise, write the full paradigm of the negated passive of خُلِقَ before you look at the following table:

Translation	الفِعْل الماضي المَنْفي	الضَمائِر	
I was not created	ما خُلِقْتُ	أنَا	مُفْرَد
you (m) were not created	ما خُلِقْتَ	أنْتَ	
you (f) were not created	ما خُلِقْتِ	أنْتِ	
he was not created	ما خُلِقَ	هُوَ	
she was not created	ما خُلِقَتْ	هِيَ	
we were not created	ما خُلِقْنَا	نَحْنُ	مُثَنَّى
you (m) were not created	ما خُلِقْتُمَا	أنْتُما (مُذَكَّر)	
you (f) were not created	ما خُلِقْتُمَا	أنْتُما (مؤنَّث)	
they (m) were not created	ما خُلِقَا	هُما (مُذَكَّر)	
they (f) were not created	ما خُلِقَتَا	هُما (مؤنَّث)	
we were not created	ما خُلِقْنَا	نَحْنُ	جَمْع
you (m) were not created	ما خُلِقْتُم	أنْتُم	
you (f) were not created	ما خُلِقْتُنَّ	أنْتُنَّ	
they (m) were not created	ما خُلِقُوا	هُم	
they (f) were not created	ما خُلِقْنَ	هُنَّ	

The Substitute of the Verb's Doer (نائِبُ الفاعِلِ)

In Arabic the common practice is to explicitly mention the verb and its subject—the فِعْل and its فاعِل.

Lesson Fifteen

See the following examples:

المَفْعول بِهِ	الفاعِل	Translation	
الإنْسانَ	اللهُ	God created man.	خَلَقَ اللهُ الإنْسانَ.
قهوةً	مَها	Maha made coffee.	عَمِلَتْ مَها قهوةً.
سَيّارةً	المُهَنْدِسُ	The engineer made a car.	صَنَعَ المُهَنْدِسُ سَيّارةً.
الزُّجاجُ	الوَلَدُ	The boy broke the glass.	كَسَرَ الوَلَدُ الزُّجاجَ.
عِظةُ	ـنا	We heard a sermon.	سَمِعْنا عِظةً.

While these five sentences demonstrate the common way to write the Arabic sentences, sometimes we remove the فاعِل and replace it with المَفْعول بِهِ. In this case, we are not concerned with the doer of the action, perhaps because the فاعِل is unimportant, unknown, or, in other cases, is very well known, such as in the example of اللهُ as the creator in the first sentence.

How will we then modify the sentence?

We must change the verb from active to passive and alter the case of the مَفْعول بِهِ from accusative to nominative. In its new nominative case, the مَفْعول بِهِ is no longer a مَفْعول بِهِ. We will call it the Substitute of the Verb's Doer, or in Arabic نائِبُ الفاعِلِ (nā'ib al-fāʿil).

Hence, the previous sentences become the following:

الفِعْل المَبْني للمَجْهول	نائِبُ الفاعِلِ	Translation	
خُلِقَ	الإنْسانُ	The man was created.	الإنْسانُ خُلِقَ.
عُمِلَتْ	قهوةٌ	A coffee was made.	قهوةٌ عُمِلَتْ.
صُنِعَتْ	سَيّارةٌ	A car was made.	سَيّارةٌ صُنِعَتْ.
كُسِرَ	الزُّجاجُ	The glass was broken.	الزُّجاجُ كُسِرَ.
سُمِعَتْ	عِظةٌ	A sermon was heard.	عِظةٌ سُمِعَتْ.

Lesson Fifteen

To create these new sentences, follow the following four steps:

1. We remove the subject (doer) of the verb: eliminate الفاعِلِ.
2. We turn the active verb into passive: the مَبْني للمَعْلوم into مَبْني للمَجْهول.
3. We change the case of the مَفْعول بِهِ from مَنْصوب (accusative) to مَرْفوع (nominative); from فَتْحَة to ضَمَّة if singular. We now call it نائِبُ الفاعِلِ.
4. We make sure that the new conjugation of the passive verb matches the نائِبُ الفاعِلِ.

There are two observations on these sentences, particularly as we compare the active voice sentences with their passive counterparts.

First, the نائِبُ الفاعِلِ is a nominative noun (مَرْفوع) in a passive sentence. Before we removed the فاعِل, this نائِبُ الفاعِلِ was initially in the accusative case and served as the direct object of an active verb. In other words, the direct object of the active voice sentence becomes the subject of the passive one. Thus, the نائِبُ الفاعِلِ is identified as an agent "taking the place of الفاعِلِ." The Arabic word نائِب refers to a deputy, representative, or delegate.

Second, you should pay attention to the gender of the نائِبُ الفاعِلِ. Compare the active voice sentence صَنَعَ المُهَنْدِسُ سَيَّارَةً to the passive one سَيَّارَةٌ صُنِعَتْ. In the former, the verb صَنَعَ is conjugated to match the masculine subject المُهَنْدِسُ. In creating the sentence using the نائِبُ الفاعِلِ, we first eliminate the فاعِل, then form the passive verb voice as صُنِعَ. However, this conjugation of the passive verb should be modified in order to agree with the gender of the نائِبُ الفاعِلِ, which is the feminine noun سَيَّارَةٌ. Thus, the passive verb will be adjusted to صُنِعَتْ.

As an exercise, study the following examples, where the نائِبُ الفاعِلِ is used:

الجُمْلة	Translation	نائِبُ الفاعِلِ	الفِعْل
الخِطابُ كُتِبَ.	The letter was written.	الخِطابُ	كُتِبَ
مَقالَةٌ دُرِسَتْ.	An article was studied.	مَقالَةٌ	دُرِسَتْ
الكِتابُ دُرِسَ.	The book was studied.	الكِتابُ	دُرِسَ
سَيَّارَةٌ سُرِقَتْ.	A car was stolen.	سَيَّارَةٌ	سُرِقَتْ
المَشروعُ عُمِلَ.	The project was done.	المَشروعُ	عُمِلَ
مَوضوعٌ بُحِثَ.	A topic was researched.	مَوضوعٌ	بُحِثَ

Lesson Fifteen

الفِعْل	نائِبُ الفاعِلِ	Translation	الجُمْلَة
بُحِثَ	مَوضوعٌ	A subject was discussed.	مَوضوعٌ بُحِثَ.
حُرِقَ	تَقْريرٌ	A report was burned.	تَقْريرٌ حُرِقَ.
قُتِلَ	صُرصورٌ	A cockroach was killed.	صُرصورٌ قُتِلَ.
ضُرِبَ	الجَرَسُ	The bell was rung.	الجَرَسُ ضُرِبَ.
سُجِنَ	السّارِقُ	The thief was imprisoned.	السّارِقُ سُجِنَ.
نُهِبَتْ	ثَروَةُ المَلِكِ	The king's wealth was plundered/looted.	ثَروَةُ المَلِكِ نُهِبَتْ.
نُشِرَ	خَبَرُ الوَفاةِ	The death's news was published.	خَبَرُ الوَفاةِ نُشِرَ.

In this table notice three main issues. First, if the نائِبُ الفاعِلِ is singular and indefinite, we use تَنْوينُ ضَمَّة instead of ضَمَّة to establish the nominative case. Second, in the last two examples, the نائِبُ الفاعِلِ is formed by *iḍāfah* constructs: ثَروَةُ المَلِكِ and خَبَرُ الوَفاةِ. Third, in this table we created the passive sentences in the form of nominal sentences, i.e., they begin with nouns. However, we can create them as verbal sentences if we simply exchange the places of the subject and the verb, i.e., كُتِبَ الخِطابُ instead of الخِطابُ كُتِبَ. The same is true for all the sentences in the table.

As an exercise, attempt to form the active sentences that correspond with the passive sentences in the table above, as in the table below:

Translation	مَبني للمَعْلوم	مَبني للمَجْهول
The father wrote the letter.	كَتَبَ الأبُ الخِطابَ.	الخِطابُ كُتِبَ.
The professor studied an article.	دَرَسَ الأُستاذُ مَقالَةً.	مَقالَةٌ دُرِسَتْ.
The student (m) studied the book.	دَرَسَ الطّالِبُ الكِتابَ.	الكِتابُ دُرِسَ.
The thief stole a car.	سَرَقَ اللِّصُ سَيّارَةً.	سَيّارَةٌ سُرِقَتْ.
The engineer made the project.	عَمِلَ المُهَنْدِسُ المَشروعَ.	المَشروعُ عُمِلَ.

The teacher researched the topic.	بَحَثَ المُعَلِّمُ مَوضوعاً.	مَوضوعٌ بُحِثَ.
Hind discussed a subject.	بَحَثَتْ هِنْدُ مَوضوعاً.	مَوضوعٌ بُحِثَ.
Khadijah burned a report.	حَرَقَتْ خَديجَةُ تَقْريراً.	تَقْريرٌ حُرِقَ.
The brother killed a cockroach.	قَتَلَ الأخُ صُرصوراً.	صُرصورٌ قُتِلَ.
The teacher rang the bell.	ضَرَبَ المُدَرِّسُ الجَرَسَ.	الجَرَسُ ضُرِبَ.
The policeman imprisoned the thief.	سَجَنَ الشُرْطِيُّ السّارِقَ.	السّارِقُ سُجِنَ.
The steward looted the wealth of the king.	نَهَبَ الوَكيلُ ثَرْوَةَ المَلِكِ.	ثَرْوَةُ المَلِكِ نُهِبَتْ.
A newspaper published news of the death.	نَشَرَتْ جَريدَةٌ خَبَرَ الوَفاةِ.	خَبَرُ الوَفاةِ نُشِرَ.

Regarding the agreement between the passive verb and its نائِبُ الفاعِلِ, it is important to review the section in Lesson Thirteen on "The Verb and Its Subject (الفِعْلُ والفاعِلُ)," in which we discussed the relationship between a verb and its subject regarding gender and plurality. The same rules apply to passive verbs. The gender of the passive verb you form must match the gender of the نائِبُ الفاعِلِ. As for plurality, if the نائِبُ الفاعِلِ is dual or plural, the verb remains singular. This resembles the treatment of the فاعِل of the active verb. As a general rule, if نائِبُ الفاعِلِ or الفاعِلِ is not singular and is explicitly mentioned after the verb, then the verb will be singular.

As an exercise, study the following passive verb examples:

نائِبُ الفاعِلِ	الفِعْل	Translation	مَبْني للمَجْهول
أطْباقٌ	كُسِرَتْ	Dishes were broken in the kitchen.	كُسِرَتْ أطْباقٌ في المَطْبَخِ.
بُيوتٌ	هُدِمَتْ	Houses were demolished in the village.	هُدِمَتْ بُيوتٌ في القَرْيَةِ.
عامِلان	طُلِبَ	Two workers were requested.	طُلِبَ عامِلانِ.

Lesson Fifteen

عِظاتٌ	سُمِعَتْ	Sermons were heard in the church.	سُمِعَتْ عِظاتٌ في الكَنيسَةِ.
الكَذّابونَ	كُرِهَ	The liars were hated.	كُرِهَ الكَذّابونَ.

In this table we notice that the نائِبُ الفاعِلِ in each sentence is either plural (أَطْباقٌ، الكَذّابونَ، عِظاتٌ، بُيوتٌ) or dual (عامِلانِ). In each example, the فِعْل is singular and either feminine (e.g., كُسِرتْ، هُدِمَتْ، سُمِعَتْ) or masculine (e.g., طُلِبَ، كُرِهَ).

Finally, it might be helpful to recapitulate: while the مَفْعول بِهِ in an active voice sentence is مَنْصوب (accusative), both the فاعِل (of an active verb) and the نائِبُ الفاعِلِ (of a passive verb) are in the مَرْفوع (nominative).

We can now summarize what we have studied so far—regarding cases of the nouns—as follows:

Possible Noun Cases		
مَجْرور	مَنْصوب	مَرْفوع
مَجْرور بحرفِ الجرِ	المَفْعول بِهِ	المُبْتَدَأ
المُضافُ إلَيهِ		الخَبَر
		الفاعِل
		نائِبُ الفاعِل

Arabic Participles (اسْمُ الفاعِلِ واسْمُ المَفْعولِ)

Since we studied the verb's subject (الفاعِل) and its direct object (المَفْعول بِهِ), it is now a good point to explore a related topic: Arabic participles. A participle is a verbal adjective—a noun built on a verb. In English, "a studying person" and "a studied topic" are formed based on the verb "to study." These are nouns (and adjectives) built upon verbs.

In Arabic there are two kinds of participles: an active participle and a passive one.

The active participle indicates the person who executes the action described by the verb (e.g., "a studying person") and is called اسْمُ الفاعِلِ. It is important to understand this label: it is اسْم, because it is a noun and الفاعِل as it refers to the doer of the verb. Thus, the اسْمُ الفاعِلِ is a noun derived from a verb and refers to the one who does, is doing, or has done the action of that verb.

The passive participle refers to the agent upon whom the action is done (e.g., "a studied topic"). We call it اسْمُ المَفْعولِ, highlighting not only that it is a noun (اسْمُ), but also that it is related to the object who received the action. Therefore, the اسْمُ المَفْعولِ is a noun derived from a verb, in order to identify the one who receives, is receiving, or has received the action of the verb.

In practice, both اسْمُ الفاعِلِ and اسْمُ المَفْعولِ often serve as subjects in sentences: a subject of a nominal sentence (مُبْتَدَأ) or a subject of a verbal sentence (فاعِل). In order to learn how to form the participles, it is recommended to review the section on الأوْزان (al-awzān) in Lesson Twelve.

To form اسْمُ الفاعِلِ of a triliteral verb, we simply follow the وَزْن of فاعِل. For instance, from the verb دَرَسَ (he studied), we form the active participle دارِس, which refers to "the one who studies," i.e., a student. We call دارِس the اسْمُ الفاعِلِ from دَرَسَ. Thus, the اسْمُ الفاعِلِ of a triliteral verb can be formed by using the pattern فاعِل of that verb. Similarly, we can build the اسْمُ الفاعِلِ of the verb ذَهَبَ as ذاهِب, meaning "the goer," or use the verb فَعَلَ (he did) to form the participle فاعِل, which refers to "the one who does" or "the doer." Study the following table for more examples:

مَعْنى اسْمُ الفاعِلِ	اسْمُ الفاعِلِ	Translation	الفِعْل
a sitter	جالِس	he sat	جَلَسَ
a creator	خالِق	he created	خَلَقَ
a hitter	ضارِب	he hit	ضَرَبَ
a prostrater (in worship)	ساجِدَ	he bowed, prostrated	سَجَدَ
a servant	خادِمَ	he served	خَدَمَ
a thief	سارِق	he stole	سَرَقَ
a maker	صانِع	he made	صَنَعَ
a winner	غالِب	he won	غَلَبَ
a kneeler (worshiper)	راكِع	he kneeled	رَكَعَ
a writer	كاتِب	he wrote	كَتَبَ
a listener	سامِع	he heard	سَمِعَ
a maker, worker	عامِل	he made	عَمِلَ

As an exercise, begin with verbs you studied earlier and attempt to form nouns which indicate a planter, server, killer, and overseer.

As with اسْمُ الفاعِلِ, to form اسْمُ المَفْعولِ of a triliteral verb, we simply follow the وَزْن of مَفْعول. So, from دَرَسَ, we form the passive participle مَدْروس, which refers to "the studied one." We call مَدْروس the اسْمُ المَفْعولِ from دَرَسَ. Compare دَرَسَ and مَدْروس in terms of their وَزْن. The former is on the pattern فَعَلَ, while the participle مَدْروس is ᶜalā wazn مَفْعول.

Study the following examples:

مَعْنى اسْمُ المَفْعولِ	اسْمُ المَفْعولِ	Translation	الفِعْلُ
a heard one	مَسْموع	he heard	سَمِعَ
a made thing	مَعْمول	he made	عَمِلَ
a planted thing (a plant)	مَزْروع	he planted	زَرَعَ
an allowed matter (permissible)	مَسْموح	he allowed	سَمَحَ
a killed person	مَقْتول	he killed	قَتَلَ
a spent (money)	مصْروف	he spent	صَرَفَ
abandoned	مَتْروك	he left	تَرَكَ
a cut item	مَقْطوع	he cut	قَطَعَ
an outrun person (loser)	مَسْبوق	he outran	سَبَقَ
a cooked (meal)	مَطْبوخ	he cooked	طَبَخَ
a drink	مَشْروب	he drank	شَرِبَ

To understand the meaning of the participles اسْمُ الفاعِلِ and اسْمُ المَفْعولِ, it is important to compare them.

Consider the verb خَدَمَ (to serve). The اسْمُ الفاعِلِ of the verb is خادِم, which refers to the person who does the action of service, i.e., a servant. The اسْمُ المَفْعولِ of the verb is مَخْدوم, which identifies the one who receives the act of service, i.e., a master.

Similarly, based on the verb قَتَلَ (to kill), we can create the noun for "a killer" as قاتِل and that of "the killed" as مَقْتول. Finally, the verb كَسَرَ (to break) can form both a كاسِر (breaker) and a مَكْسور (broken).

Finally, there are more complex ways of forming the participles اسْمُ الفاعِلِ and اسْمُ المَفْعولِ, especially with unique and sophisticated verbs. In this introductory course, we focus only on the basic ways to form these participles.

Nouns of Intensiveness and Exaggeration (اسْمُ المُبالَغة)

Arabic uses various noun forms to describe intensiveness and exaggeration. These are nouns derived from verbs, and they indicate the frequency and quality of the action denoted by the verb. These nouns point to a subject (person) who possesses a high level of the verb's core meaning or who performs it intensively and repeatedly. Thus, they make great adjectives. Some call them صِيَغْ المُبالَغة, referring to them as exaggeration forms or hyperbolic participles. Since they are also nouns, the term is also called اسْمُ المُبالَغة.

Consider the verb "to break." Its exaggeration noun اسْمُ المُبالَغة would mean "the one who breaks (things) repeatedly" or "a repeated breaker," which may refer to a person whose profession requires breaking things. The verb "to kill" can form اسْمُ المُبالَغة to describe "the one who kills quite often and repeatedly," or "a serial killer."

To form اسْمُ المُبالَغة (a noun of intensiveness), again we rely on the أَوْزان. However, at the outset, four important matters should be mentioned: (1) there are various أَوْزان which we can follow in order to form a noun of intensiveness; (2) not all possible أَوْزان are suitable for every verb, and there is no specific formula to discern which وَزْن can be used with each specific verb; (3) we can only form the اسْمُ المُبالَغة from a triliteral verb; and (4) not every verb can establish a corresponding اسْمُ المُبالَغة.

Four of the most common أَوْزان to form اسْمُ المُبالَغة are as follows:

فَعول

فَعيل

فَعَّال

مِفْعال

See the following examples:

<div align="center" colspan="4">عَلَى وَزْن: فَعُوْل</div>			
a big eater	أكول	to eat	أَكَلَ
a liar	كَذوب	to lie	كَذَبَ
a patient (enduring) person	صَبور	to be patient	صَبَرَ
an envious person	حَسود	to envy	حَسَدَ
a thankful one	شَكور	to thank	شَكَرَ
all forgiving	غفور	to forgive	غَفَرَ
<div align="center" colspan="4">عَلَى وَزْن: فَعيل</div>			
a huge listener	سَميع	to hear	سَمِعَ
an all merciful	رَحيم	to be merciful	رَحِمَ
an all knower	عَليم	to know	عَلِمَ
a warner	نَذير	to warn	نَذَرَ
an almighty	قَدير	to be able	قَدِرَ
a generous one	كَريم	to be generous	كَرُمَ
a huge one	كَبير	to become bigger	كَبُرَ
an anointed one	مَسيح	to anoint	مَسَحَ
a praiseworthy one	حَميد	to praise	حَمَدَ
<div align="center" colspan="4">عَلَى وَزْن: فَعَّال</div>			
a smiling one	بَسَّام	to smile	بَسَمَ
all knowing	عَلَّام	to know	عَلِمَ
all forgiving	غَفَّار	to forgive	غَفَرَ
a murderous one	قَتَّال	to kill	قَتَلَ
a blood-shedder	سَفَّاك	to shed blood	سَفَكَ

an often swearer	حَلَّاف	to swear	حَلَفَ
a serial killer	سَفَّاح	to pour out	سَفَحَ
a porter	حَمَّال	to carry	حَمَلَ
a drinker	شَرَّاب	to drink	شَرِبَ
a cook	طَبَّاخ	to cook	طَبَخَ
a perfume seller	عَطَّار	to perfume	عَطِرَ
a carpenter	نَجَّار	to trim (wood)	نَجَرَ
a farmer	فَلَّاح	to till the soil	فَلَحَ
an opener	فَتَّاح	to open	فَتَحَ
عَلَى وَزْن: مِفْعَال			
an adventurous person	مِقْدَام	to come forth	قَدَمَ
a humorist joker	مِهْذَار	to joke	هَذَرَ

From this table, there are several observations.

First, the verb غَفَرَ can establish two different exaggeration forms: غَفُور and غَفَّار. Both forms describe a person who performs the act of "forgiving" repeatedly, excessively, or in a high quality. This is the core idea behind اسْمُ المُبَالَغَة.

Second, if you compare the examples under فَعِيل with those under فَعَّال, you will notice a pattern concerning the meanings they provide. The exaggeration forms following فَعِيل mostly reflect divine attributes, i.e., characteristics of God. As for those following فَعَّال, their meanings usually relate to professions and jobs.

Third, these exaggeration forms are built on verbs, yet we cannot really specify a formula as to which وَزْن should be used with each verb. For instance, from the verb سَفَحَ, we can establish اسْمُ المُبَالَغَة as سَفَّاح, but not سَفِيح. There is no specific reason, except that Arabic-speakers pronounce it this way. Similarly, from the verb هَذَرَ, the اسْمُ المُبَالَغَة is مِهْذَار, but not هَذِير nor هَذُور.

Fourth, both اسْمُ المُبَالَغَة and اسْمُ الفَاعِل are not only derived from a verb but also share comparable and close meanings, with the exception that اسْمُ المُبَالَغَة indicates that the agent (subject or actor) executes the verb repeatedly and in an intensive manner.

In concluding this section, we will examine how اسْمُ المُبَالَغَة functions in a sentence.

Lesson Fifteen

Consider the sentence اللهُ غَفورٌ. It means "God is all forgiving." This is a nominal sentence, in which the noun اللهُ is the مُبْتَدَأ, while غَفورٌ is the خَبَر. Both the مُبْتَدَأ and the خَبَر are مَرْفوع (nominative). The اسْمُ المُبالَغة functions as the خَبَر of the nominative sentence.

Consider the following sentences. Try to determine the وَزْن of اسْمُ المُبالَغة before you look at the last column:

عَلى وَزْن	اسْمُ المُبالَغة	Translation	
فَعول فَعيل	غَفورٌ رَحيمٌ	God is all forgiving, all merciful.	اللهُ غَفورٌ رَحيمٌ.
فَعّال	عَلّامٌ	God is all knowing of the unseen.	اللهُ عَلّامُ الغَيْبِ.
مِفْعال	مِقْدامٌ	This is an adventurous man.	هذا رَجُلٌ مِقْدامٌ.
فَعولة	صَبورةٌ	This is a (strongly) patient woman.	هَذِهِ امْرَأَةٌ صَبورةٌ.
فَعيلات	كَريماتٌ	They (fp) are (quite) generous.	هُنَّ كَريماتٌ.

From this table we deduce one additional piece of information: The اسْمُ المُبالَغة can be definite or indefinite, and it can be singular, dual, or plural. However, it must follow one of the abovementioned patterns (أَوْزان).

Vocabulary

In this lesson, we encountered plenty of new words. Here is your vocabulary list.

a sitter	جالِس	article	مَقالَة
a creator	خالِق	book	كِتاب
a hitter	ضارِب	car	سَيَّارَة
a prostrater	ساجِدَ	project	مَشْروع
a servant	خادِمَ	topic	مَوضوع
a thief	سارِق	subject	مَوضوع

a maker	صَانِع	report	تَقْرِير
a winner	غَالِب	cockroach	صُرصور
a kneeler	رَاكِع	bell	جَرَس
a writer	كَاتِب	wealth	ثَرْوَة
a listener	سَامِع	death's news	خَبَرُ الوَفاةِ
a maker, worker	عَامِل	a left aside matter/person	مَتْروك
a heard one (audible)	مَسْموع	a cut item	مَقْطوع
a made thing	مَعْمول	an outrun person (loser)	مَسْبوق
a planted thing (a plant)	مَزْروع	a cooked (meal)	مَطْبوخ
an allowed matter	مَسْموح	a drink	مَشْروب
a killed person	مَقْتول	a big eater	أَكول
a spent (money)	مَصْروف	a liar	كَذوب
a smiling one	بَسَّام	a patient (enduring) person	صَبور
all knowing	عَلَّام	an envious person	حَسود
all forgiving	غَفَّار	a thankful one	شَكور
a murderous one	قَتَّال	all forgiving	غَفور
a blood-shedder	سَفَّاك	a huge listener	سَميع
an often swearer	حَلَّاف	an all-merciful one	رَحيم
a serial killer	سَفَّاح	an all-knower	عَليم
a porter	حَمَّال	a warner	نَذير
a drinker	شَرَّاب	an almighty one	قَدير

Lesson Fifteen

a cook	طَبَّاخ	a generous one	كَريم
a perfume seller	عَطَّار	a huge one	كَبير
a carpenter	نَجَّار	an anointed one	مَسيح
a farmer	فَلَّاح	a praiseworthy one	حَميد
an opener	فَتَّاح	exaggeration	مُبالَغَة
an adventurous person	مِقْدام	man (a human)	إنْسان
a humorist joker	مِهذار	lady	سَيِّدَة
thief	سارِق	coffee	قَهْوَة
thief	لِص	boy	وَلَد
a piece of news	خَبَر	glass	زُجاج
news of death	خَبَرُ الوَفاةِ	sermon	عِظَة
king	مَلِك	sermons	عِظاتُ
policeman	شُرْطِيّ	letter, speech	خِطابُ
a steward, agent	وَكيل	kitchen	مَطْبَخ
newspaper	جَريدَة	village	قَرْيَة
dishes	أطْباق	liars	كَذَّابونَ

Exercises

Exercise 15.1

Negate the following sentences.

1. كُسِرَ الزُّجاجُ.

2. صَنَعَ المُهَنْدِسُ السَّيَّارَةَ.

3. كَسَرَ الوَلَدُ الزُّجاجَ.

4. مَوضوعٌ بُحِثَ.

5. المُعَلِّمُ كَتَبَ الدرسَ.

6. سَمِعْنا العِظةَ.

7. قَتَلَ الأخُ صُرصوراً.

8. المُدَرِّسُ ضَرَبَ الجَرَسَ.

9. ثَرْوَةُ المَلِكِ نُهِبَتْ.

10. نُشِرَ خَبَرُ الوَفاةِ.

Exercise 15.2

Here are active sentences. Make them passive and identify the نائِبُ الفاعِلِ.

1. طَبَخَتْ سُعادُ وفاطِمَةُ الوَجْبَةَ.

2. طَبَخَ الوالِدُ الوَجْبَةَ.

3. كَتَبَ المُعَلِّمُ الاخْتِبارَ.

4. شَرَحَ الكاهِنُ الدَرْسَ.

5. بَحَثَ الطالبانِ المَشْروعَ.

6. قَتَلْنا الصُّرصورَ.

7. كَسَرْتُم الزُّجاجَ.

Exercise 15.3

In the following set of nouns, determine اسْمُ الفاعِلِ, اسْمُ المَفْعولِ, and اسْمُ المُبالَغَة.

مَقْطوع	صابِر	سامِع	ضارِب	عابِر
كَبير	عامِل	مَعْمول	مَقْتول	مَطْبوخ
كَذّاب	غالِب	شَكور	رَحيم	قَدير

Exercise 15.4

Translate the following sentences into Arabic.

1. Dishes were broken.

2. God is all knowing of the unseen.

3. This is an adventurous girl.

4. This is a (strongly) patient man.

5. Houses were demolished.

6. The killer (f) was imprisoned.

7. A worker (m) was requested.

8. The master (m) exited from the gate.

9. A writer entered the house.

10. I want a drink.

Lesson Sixteen
سِتَّةَ عَشَرَ

Present Simple Verbs

In this lesson we focus on the forms of present tense verbs, including both active and passive voices. Afterward, we will examine the future tense and various ways to negate present and future.

Present Active Tense (الفِعْل المُضارع)

If the past tense is perfective, present tense is imperfective. The words "imperfect" and "present" should be viewed as grammatically synonymous. The action of the present tense has not yet finished. It is ongoing during the speech. The present tense is called الفِعْل المُضارع. We will now examine the active voice (المَعْلوم), before later discussing the passive (المَجْهول).

Consider the full paradigm of the active voice of the present simple tense of دَرَسَ. Examine each conjugation, and expect important observations to follow:

I study	أَدْرُسُ	أَنَا	مُفْرَد
you (m) study	تَدْرُسُ	أَنْتَ	
you (f) study	تَدْرُسِينَ	أَنْتِ	
he studies	يَدْرُسُ	هُوَ	
she studies	تَدْرُسُ	هِيَ	
we study	نَدْرُسُ	نَحْنُ	مُثَنّى
you (m) study	تَدْرُسانِ	أَنْتُما (مُذَكَّر)	
you (f) study	تَدْرُسانِ	أَنْتُما (مؤَنَّث)	
they (m) study	يَدْرُسانِ	هُما (مُذَكَّر)	
they (f) study	تَدْرُسانِ	هُما (مؤَنَّث)	

	نَحْنُ	نَدْرُسُ	we study
	أَنْتُمْ	تَدْرُسُونَ	you (m) study
جَمْع	أَنْتُنَّ	تَدْرُسْنَ	you (f) study
	هُمْ	يَدْرُسُونَ	they (m) study
	هُنَّ	يَدْرُسْنَ	they (f) study

There are five observations to make regarding this verb paradigm.

First, each item is translated as present simple tense (e.g., I study), although it can also be translated in a present continuous manner (e.g., I am studying). The context is key.

Second, there is an obvious difference between الفِعْل المُاضي and الفِعْل المُضارع. Unlike الماضي, which has only suffixes, the paradigm of المُضارع has both prefixes and suffixes. This is, in a way, very helpful and makes distinguishing between the tenses easier.

Third, observe the prefixes. Notice that every prefix is one of the following letters: أ، تَـ، يَـ، نَـ. It is also associated with a فَتْحَة. These prefixes are helpful in determining that we are dealing with المُضارع, and they point us to the gender of the verb's subject. As with the perfect tense, in the imperfect the فاعِل (the subject, the verb's actor) is part of the conjugation.

Fourth, examine the conjugations again and focus on identifying similarities. You will quickly notice that a couple of conjugations are identical. In the singular section, the conjugation تَدْرُسُ is found with the pronouns أَنْتَ and هِيَ. Both pronouns conjugate the verb in the same way. In the dual section, the conjugation تَدْرُسَانِ is identical to masculine/feminine أَنْتُما and feminine هُما. This is an important feature in the present tense.

Fifth, just as we did in the past tense, we will refer to this paradigm with the third-person singular masculine. So, this is verb يَدْرُسُ. In fact, Arabic linguists label verbs in a unique way, by referring to past and present conjugations of third-person masculine singular consecutively. So they label this verb as دَرَسَ يَدْرُسُ (verb *darasa yadrusu*, in this particular sequence, i.e., past followed by present).

Follow the example of يَدْرُسُ and write the full paradigm of the present tense conjugations of the verb يَخْلُقُ before looking at the following table:

I create	أَخْلُقُ	أَنَا	
you (m) create	تَخْلُقُ	أَنْتَ	
you (f) create	تَخْلُقِينَ	أَنْتِ	مُفْرَد
he creates	يَخْلُقُ	هُوَ	
she creates	تَخْلُقُ	هِيَ	
we create	نَخْلُقُ	نَحْنُ	
you (m) create	تَخْلُقَانِ	أَنْتُما (مُذَكَّر)	
you (f) create	تَخْلُقَانِ	أَنْتُما (مؤنَّث)	مُثَنَّى
they (m) create	يَخْلُقَانِ	هُما (مُذَكَّر)	
they (f) create	تَخْلُقَانِ	هُما (مؤنَّث)	
we create	نَخْلُقُ	نَحْنُ	
you (m) create	تَخْلُقُونَ	أَنْتُمْ	
you (f) create	تَخْلُقْنَ	أَنْتُنَّ	جَمْع
they (m) create	يَخْلُقُونَ	هُمْ	
they (f) create	يَخْلُقْنَ	هُنَّ	

The paradigm of the verb خَلَقَ يَخْلُقُ is straightforward. By comparing the conjugations of the verbs يَدْرُسُ and يَخْلُقُ, you will notice no irregularities at all. You can be certain that the paradigm of المُضارع will always use the same prefixes and suffixes. This should be comforting. However, there is still more to learn about the imperfect verb conjugations. In order to move an additional step further in understanding these conjugations and the way other imperfect verb paradigms operate, let's form the conjugations of the present verbs يَذْهَبُ (to go) and يَفْعَلُ (to do), and then compare them with those we formed earlier, يَدْرُسُ and يَخْلُقُ.

Lesson Sixteen

Here are the conjugations of يَذْهَبُ and يَفْعَلُ:

الضَّمائِر		الفِعْل المُضارِع يَذْهَبُ	الفِعْل المُضارِع يَفْعَلُ
مُفْرَد	أَنَا	أَذْهَبُ	أَفْعَلُ
	أَنْتَ	تَذْهَبُ	تَفْعَلُ
	أَنْتِ	تَذْهَبِينَ	تَفْعَلِينَ
	هُوَ	يَذْهَبُ	يَفْعَلُ
	هِيَ	تَذْهَبُ	تَفْعَلُ
مُثَنَّى	نَحْنُ	نَذْهَبُ	نَفْعَلُ
	أَنْتُما (مُذَكَّر)	تَذْهَبَانِ	تَفْعَلَانِ
	أَنْتُما (مؤَنَّث)	تَذْهَبَانِ	تَفْعَلَانِ
	هُما (مُذَكَّر)	يَذْهَبَانِ	يَفْعَلَانِ
	هُما (مؤَنَّث)	تَذْهَبَانِ	تَفْعَلَانِ
جَمْع	نَحْنُ	نَذْهَبُ	نَفْعَلُ
	أَنْتُم	تَذْهَبُونَ	تَفْعَلُونَ
	أَنْتُنَّ	تَذْهَبْنَ	تَفْعَلْنَ
	هُمْ	يَذْهَبُونَ	يَفْعَلُونَ
	هُنَّ	يَذْهَبْنَ	يَفْعَلْنَ

If you compare the conjugations of يَدْرُسُ and يَخْلُقُ against those of يَذْهَبُ and يَفْعَلُ, you will quickly notice one unexpected feature: while all of these verbs are on the pattern فَعَلَ in the perfect tense and use the exact prefixes and suffixes in the imperfect tense, the second letter of the root takes a ضَمَّة in the first pair and a فَتْحَة in the second.

This feature can confuse non-Arabic speakers, but there is a helpful linguistic rule which can explain why verbs act this way. In regular triliteral verbs, if the second letter of the root (remember it is also called "second radical") uses a فَتْحَة in the past tense, it may switch to a ضَمَّة or كَسْرَة in the present tense. This is usually true, as in

يَدْرُسُ and يَخْلُقُ. One exception to this rule is when the second letter is a guttural, as in the case of يَذْهَبُ and يَفْعَلُ, where we have the gutturals ـهَـ and ـعَـ, respectively. In this exceptional case, the فَتْحَة remains in the imperfect verb conjugations.[1] This rule clarifies why the verbs يَذْهَبُ and يَفْعَلُ did not operate in the same way as يَدْرُسُ and يَخْلُقُ in switching to a ضَمَّة on the root's second letter. Both يَذْهَبُ and يَفْعَلُ retain the فَتْحَة from their perfect tenses ذَهَبَ and فَعَلَ. Therefore, in regular triliteral verbs عَلَى وَزْن فَعَلَ, the second radical will switch its short vowel from a فَتْحَة in the past tense to a ضَمَّة or كَسْرَة in the present, unless that letter was a guttural.

Let's further examine present verb paradigms. What do you expect the imperfect tense conjugations of قَتَلَ (to kill) and ضَرَبَ (to hit) to be? At the outset, both verbs are عَلَى وَزْن فَعَلَ, and their second radicals are not gutturals. Here are their conjugations:

	الضَّمائِر	الفِعْل المُضارِع يَقْتُلُ	الفِعْل المُضارِع يَضْرِبُ
مُفْرَد	أَنَا	أَقْتُلُ	أَضْرِبُ
	أَنْتَ	تَقْتُلُ	تَضْرِبُ
	أَنْتِ	تَقْتُلِينَ	تَضْرِبِينَ
	هُوَ	يَقْتُلُ	يَضْرِبُ
	هِيَ	تَقْتُلُ	تَضْرِبُ
مُثَنَّى	نَحْنُ	نَقْتُلُ	نَضْرِبُ
	أَنْتُما (مُذَكَّر)	تَقْتُلَانِ	تَضْرِبَانِ
	أَنْتُما (مُؤَنَّث)	تَقْتُلَانِ	تَضْرِبَانِ
	هُما (مُذَكَّر)	يَقْتُلَانِ	يَضْرِبَانِ
	هُما (مُؤَنَّث)	تَقْتُلَانِ	تَضْرِبَانِ

---

1. To feed the inquiring minds of some students, see more on this point in William Wright, *A Grammar of the Arabic Language*, new impression, 3 vols. (Beirut: Librairie de Liban, 1996), 1:57ff.

جَمْع	نَحْنُ	نَقْتُلُ	نَضْرِبُ
	أَنْتُمْ	تَقْتُلُونَ	تَضْرِبُونَ
	أَنْتُنَّ	تَقْتُلْنَ	تَضْرِبْنَ
	هُمْ	يَقْتُلُونَ	يَضْرِبُونَ
	هُنَّ	يَقْتُلْنَ	يَضْرِبْنَ

As expected, since both verbs قَتَلَ and ضَرَبَ have فَتْحَة on the root's second letter in the past tense and since that letter is not a guttural, the فَتْحَة on the second letter switches to a كَسْرَة or ضَمَّة when we create imperfect verb conjugations. Here, it is a ضَمَّة in the case of verb قَتَلَ يَقْتُلُ, and a كَسْرَة in that of ضَرَبَ يَضْرِبُ. Still, the prefixes and suffixes are consistent with the imperfect tense paradigm initially given.

As an exercise, attempt to form the imperfect conjugations of the verbs كَتَبَ (to write) and جَلَسَ (to sit). Note that their second radicals are not gutturals, and both use a فَتْحَة:

	الضَّمائِر	الفِعْل المُضارِع يَكْتُبُ	الفِعْل المُضارِع يَجْلِسُ
مُفْرَد	أَنَا	أَكْتُبُ	أَجْلِسُ
	أَنْتَ	تَكْتُبُ	تَجْلِسُ
	أَنْتِ	تَكْتُبِينَ	تَجْلِسِينَ
	هُوَ	يَكْتُبُ	يَجْلِسُ
	هِيَ	تَكْتُبُ	تَجْلِسُ
مُثَنَّى	نَحْنُ	نَكْتُبُ	نَجْلِسُ
	أَنْتُما (مُذَكَّر)	تَكْتُبانِ	تَجْلِسانِ
	أَنْتُما (مؤَنَّث)	تَكْتُبانِ	تَجْلِسانِ
	هُما (مُذَكَّر)	يَكْتُبانِ	يَجْلِسانِ
	هُما (مؤَنَّث)	تَكْتُبانِ	تَجْلِسانِ

	الضمائر			
جَمْع	نَحْنُ	نَكْتُبُ	نَجْلِسُ
	أَنْتُمْ	تَكْتُبُونَ	تَجْلِسُونَ
	أَنْتُنَّ	تَكْتُبْنَ	تَجْلِسْنَ
	هُمْ	يَكْتُبُونَ	يَجْلِسُونَ
	هُنَّ	يَكْتُبْنَ	يَجْلِسْنَ

Again, as expected, since both verbs كَتَبَ and جَلَسَ have فَتْحَة on the second letter of their roots and since that letter is not a guttural, the فَتْحَة on the second radical switches to a ضَمَّة or كَسْرَة in the present. It is a ضَمَّة in the verb كَتَبَ يَكْتُبُ and a كَسْرَة in the case of جَلَسَ يَجْلِسُ. It is important to reiterate, however, that all the prefixes and suffixes are consistent with what we learned earlier in the lesson.

But what if the root's second radical is a guttural with a فَتْحَة? As we discussed earlier, this فَتْحَة will remain in the present tense conjugations and will not switch to a ضَمَّة or كَسْرَة.

Consider the verbs قَهَرَ (to beat or defeat), سَحَرَ (to bewitch someone), and طَحَنَ (to crush or pound something). All of them have roots with a guttural as the second radical. What should we expect when we form their imperfect verb conjugations? They should retain the فَتْحَة on the second radical in the imperfect. See the table below:

	الضمائر	الفِعْل المُضارع يَقْهَرُ	الفِعْل المُضارع يَسْحَرُ	الفِعْل المُضارع يَطْحَنُ
مُفْرَد	أَنَا	أَقْهَرُ	أَسْحَرُ	أَطْحَنُ
	أَنْتَ	تَقْهَرُ	تَسْحَرُ	تَطْحَنُ
	أَنْتِ	تَقْهَرِينَ	تَسْحَرِينَ	تَطْحَنِينَ
	هُوَ	يَقْهَرُ	يَسْحَرُ	يَطْحَنُ
	هِيَ	تَقْهَرُ	تَسْحَرُ	تَطْحَنُ

Lesson Sixteen

نَطْحَنُ	نَسْحَرُ	نَقْهَرُ	نَحْنُ	
تَطْحَنَانِ	تَسْحَرَانِ	تَقْهَرَانِ	أَنْتُما (مُذَكَّر)	
تَطْحَنَانِ	تَسْحَرَانِ	تَقْهَرَانِ	أَنْتُما (مؤَنَّث)	مُثَنَّى
يَطْحَنَانِ	يَسْحَرَانِ	يَقْهَرَانِ	هُما (مُذَكَّر)	
تَطْحَنَانِ	تَسْحَرَانِ	تَقْهَرَانِ	هُما (مؤَنَّث)	
نَطْحَنُ	نَسْحَرُ	نَقْهَرُ	نَحْنُ	
تَطْحَنُونَ	تَسْحَرُونَ	تَقْهَرُونَ	أَنْتُمْ	
تَطْحَنَّ	تَسْحَرْنَ	تَقْهَرْنَ	أَنْتُنَّ	جَمْع
يَطْحَنُونَ	يَسْحَرُونَ	يَقْهَرُونَ	هُمْ	
يَطْحَنَّ	يَسْحَرْنَ	يَقْهَرْنَ	هُنَّ	

In this table, notice that none of the three verbs switch from the فَتْحَة on the root's second radical in the past tense to a ضَمَّة or كَسْرَة in the present, because their roots have gutturals as their second radicals. The result is يَطْحَنُ، يَسْحَرُ، يَقْهَرُ. This should clarify the rule regarding the second radical of the root and whether its فَتْحَة should switch to a ضَمَّة or كَسْرَة when forming the imperfect.[2]

There is one more matter to discuss regarding the conjugations of the imperfect tense. You will recall that in the past tense of triliteral verbs there are three different patterns: فَعَلَ، فَعِلَ، فَعُلَ. Each pattern differs only in the vowel of the second radical of the root. What will occur when we form their present tense conjugations?

Triliteral verbs following the pattern فَعِلَ (in the past tense) often form their present verb conjugations as يَفْعَلُ, i.e., their second radical alters the كَسْرَة into a فَتْحَة when forming the present. As for triliteral verbs following the pattern فَعُلَ (in the

---

2. A student may ask, though, are there exceptions? Should we always expect the second radical of the root to retain a فَتْحَة in the imperfect as long as it is a guttural? While this is the rule in most cases, there are a few exceptions. For example, the verbs فَعَدَ يَقْعُدُ (to sit) and رَعَدَ يَرْعُدُ (to thunder) both have gutturals as their root second radical, but they do not retain a فَتْحَة over that guttural in the present. Again, this is a rare exception to the rule. Since this is an introductory course, it should suffice to adhere to the rule mentioned above regarding gutturals. See more in Wright, *A Grammar of the Arabic Language*, 1:57ff.

perfect tense), they adopt the pattern يَفْعُلُ for their present verb conjugations, i.e., they retain the ضَمَّة in the imperfect tense.

Study the examples in the table below:

Translation	المُضارع	الماضي	وَزْن الفِعْل
to make	يَعْمَلُ	عَمِلَ	فَعِلَ
to hear	يَسْمَعُ	سَمِعَ	فَعِلَ
to bear witness	يَشْهَدُ	شَهِدَ	فَعِلَ
to get sick	يَمْرَضُ	مَرِضَ	فَعِلَ
to get angry	يَغْضَبُ	غَضِبَ	فَعِلَ
to become small	يَصْغُرُ	صَغُرَ	فَعُلَ
to be complete	يَكْمُلُ	كَمُلَ	فَعُلَ

While exercises are usually left to the end of the lesson, it is good to stop here for a moment and practice present tense verbs. Attempt to translate the following passage into Arabic before checking the answer. Note that we used many of the previously learned verbs, except when we needed to add a verb or adverb from outside of the list.

> "Grace and peace to you. My name is Ibrahim. I am Egyptian and American. I live in Louisville, Kentucky. I am a history teacher at my school. I love my students. They are smart. They study Arabic, history, and theology. They succeed in their exams. My wife is also a teacher. She teaches Spanish to children. We are Christians. We go to church on Sunday. Our friend and his wife go with us. We ride in a car and cross the river to go to our church. The grace of God appears in our church. We always worship, kneel, and listen to sermons from the Bible. The pastor of the church is a good and kind man. His wife is our friend. She and my wife go running every Friday. Every Wednesday we have a party. Our wives cook a great meal. We sit, eat, and play together. We love our friends. Our neighbor is Muslim. His name is Mohammad. He is the imam of the mosque in our region. His wife's name is Fatima. He and his wife and his children attend our party every Wednesday. They live in a big and new house with their son Ali, and daughter Mona. We love our neighbors."

Here is the translation:

نِعْمَةٌ وسَلامٌ لَكُمْ. اسمي إبْراهيم. أنا مِصْريٌّ وأَمْريكيٌّ. أنا أَسْكُنُ في لوِيفيل، كِنْتاكي. أنا مُدَرِّسُ تاريخٍ في مَدْرَسَتي. أنا أُحِبُّ طُلّابي. هُمْ أذكياء ويَدْرُسُونَ العَرَبيَّة والتّاريخَ واللّاهوتَ. هُمْ يَنْجَحُونَ في اِمْتِحانِهم. زَوجَتي أَيْضاً مُعَلِّمَةٌ. هِيَ تُعَلِّمُ الإسْبانيَّة للأطْفال. نَحْنُ مَسيحيّان. نَحْنُ نَذْهَبُ إلى الكنيسةِ يَوم الأحَدِ. صَديقُنا وزَوجَتُهُ يَذْهَبانِ مَعْنا. نَرْكَبُ سَيّارَةً ونَعْبُرُ النَهْرَ لَنَذْهَبَ إلى كَنيسَتِنا. نعمةُ اللهِ تَظْهَرُ في كَنيسَتِنا. نَحْنُ دائِماً نَعْبُدُ ونَرْكَعُ ونَسْمَعُ عِظاتٍ من الكتابِ المُقَدَّس. قِسِّيسُ الكَنيسَةِ رَجُلٌ طَيِّبٌ ولَطيفٌ. زَوجَتُهُ صَديقَتُنا. هِيَ وزوجَتي تَذْهَبانِ إلى الرَكْضِ كل جُمعةٍ. كُل يَوم أرْبَعاءٍ عِنْدَنا حَفْلَةٌ. زَوجاتُنا يَطْبُخْنَ وَجْبَةً رائِعَةً. نَجْلِسُ ونَأكُلُ و نَلْعَبُ معاً. نَحْنُ نُحِبُّ أصْدِقائَنا. جارُنا مُسْلِمٌ. اسمُهُ مُحَمَّد. هو إمامُ المسجد في مَنْطِقَتِنا. اسمُ زَوجَتِهِ فاطِمَة. هُوَ وزَوْجَتُهُ وأطْفالُهُ يَحْضُرُونَ حَفلَتِنا كل أَرْبَعاء. هُمْ يَسْكُنونَ في مَنْزِلٍ كَبيرٍ وجَديدٍ مِعَ ابْنِهِما عَلي وابْنَتِهِما مُنَى. نَحْنُ نُحِبُّ جيرانَنا.

By reading the passage and the translation, you can both practice the conjugation of present tense verbs and identify the meaning of old and new words.

At this stage it is important to practice parsing some present verbs. Use the same sequence of parsing we used in past simple tense: tense, person, gender, number, root, and meaning. Attempt to parse the word in the right column before you check the answer:

الإعْراب	الكَلِمَة
Present, 3mp, ح.م.ل, they carry	يَحْمِلُونَ
Present, 2md/2fd, د.ف.ع, you pay/push, or Present, 3fd, د.ف.ع, they pay/push	تَدْفَعانِ
Present, 1mp/1fp, (or dual), ف.ه.م, we understand	نَفْهَمُ
Present, 2fs, س.ه.ل, you become easy	تَسْهُلِينَ
Present, 3fp, ك.ب.ر, they become big	يَكْبُرْنَ
Present, 2md/2fd, د.ر.س, you study, or Present, 3fd, د.ر.س, they study	تَدْرُسانِ

تَفْعَلُ	Present, 2ms, ف.ع.ل, you do, or Present, 3fs, ف.ع.ل, she does
تَقْتُلانِ	Present, 2md/2fd, ق.ت.ل, you kill, or Present, 3fd, ق.ت.ل, they kill
تَعْبُدْنَ	Present, 2fp, ع.ب.د, you worship
تَشْرَبُ	Present, 2ms, ش.ر.ب, you drink, or Present, 3fs, ش.ر.ب, she drinks

One final note regarding the verb-subject agreement: You recall from the previous lesson on the past simple tense (Lesson Thirteen) that, when it comes to gender, the verb agrees with its subject. As for number, the verb remains singular whether the subject is singular, dual, or plural, unless the subject precedes the verb, such as in nominal sentences. The same rule applies in the present tense.

For example, consider the verb عَبَدَ يَعْبُدُ, meaning "to worship." The following sentences are all correct. Notice the number of the subjects and whether they precede or follow the verb:

يَعْبُدُ الرَّجُلُ في الكَنيسَةِ.

يَعْبُدُ الرَّجُلانِ في الكَنيسَةِ.

يَعْبُدُ الرِّجالُ في الكَنيسَةِ.

تَعْبُدُ السَّيِّدَةُ في الكَنيسَةِ.

تَعْبُدُ السَّيِّدَتانِ في الكَنيسَةِ.

تَعْبُدُ السَّيِّداتُ في الكَنيسَةِ.

الرَّجُلانِ يَعْبُدانِ.

السَّيِّدَتانِ تَعْبُدانِ.

السَّيِّداتُ يَعْبُدْنَ في الكَنيسَةِ.

الرِّجالُ يَعْبُدونَ في الكَنيسَةِ.

To summarize, in verbal sentences the verb is always singular. In nominal sentences the verb takes the number of its subject. As for gender, the verb always agrees with its subject. After exploring the present active tense المُضارع المَعلوم, we will now turn to its passive voice.

Lesson Sixteen

Present Passive Tense (المُضارع المَجْهول)

In the imperfect passive, every prefix takes ضَمَّة, while the root's second radical takes a فَتْحَة, and the rest remains the same. This is the simplest way to explain the directions to change present active to passive. For more detail, there are four steps to create the imperfect:

1. Give the prefix a ضَمَّة.

2. The first radical and its سُكون remain the same.

3. The second radical takes a فَتْحَة.

4. The last radical, its vowel, and the suffix remain the same.

To apply these steps, we will now form the present passive paradigm of the verb خَلَقَ يَخْلُقُ:

	الضَّمائر	المَعْلوم	المَجْهول
مُفْرَد	أنَا	أخْلُقُ	أُخْلَقُ
	أنْتَ	تَخْلُقُ	تُخْلَقُ
	أنْتِ	تَخْلُقِينَ	تُخْلَقِينَ
	هُوَ	يَخْلُقُ	يُخْلَقُ
	هِيَ	تَخْلُقُ	تُخْلَقُ
مُثَنَّى	نَحْنُ	نَخْلُقُ	نُخْلَقُ
	أنْتُما (مُذَكَّر)	تَخْلُقَانِ	تُخْلَقَانِ
	أنْتُما (مؤنَّث)	تَخْلُقَانِ	تُخْلَقَانِ
	هُما (مُذَكَّر)	يَخْلُقَانِ	يُخْلَقَانِ
	هُما (مؤنَّث)	تَخْلُقَانِ	تُخْلَقَانِ

		المَعْلوم	المَجْهول
جَمْع	نَحْنُ	نَخْلُقُ	نُخْلَقُ
	أَنْتُمْ	تَخْلُقُونَ	تُخْلَقُونَ
	أَنْتُنَّ	تَخْلُقْنَ	تُخْلَقْنَ
	هُمْ	يَخْلُقُونَ	يُخْلَقُونَ
	هُنَّ	يَخْلُقْنَ	يُخْلَقْنَ

Notice in this table that letters do not change between active and passive; only certain vowels do.

Compare المَعْلوم (the active voice) to المَجْهول (the passive). For instance, compare أَخْلُقُ to أُخْلَقُ; يَخْلُقُ to يُخْلَقُ; and تَخْلُقْنَ to تُخْلَقْنَ. It is noticeable that the passive is formed by applying the four steps: the prefix takes ضَمَّة; the first radical خ and its سُكون do not change, the second radical ل takes فَتْحَة; and the last radical ق, its vowel, and the suffix remain the same.

These four steps apply in every case, even those cases with the guttural as the second radical of the root, as well as those on the patterns فَعِلَ and فَعُلَ.

For one final practice, write the present passive of the verb ذَهَبَ يَذْهَبُ:

	الضَّمائِر	المَعْلوم	المَجْهول
مُفْرَد	أَنَا	أَذْهَبُ	أُذْهَبُ
	أَنْتَ	تَذْهَبُ	تُذْهَبُ
	أَنْتِ	تَذْهَبِينَ	تُذْهَبِينَ
	هُوَ	يَذْهَبُ	يُذْهَبُ
	هِيَ	تَذْهَبُ	تُذْهَبُ
مُثَنَّى	نَحْنُ	نَذْهَبُ	نُذْهَبُ
	أَنْتُما (مُذَكَّر)	تَذْهَبانِ	تُذْهَبانِ
	أَنْتُما (مؤنَّث)	تَذْهَبانِ	تُذْهَبانِ
	هُما (مُذَكَّر)	يَذْهَبانِ	يُذْهَبانِ
	هُما (مؤنَّث)	تَذْهَبانِ	تُذْهَبانِ

Lesson Sixteen

جَمْع	نَحْنُ	نَذْهَبُ	نُذْهَبُ
	أَنْتُمْ	تَذْهَبُونَ	تُذْهَبُونَ
	أَنْتُنَّ	تَذْهَبْنَ	تُذْهَبْنَ
	هُمْ	يَذْهَبُونَ	يُذْهَبُونَ
	هُنَّ	يَذْهَبْنَ	يُذْهَبْنَ

The table shows how straightforward forming the passive is. Follow the four steps: the prefix takes ضَمَّة; the first radical ذ and its سُكون do not change; the second radical هـ takes فَتْحَة; and the third radical ب, its vowel, and the suffix remain the same.

Now, let's practice forming present passive sentences from their active counterparts:

المَعْلوم	المَجْهول
كَريمَةُ تَصْرِفُ المالَ.	المالُ يُصْرَفُ.
طالِبُ المَدْرَسَةِ يَسْرِقُ القَلَمَ.	القَلَمُ يُسْرَقُ.
خديجة ومنى وسعاد يَصْنَعْنَ كُرْسِيّاً جَديداً.	كُرْسِيٌّ جديدٌ يُصْنَعُ.
الطَّالِبُ يَسْمَعُ الدَّرْسَ.	الدَّرْسُ يُسْمَعُ.
المُعَلِّمُ يَذْكُرُ القِصَّةَ.	القِصَّةُ تُذْكَرُ.
إمامُ المَسْجِدِ يَفْتَحُ البَوَّابَةَ.	البَوَّابَةُ تُفْتَحُ.
الحِصانُ يَدْفَعُ العَرَبَةَ.	العَرَبَةُ تُدْفَعُ.
فاطِمَةُ تَقْطَعُ الخُبْزَ.	الخُبْزُ يُقْطَعُ.
حَسَنُ يَزْرَعُ شَجَرَةً.	شَجَرَةٌ تُزْرَعُ.

From these examples, one can make several observations.

First, in order to form the passive, we simply follow the aforementioned steps. These steps apply to all of the examples in the table.

Second, as explained in the previous lesson on past passive, when we create the passive voice, we must pay attention to the gender of the *new* verb's subject. For example, consider the last sentence in the table. The active voice is حَسَنُ يَزْرَعُ شَجَرَةً (Hasan plants a tree). Here, شَجَرَةً is accusative, as it is the direct object of the verb يَزْرَعُ, and since Hasan is masculine, the verb يَزْرَعُ is masculine also. The passive voice sentence is شَجَرَةٌ تُزْرَعُ, where شَجَرَةٌ becomes the new subject (the نائِبُ الفاعِلِ).

The noun شَجَرَة is feminine and singular. The passive verb must take a feminine conjugation and thus becomes تُزْرَعُ (compare this with the masculine singular form of the present active voice يَزْرَعُ).

Finally, the passive voice exists only with past and present tenses, not with imperative (which we will explain in the following lesson). Because of this, by completing the passive voice in the present tense, we have studied everything we need to cover regarding the passive voice. Since we have examined the present active and passive forms, we will turn next to a related tense: the future tense. Luckily, the future tense is quite straightforward and is built upon the present tense.

Vocabulary

Here are the words we used in this lesson; some are new.

I love …	أنا أُحِبُّ	singular	مُفْرَد
we love …	نَحْنُ نُحِبُّ	dual	مُثَنَّى
smart people	أذْكِياء	plural	جَمْع
theology	اللّاهوت	masculine	مُذَكَّر
also, as well	أَيْضاً	feminine	مؤَنَّث
Spanish (language)	الإسْبانِيَّة	to beat, defeat	قَهَرَ
Christians	مَسيحِيّون	to bewitch	سَحَرَ
Muslim	مُسْلِم	to crush	طَحَنَ
church's pastor	قِسّيسُ الكَنيسَةِ	to sit down	قَعَدَ
running (sport)	رَكْض	to thunder	رَعَدَ
Wednesday	الأرْبَعاء	to cut	قَطَعَ
party	حَفْلَة	to commence	شَرَعَ
neighbor	جار	to allow, permit	سَمَحَ
son	ابن	to make, do	عَمِلَ
district, region	مَنْطِقَة	grace	نِعْمَة
peace	سَلام	grace of God	نِعْمَةُ الله

Lesson Sixteen

Exercises

Exercise 16.1

Translate the following sentences into Arabic.

1. We love our neighbor.

2. They (fp) are studying an article.

3. We sit on the new chair.

4. She sits on a new chair.

5. Do you (mp) go to the school or the university?

6. She writes the article at her class.

7. They (fd) cut the bread in the kitchen.

8. We listen to the sermon from the church's priest.

9. The lesson is heard.

10. The article is researched and the story studied.

Exercise 16.2

Translate the following sentences into English.

1. طالبُ المدرسةِ يَسْمَعُ الدَرْسَ.

2. فاطِمَةُ تَفْتَحُ البابَ.

3. إمامُ المَسْجِدِ يَشْكُرُ قِسّيسَ الكَنيسَةِ.

4. الفَنّاناتُ يَصْنَعْنَ كُرْسِيّاً جَميلاً.

5. اللِّصُّ يَسْرِقُ العَرَبَةَ.

6. مُحَمَّدٌ يَزْرَعُ الشَّجَرَةَ.

7. فاطِمَةُ تَدْفَعُ المالَ.

Exercise 16.3

The phrases in the previous exercise (16.2) are all active voice. Make them passive.

1.

2.

3.

4.

5.

6.

7.

Exercise 16.4

Parse the following verbs.

1. تَسْمَحُونَ

2. يَسْمَحُونَ

3. تَذْكُرِينَ

4. يَقْطَعْنَ

5. أَقْطَعُ

6. تَزْرَعِينَ

7. تَزْرَعُ

8. تَنْجَحَانِ

9. تَذْكُرُ

10. تَشْرَبَانِ

Note that the last four have more than one parsing option.

Exercise 16.5

State whether the phrase is correct or inaccurate. Fix the mistake(s).

يَسجدانِ الرَجُلانِ في المَسْجدِ.

تَعْبُدُ الرَجُلُ في الكَنيسَةِ.

الرِجالُ يَدْرُسُ في الجامعةِ.

يَطْبُخْنَ السَّيداتُ في المطبخِ.

أَحْمَدُ تَشْكُرُ الرَجُلَ.

Lesson Seventeen
سَبْعَةَ عَشَرَ

Future Simple Tense (الزَّمَنُ المُستَقْبَل)

Future in Arabic is called المُستَقْبَل. In English to create a future tense you add "will" or "shall" before the present verb. It is similar in Arabic. The مُضارع (present) and مُستَقْبَل (future) tenses are closely linked, as the latter is built on the conjugations of the former, with the addition of a simple indicator of the future tense.

Forming the conjugations of المُستَقْبَل is straightforward. You have two options:

1. Add the prefix سَـ to the present tense conjugation.
2. Add the particle سَوْفَ before the present tense conjugation.

Let's form المُستَقْبَل of the verb دَرَسَ:

	الضَّمائِر	المُضارِع	المُستَقْبَل	المُستَقْبَل
مُفْرَد	أَنَا	أَدْرُسُ	سَأَدْرُسُ	سَوْفَ أَدْرُسُ
	أَنْتَ	تَدْرُسُ	سَتَدْرُسُ	سَوْفَ تَدْرُسُ
	أَنْتِ	تَدْرُسِينَ	سَتَدْرُسِينَ	سَوْفَ تَدْرُسِينَ
	هُوَ	يَدْرُسُ	سَيَدْرُسُ	سَوْفَ يَدْرُسُ
	هِيَ	تَدْرُسُ	سَتَدْرُسُ	سَوْفَ تَدْرُسُ
مُثَنَّى	نَحْنُ	نَدْرُسُ	سَنَدْرُسُ	سَوْفَ نَدْرُسُ
	أَنْتُما (مُذَكَّر)	تَدْرُسَانِ	سَتَدْرُسَانِ	سَوْفَ تَدْرُسَانِ
	أَنْتُما (مؤنَّث)	تَدْرُسَانِ	سَتَدْرُسَانِ	سَوْفَ تَدْرُسَانِ
	هُما (مُذَكَّر)	يَدْرُسَانِ	سَيَدْرُسَانِ	سَوْفَ يَدْرُسَانِ
	هُما (مؤنَّث)	تَدْرُسَانِ	سَتَدْرُسَانِ	سَوْفَ تَدْرُسَانِ

سَوْفَ نَدْرُسُ	سَنَدْرُسُ	نَدْرُسُ	نَحْنُ	
سَوْفَ تَدْرُسُونَ	سَتَدْرُسُونَ	تَدْرُسُونَ	أَنْتُمْ	
سَوْفَ تَدْرُسْنَ	سَتَدْرُسْنَ	تَدْرُسْنَ	أَنْتُنَّ	جَمْع
سَوْفَ يَدْرُسُونَ	سَيَدْرُسُونَ	يَدْرُسُونَ	هُمْ	
سَوْفَ يَدْرُسْنَ	سَيَدْرُسْنَ	يَدْرُسْنَ	هُنَّ	

From this table you can see that the future tense is formed from the present, with no irregularities. We simply add ـسَ or سَوْفَ to the present tense conjugation in order to produce the future tense. The meaning of the future tense is comparable whether you use ـسَ or سَوْفَ. However, it is suggested that ـسَ indicates the near future, while سَوْفَ conveys the more distant future. Therefore, the phrase أَنَا سَأَدْرُسُ can be rendered "I will [soon] study," while أَنَا سَوْفَ أَدْرُسُ translates as "I will study."

As an exercise, form المُستَقْبَل of ذَهَبَ and فَعَلَ. You will first need to form the present tense, then the future. Use near future with يَذْهَبُ and distant future with يَفْعَلُ. Attempt to form the full chart before checking the following table:

المُستَقْبَل مِن يَفْعَلُ	المُستَقْبَل مِن يَذْهَبُ	الضَّمائِر	
سَوْفَ أَفْعَلُ	سَأَذْهَبُ	أَنَا	
سَوْفَ تَفْعَلُ	سَتَذْهَبُ	أَنْتَ	
سَوْفَ تَفْعَلِينَ	سَتَذْهَبِينَ	أَنْتِ	مُفْرَد
سَوْفَ يَفْعَلُ	سَيَذْهَبُ	هُوَ	
سَوْفَ تَفْعَلُ	سَتَذْهَبُ	هِيَ	
سَوْفَ نَفْعَلُ	سَنَذْهَبُ	نَحْنُ	
سَوْفَ تَفْعَلَانِ	سَتَذْهَبَانِ	أَنْتُما (مُذَكَّر)	
سَوْفَ تَفْعَلَانِ	سَتَذْهَبَانِ	أَنْتُما (مؤَنَّث)	مُثَنَّى
سَوْفَ يَفْعَلَانِ	سَيَذْهَبَانِ	هُما (مُذَكَّر)	
سَوْفَ تَفْعَلَانِ	سَتَذْهَبَانِ	هُما (مؤَنَّث)	

سَوْفَ نَفْعَلُ	سَنَذْهَبُ	نَحْنُ	
سَوْفَ تَفْعَلُونَ	سَتَذْهَبُونَ	أَنْتُمْ	
سَوْفَ تَفْعَلْنَ	سَتَذْهَبْنَ	أَنْتُنَّ	جَمْع
سَوْفَ يَفْعَلُونَ	سَيَذْهَبُونَ	هُمْ	
سَوْفَ يَفْعَلْنَ	سَيَذْهَبْنَ	هُنَّ	

This chart demonstrates that there are no irregularities in forming the future tense from the present. Now we will study the ways to negate present and future tenses.

Negating Present Tense

To negate present verbs simply place the particle لا before the verb. This applies on active and passive verbs. By adding the particle لا, the conjugation of the verb does not incur any changes. It is important to state this here, because in later discussions on other forms of negation, the verb will change once we add the negating particle.

Read these present tense sentences. Some are active and some are passive:

أَنَا لا أَدْرُسُ.	أَنَا أَدْرُسُ.
هِيَ لا تَخْلُقُ.	هِيَ تَخْلُقُ.
نَحْنُ لا نَفْعَلُ.	نَحْنُ نَفْعَلُ.
أَنْتُما لا تَجْلِسَانِ.	أَنْتُما تَجْلِسَانِ.
نَحْنُ لا نَذْهَبُ.	نَحْنُ نَذْهَبُ.
نَحْنُ لا نَخْلُقُ.	نَحْنُ نَخْلُقُ.
نَحْنُ لا نُخْلَقُ.	نَحْنُ نُخْلَقُ.
أَنْتُما لا تَكْتُبَانِ.	أَنْتُما تَكْتُبَانِ.
المالُ لا يُصْرَفُ.	المالُ يُصْرَفُ.
كَرِيمَة لا تَصْرِفُ المالَ.	كَرِيمَة تَصْرِفُ المالَ.
المُعَلِّمُ لا يَذْكُرُ القِصَّةَ.	المُعَلِّمُ يَذْكُرُ القِصَّةَ.
القِصَّةُ لا تُذْكَرُ.	القِصَّةُ تُذْكَرُ.
حَسَن لا يَزْرَعُ الشَجَرَةَ.	حَسَن يَزْرَعُ الشَجَرَةَ.
الشَجَرَةُ لا تُزْرَعُ.	الشَجَرَةُ تُزْرَعُ.

Lesson Seventeen

The table shows that negating the present tense is straightforward, with no irregularities. Simply add the particle *lām-alif* (لا) before the present tense verb.

Negating Future Tense: Introducing Subjunctive Mood

In order to negate a future tense verb, a specific particle is used: لَنْ. The negation process follows three steps:

1. Remove the future marker, whether it is ـسَ or سَوْفَ. This basically returns the future verb to its present tense form.

2. Add the particle لَنْ before the updated verb (i.e., the present).

3. Modify the verb by changing the conjugations as follows: (a) for those ending with ضَمَّة, make it فَتْحَة; (b) for conjugations ending with نَ, keep them as they are; and (c) for those ending with ـون، ـان، ـين, simply delete the ن. This "modification" step is important. It actually changes the indicative mood to subjunctive. If the indicative mood indicates factual statements, the subjunctive mood reflects conditional, wishful, or imaginary statements.

See this table, which clarifies negating future simple tense, before we discuss important comments afterwards:

Negated Sentence	Modified Verb	Future Sentence	
أَنَا لَنْ أَدْرُسَ	أَدْرُسَ	أَنَا سَوْفَ أَدْرُسُ	مُفْرَد
أَنْتَ لَنْ تَدْرُسَ	تَدْرُسَ	أَنْتَ سَوْفَ تَدْرُسُ	
أَنْتِ لَنْ تَدْرُسِي	تَدْرُسِي	أَنْتِ سَوْفَ تَدْرُسِينَ	
هُوَ لَنْ يَدْرُسَ	يَدْرُسَ	هُوَ سَوْفَ يَدْرُسُ	
هِيَ لَنْ تَدْرُسَ	تَدْرُسَ	هِيَ سَوْفَ تَدْرُسُ	
نَحْنُ لَنْ نَدْرُسَ	نَدْرُسَ	نَحْنُ سَوْفَ نَدْرُسُ	مُثَنَّى
أَنْتُما لَنْ تَدْرُسَا	تَدْرُسَا	أَنْتُما سَوْفَ تَدْرُسَانِ	
أَنْتُما لَنْ تَدْرُسَا	تَدْرُسَا	أَنْتُما سَوْفَ تَدْرُسَانِ	
هُما لَنْ يَدْرُسَا	يَدْرُسَا	هُما سَوْفَ يَدْرُسَانِ	
هُما لَنْ تَدْرُسَا	تَدْرُسَا	هُما سَوْفَ تَدْرُسَانِ	

	نَحْنُ سَوْفَ نَدْرُسُ	نَدْرُسَ	نَحْنُ لَنْ نَدْرُسَ
	أَنْتُمْ سَوْفَ تَدْرُسُونَ	تَدْرُسُوا	أَنْتُمْ لَنْ تَدْرُسُوا
جَمْع	أَنْتُنَّ سَوْفَ تَدْرُسْنَ	تَدْرُسْنَ	أَنْتُنَّ لَنْ تَدْرُسْنَ
	هُمْ سَوْفَ يَدْرُسُونَ	يَدْرُسُوا	هُمْ لَنْ يَدْرُسُوا
	هُنَّ سَوْفَ يَدْرُسْنَ	يَدْرُسْنَ	هُنَّ لَنْ يَدْرُسْنَ

In this table you will notice a few things.

First, the negation of the future tense by the particle لَنْ is not as straightforward as it is with past or present tenses. There are several steps to negate the future tense. Not only do we replace the future marker with the particle لَنْ, which essentially returns the future form to its present conjugation, but we also modify this conjugation.

The fifteen conjugations in the table above are modified in different ways. There are six that end with ضَمَّة. We change it to فَتْحَة. There are two which end with نَ. We keep them as they are. There are seven which end with ـون، ـان، ـين. We drop off the ن, with one caveat: When we delete the ن in conjugations ending with ـون, we are left with ـو alone, which is not a real conjugation, so we must add an *alif* to make it ـوا.

Second, it is necessary to study this modified verb in some detail. It is called الْمُضارِعُ الْمَنْصوبُ (*al-muḍāriʿ al-manṣūb*) and is known as the subjunctive mood. It expresses a wishful possibility or imaginary activity. In a sense, it is built on the indicative mood, which we have been studying and is called الْمُضارِعُ الْمَرْفوعُ (*al-muḍāriʿ al-marfūʿ*), clearly marked by the ضَمَّة at the end of most of its conjugations. If the indicative is mostly marked by ضَمَّة, the subjunctive is marked by فَتْحَة. We should note here that الْمُضارِعُ الْمَنْصوبُ not only has a future sense to it but also appears after various particles such as the following:

Translation	Subjunctive Particle
not, negating future	لَنْ
to (as in "I want to")	أَنْ
to, in order to	كَي
to, in order to	لِكَي
to, in order to	حَتَّى
to, in order to	لـ

Lesson Seventeen

These particles indicate subjunctive mood. Present verbs following any of these particles must be conjugated as مَنْصوبُ. It is obvious that the last four reflect almost the same meaning.

Here are several examples to demonstrate the difference between the conjugations of المَرْفوعُ (indicative) and المَنْصوبُ (subjunctive) and the way they appear in sentences.

I go to school.	أنا أَذْهَبُ إلى المَدْرَسَةِ.
I will go to school.	أنا سَأَذْهَبُ إلى المَدْرَسَةِ.
I will not go to school.	أنا لَنْ أَذْهَبَ إلى المَدْرَسَةِ.
The students will listen to the lecture.	الطُّلّابُ سَوْفَ يَسْمَعُونَ المُحاضَرَةَ.
The students will not listen to the lecture.	الطُّلّابُ لَنْ يَسْمَعُوا المُحاضَرَةَ.
She opens the gate in order to enter the house.	هِيَ تَفْتَحُ البَوّابَةَ كَي تَدْخَلَ المَنْزِلَ.
The man and his wife kneel at the mosque, in order to worship.	الرَّجُلُ وزوجَتُهُ يَرْكَعانِ في المسجدِ لِـيَعْبُدَا.
I want to study history.	أنا أُريدُ أَنْ أَدْرُسَ التّاريخَ.
I want to go to church.	أنا أُريدُ أَنْ أَذْهَبَ إلى الكَنيسَةِ.
She wants to cook.	هِيَ تُريدُ أَنْ تَطْبُخَ.
I go to the university to study.	أنا أَذْهَبُ إلى الجامِعَةِ حَتّى أَدْرُسَ.
I read my books to succeed.	أنا أَقْرَأُ كُتُبي كَي أَنْجَحَ.
The policeman will not allow…	الشُرطِيّ لن يَسْمَحَ...

Let's study some of the sentences in this table.

First, compare the first three sentences أنا أَذْهَبُ إلى المَدْرَسَةِ, أنا سَأَذْهَبُ إلى المَدْرَسَةِ, and أنا لَنْ أَذْهَبَ إلى المَدْرَسَةِ, particularly the way the verbs are conjugated. In the first sentence we have an indicative present verb أَذْهَبُ, while in the second the verb is indicative future سَأَذْهَبُ. In the third sentence we have a negated future in the subjunctive mood أَذْهَبَ following the negating particle لَنْ. The subjunctive verb أَذْهَبَ is marked by فَتْحَة, while the indicative أَذْهَبُ is marked by ضَمَّة.

Similarly, if you compare the fourth and fifth sentences in the table, you find that الطُّلَّابُ سَوْفَ يَسْمَعُونَ المُحاضَرَةَ is indicative with a future verb سَوْفَ يَسْمَعُونَ, while الطُّلَّابُ لَنْ يَسْمَعُوا المُحاضَرَةَ is a negated future with a subjunctive verb يَسْمَعُوا. We transform the indicative of the former sentence into the subjunctive in the latter by using the particle لَنْ. It is noteworthy to mention that verbs negated with the particle لَنْ are emphatically strong. To indicate this, we may render the negation "The students will *never* listen to the lecture."

Second, consider the sentence هِيَ تَفْتَحُ البَوَّابَةَ كَي تَدْخُلَ المَنْزِلَ. It has two parts, one indicative and the other subjunctive. The indicative portion (هِيَ تَفْتَحُ البَوَّابَةَ) includes the verb تَفْتَحُ, while the subjunctive part (كَي تَدْخُلَ المَنْزِلَ) has the verb تَدْخُلَ immediately following the particle كَي. The indicative verb تَفْتَحُ is clearly marked by the ضَمَّة, while the subjunctive تَدْخُلَ by the فَتْحَة. This sentence is a good example of how indicative and subjunctive verbs operate in sentences. The subjunctive often occurs in subordinate clauses and provides clues on actions dependent on previously mentioned verbs. The subjunctive clause in this structure always indicates something that will occur in the future and only after the completion of the indicative clause.

Similarly, consider the sentence الرَّجُلُ وزوجَتُهُ يَرْكَعانِ في المسجدِ لِـيَعْبُدَا in the table. Its two parts are الرَّجُلُ وزوجَتُهُ يَرْكَعانِ في المسجدِ and لِـيَعْبُدَا. The former is indicative with the verb يَرْكَعانِ and the latter is subjunctive with يَعْبُدَا immediately occurring after the subjunctive particle لِـ. The subjunctive form يَعْبُدَا is from the indicative imperfect يَعْبُدَانِ after dropping the ن. The same is true for the sentence أنا أَذْهَبُ إلى الجامِعَةِ حَتَّى أَدْرُسَ.

Third, the three sentences هِيَ تُرِيدُ, أنا أُرِيدُ أَنْ أَذْهَبَ إلى الكَنيسَةِ, أنا أُرِيدُ أَنْ أَدْرُسَ التَّارِيخَ and أُرِيدُ أَنْ تَطْبُخَ introduce us to the verbal form usually translated as "I want to," where the verb أُرِيدُ, meaning "I want," is quadrilateral. In the three sentences, you notice that immediately after تُرِيدُ أَنْ or أُرِيدُ أَنْ the verbs come in subjunctive conjugation أَدْرُسَ, تَطْبُخَ, and أَذْهَبَ, respectively. The particle أَنْ transforms indicative to subjunctive. For example, we write أنا أُرِيدُ أَنْ أَدْرُسُ التَّارِيخَ in the indicative mood, but أنا أُرِيدُ أَنْ أَدْرُسَ التَّارِيخَ in the subjunctive. The subjunctive sentence reflects a wish, possibility, or imaginary hope.

Since we refer here to the quadrilateral verb أَرَادَ يُرِيدَ, it would be helpful to conjugate its past and present forms:

المُضارِعُ المَنْصوبُ	المُضارِعُ المَرْفوعُ	الماضي	الضّمائر	
أُريدَ	أُريدُ	أَرَدْتُ	أنا	مُفْرَد
تُريدَ	تُريدُ	أَرَدْتَ	أنْتَ	
تُريدي	تُريدينَ	أَرَدْتِ	أنْتِ	
يُريدَ	يُريدُ	أَرادَ	هُوَ	
تُريدَ	تُريدُ	أَرادَتْ	هِيَ	
نُريدَ	نُريدُ	أَرَدْنا	نَحْنُ	مُثَنّى
تُريدا	تُريدانِ	أَرَدْتُما	أنْتُما (مُذَكَّر)	
تُريدا	تُريدانِ	أَرَدْتُما	أنْتُما (مؤَنَّث)	
يُريدا	يُريدانِ	أَرادا	هُما (مُذَكَّر)	
تُريدا	تُريدانِ	أَرادَتا	هُما (مؤَنَّث)	
نُريدَ	نُريدُ	أَرَدْنا	نَحْنُ	جَمْع
تُريدوا	تُريدونَ	أَرَدْتُم	أنْتُم	
تُرِدْنَ	تُرِدْنَ	أَرَدْتُنَّ	أنْتُنَّ	
يُريدوا	يُريدونَ	أَرادوا	هُمْ	
يُرِدْنَ	يُرِدْنَ	أَرَدْنَ	هُنَّ	

If you compare the conjugations of المُضارِعُ المَرْفوعُ to those of المُضارِعُ المَنْصوبُ, you will notice that we followed the rules of the triliteral verbs. The past tense is straightforward, too.

To practice, see these four sentences:

أنا أَرَدْتُ النَجاحَ. أنا أُريدُ القَلَمَ. أنا لَنْ أُريدَ الكِتابَ. أنا لا أُريدُ الكِتابَ.

We translate them as "I wanted success. I want the pen. I will not want the book. I do not want the book." The verb أَرَدْتُ is past, أُريدُ is present indicative, and أُريدَ is subjunctive. Notice that the subjunctive has a future sense embedded in it, which appears clearly in our translation.

Since we are exploring the quadrilateral verb أَرَادَ يُرِيدَ, there is another Arabic verb that is both quadrilateral and frequently used. It is the verb "I love" or "I would love," أَحَبَّ يُحِبُّ. Although it is not triliteral, we should be familiar with its conjugations not only to recognize them but also to use them in conversations:

	الضَّمائِر	الماضي	المُضارِعُ المَرْفوعُ	المُضارِعُ المَنْصوبُ
مُفْرَد	أَنَا	أَحْبَبْتُ	أُحِبُّ	أُحِبَّ
	أَنْتَ	أَحْبَبْتَ	تُحِبُّ	تُحِبَّ
	أَنْتِ	أَحْبَبْتِ	تُحِبِّينَ	تُحِبِّي
	هُوَ	أَحَبَّ	يُحِبُّ	يُحِبَّ
	هِيَ	أَحَبَّتْ	تُحِبُّ	تُحِبَّ
مُثَنَّى	نَحْنُ	أَحْبَبْنَا	نُحِبُّ	نُحِبَّ
	أَنْتُما (مُذَكَّر)	أَحْبَبْتُما	تُحِبَّانِ	تُحِبَّا
	أَنْتُما (مؤَنَّث)	أَحْبَبْتُما	تُحِبَّانِ	تُحِبَّا
	هُما (مُذَكَّر)	أَحَبَّا	يُحِبَّانِ	يُحِبَّا
	هُما (مؤَنَّث)	أَحَبَّتَا	تُحِبَّانِ	تُحِبَّا
جَمْع	نَحْنُ	أَحْبَبْنَا	نُحِبُّ	نُحِبَّ
	أَنْتُمْ	أَحْبَبْتُم	تُحِبُّونَ	تُحِبُّوا
	أَنْتُنَّ	أَحْبَبْتُنَّ	تُحْبِبْنَ	تُحْبِبْنَ
	هُمْ	أَحَبُّوا	يُحِبُّونَ	يُحِبُّوا
	هُنَّ	أَحْبَبْنَ	يُحْبِبْنَ	يُحْبِبْنَ

Lesson Seventeen

Let's conclude this section with some more sentences as an exercise:

Ahmad wants happiness.	أَحْمَدُ يُرِيدُ السَّعادَةَ.
Yusuf wants to drink.	يوسُف يُرِيدُ أَنْ يَشْرَبَ.
Aisha loves life.	عائِشَةُ تُحِبُّ الحَياةَ.
Fatima loves to cook.	فاطِمَةُ تُحِبُّ أَنْ تَطْبُخَ.
They want the money to play soccer.	هُما يُرِيدانِ المالَ كَي يَلْعَبا الكُرَةَ.

Another Way to Negate Past Tense: Introducing Jussive Mood

In a previous lesson we studied one way to negate the past simple tense—by placing the particle ما before the verb. We indicated that there is a second way to negate the past. Since this second way is linked with the present simple tense, we postponed it until this section. We will discuss this second method here, as it not only parallels with negating the future tense but also introduces us to an additional mood in Arabic sentences, which is called jussive.

To negate an affirmative past simple tense verb, we use the particle لَمْ. This particle negates the past tense, but it must be followed by the present tense verb conjugation in its jussive mood. In other words, we can negate a past simple tense by using لَمْ before the jussive imperfect form of the past tense verb. The imperfect jussive is called المُضارِعُ المَجْزومُ (al-muḍāriᶜ al-majzūm).

Just as the subjunctive mood is marked by a فَتْحَة on the final letter of most of its conjugations, the jussive is distinguished by the absence of any vowels, i.e., سُكون. In fact, the Arabic notion of jussive simply means cutting the verb short at its end, meaning to create a سُكون instead of a vowel at its final letter. Thus, the particle لَمْ can negate a past tense verb, but it must be followed by the imperfect jussive. See these examples:

Negated Sentence	Affirmative Past
أنا لَمْ أَدْرُسْ.	أنا دَرَسْتُ.
لَمْ أَعْرِفْ صَديقاً.	عَرَفْتُ صَديقاً.
المُعَلِّمُ لَمْ يَسْمَعْ عِظَةً.	المُعَلِّمُ سَمِعَ عِظَةً.

The verbs يَسْمَعْ, أَعْرِفْ, and أَدْرُسْ are all in the jussive form. Notice they have the form of the present indicative, only with a سُكون as the final letter. The particle لَمْ forces the following verb into the jussive mood, i.e., مَجْزومٌ (majzūm); thus, each verb takes a سُكون. The negated sentences in the table denote an action which did not occur in the past. So how do we form the jussive conjugations? Examine this table for the jussive forms, comparing them to their subjunctive and indicative counterparts:

		Indicative المَرْفوع	Subjunctive المنصوب	Jussive المجزوم
مُفْرَد	أَنَا	أَدْرُسُ	أَدْرُسَ	أَدْرُسْ
	أَنْتَ	تَدْرُسُ	تَدْرُسَ	تَدْرُسْ
	أَنْتِ	تَدْرُسِينَ	تَدْرُسِي	تَدْرُسِي
	هُوَ	يَدْرُسُ	يَدْرُسَ	يَدْرُسْ
	هِيَ	تَدْرُسُ	تَدْرُسَ	تَدْرُسْ
مُثَنَّى	نَحْنُ	نَدْرُسُ	نَدْرُسَ	نَدْرُسْ
	أَنْتُما (مُذَكَّر)	تَدْرُسانِ	تَدْرُسا	تَدْرُسا
	أَنْتُما (مؤَنَّث)	تَدْرُسانِ	تَدْرُسا	تَدْرُسا
	هُما (مُذَكَّر)	يَدْرُسانِ	يَدْرُسا	يَدْرُسا
	هُما (مؤَنَّث)	تَدْرُسانِ	تَدْرُسا	تَدْرُسا
جَمْع	نَحْنُ	نَدْرُسُ	نَدْرُسَ	نَدْرُسْ
	أَنْتُمْ	تَدْرُسُونَ	تَدْرُسُوا	تَدْرُسُوا
	أَنْتُنَّ	تَدْرُسْنَ	تَدْرُسْنَ	تَدْرُسْنَ
	هُمْ	يَدْرُسُونَ	يَدْرُسُوا	يَدْرُسُوا
	هُنَّ	يَدْرُسْنَ	يَدْرُسْنَ	يَدْرُسْنَ

In this table compare the jussive and the subjunctive columns. They are almost identical, with the exception of replacing the فَتْحَة of the subjunctive with the سُكون of the jussive. The rest of the forms are the same. You also notice that the second-person feminine plural تَدْرُسْنَ is identical in the indicative, subjunctive, and jussive. The same goes for the third person feminine plural يَدْرُسْنَ.

Lesson Seventeen

Like the subjunctive, the jussive conjugations are built on the indicative ones, but the سُكون distinguishes the jussive. Earlier, we formed the subjunctive from the indicative; the same applies here to form the jussive from the indicative—only use سُكون instead of فَتْحَة. While there are various situations where a verb is forced to take a jussive form, we are only concerned with the forms following the particle لَمْ as a negating article of the past tense.

Thus, a present tense verb can have one of three grammatical moods: المَرْفوعُ (indicative), المَنْصوبُ (subjunctive), or المَجْزومُ (jussive). The indicative verb is marked by a ضَمَّة, the subjunctive by a فَتْحَة, and the jussive by a سُكون at their final letter.

See the following examples of negating the past tense using لَمْ:

Translation of the Negated	Negated Sentence	Affirmative Past
They (fd) did not leave the lecture.	لَمْ تَتْرُكَا المُحاضَرَةَ.	تَرَكَتَا المُحاضَرَةَ.
The doctors did not thank the team.	الأطِبّاءُ لَمْ يَشْكُروا الفَريقَ.	الأطِبّاءُ شَكَروا الفَريقَ.
She did not succeed in the exam.	لَمْ تَنْجَحْ في الامتحانِ.	قَدْ نَجَحَتْ في الامتحانِ.
The donkey did not push a cart.	الحِمارُ لَمْ يَدْفَعْ عَرَبَةً.	الحِمارُ دَفَعَ عَرَبَةً.
He did not understand a lesson.	لَمْ يَفْهَمْ دَرْساً.	قَدْ فَهِمَ دَرْساً.
The artists (m) did not rejoice in the party.	الفَنّانونَ لَمْ يَفْرَحوا في الحَفْلَةِ.	الفَنّانونَ فَرِحوا في الحَفْلَةِ.
The students (f) did not fail in the exam.	الطّالِباتُ لَمْ يَفْشِلْنَ في الاخْتِبارِ.	الطّالِباتُ فَشِلْنَ في الاخْتِبارِ.
The student (f) did not get sick.	الطّالِبَةُ لَمْ تَمْرَضْ.	الطّالِبَةُ مَرِضَتْ.
We did not drink tea.	لَمْ نَشْرَبْ شاياً.	شَرِبْنا شاياً.
The road did not become easy.	الطَّريقُ لَمْ يَسْهُلْ.	الطَّريقُ سَهُلَ.

Negating Nominal Sentences

Negating Arabic nominal sentences is usually accomplished by using لَيْسَ and its various forms. The word لَيْسَ conveys the meaning "is not," or generally "[be] not." For instance, the phrase الرَّجُلُ هُنا (the man is here) is negated as لَيْسَ الرَّجُلُ هُنا or الرَّجُلُ لَيْسَ هُنا. Thus, the word لَيْسَ is added to a nominal sentence (subject and predicate) and negates it.

However, the matter is more complex than it initially appears: لَيْسَ is not a particle. It is a verb. Unlike previously studied particles, including لأَنْ، ما، لا, the verb لَيْسَ is unique and can operate in different ways, which is, in a sense, advanced for this introductory course. It is necessary, nonetheless, to study its effect as a negating tool in nominal sentences.

Earlier in this course we explained that a nominal sentence consists of two main components: the مُبْتَدَأ (subject) and the خَبَر (predicate). Both are generally in the nominative case. When لَيْسَ precedes a nominal sentence, it not only negates it but also alters the case of the خَبَر (predicate) from nominative to accusative. This is why linguists often call لَيْسَ "the abrogating tool," as it transforms the usual case of the predicate. Grammatically, لَيْسَ divorces the مُبْتَدَأ from the خَبَر. Before لَيْسَ enters into a nominal sentence, the مُبْتَدَأ and the خَبَر are closely related—the latter provides details about the former. After لَيْسَ, the خَبَر no longer conveys details of the مُبْتَدَأ. Finally, since لَيْسَ is a verb, it has conjugations. It is a past tense verb, so its conjugations will appear familiar in some aspects. Here is the chart:

	الضَّمائِر	الفِعْل لَيْسَ
مُفْرَد	أَنَا	لَسْتُ
	أَنْتَ	لَسْتَ
	أَنْتِ	لَسْتِ
	هُوَ	لَيْسَ
	هِيَ	لَيْسَتْ

Lesson Seventeen

مُثَنّى	نَحْنُ	لَسْنا	
	أنْتُما (مُذَكَّر)	لَسْتُما	
	أنْتُما (مؤَنَّث)	لَسْتُما	
	هُما (مُذَكَّر)	لَيْسا	
	هُما (مؤَنَّث)	لَيْسَتا	
جَمْع	نَحْنُ	لَسْنا	
	أنْتُمْ	لَسْتُمْ	
	أنْتُنَّ	لَسْتُنَّ	
	هُمْ	لَيْسوا	
	هُنَّ	لَسْنَ	

For example, a nominal sentence like المُهَنْدِسُ نَشيطٌ means "the engineer is energetic." When لَيْسَ enters the sentence, it becomes لَيْسَ المُهَنْدِسُ نَشيطاً. Notice the case of the مُبْتَدَأ remains the same, while that of the خَبَر is altered to accusative.

Consider another example. The sentence الصَّبْرُ جَميلٌ means "patience is good (or beautiful)." The negated sentence is لَيْسَ الصَّبْرُ جَميلاً. Similarly, the feminine sentence سارَةُ مُهَنْدِسَةٌ (Sarah is an engineer) is negated as لَيْسَتْ سارَةُ مُهَنْدِسَةً or سارَةُ لَيْسَتْ مُهَنْدِسَةً. Moreover, the dual sentence العامِلانِ نَشيطانِ is negated as العامِلانِ لَيْسا نَشيطينِ. Note how نَشيطانِ is nominative and نَشيطينِ is accusative. Finally, the sentence أنتَ طالبٌ (you are a student) is negated as أنتَ لَسْتَ طالباً or simply لَسْتَ طالباً. As for نَحْنُ مِنْ أَمْريكا, it is negated as نَحْنُ لَسْنا مِنْ أَمْريكا or simply لَسْنا مِنْ أَمْريكا.

Practice with the following examples:

Nominal Sentence	مُبْتَدَأ	خَبَر	Negated Nominal Sentence
القَمرُ جَميلٌ.	القَمرُ	جَميلٌ	لَيْسَ القَمرُ جَميلاً.
الشَّمْسُ جَميلةٌ.	الشَّمْسُ	جَميلةٌ	لَيْسَت الشَّمْسُ جَميلةً.
القَمرُ والشَّمْسُ جَميلانِ.	القَمرُ والشَّمْسُ	جَميلانِ	القَمرُ والشَّمْسُ لَيْسا جَميلَينِ.
هَذِه سيّارةٌ.	هَذِه	سيّارةٌ	لَيْسَت هَذِه سيّارةً.

لَيْسَتْ فَنَّانَةً.	فَنَّانَةٌ	هِيَ	هِيَ فَنَّانَةٌ.
لَيْسَ هذا رَجُلاً طيباً.	رَجُلٌ	هذا	هذا رَجُلٌ طيبٌ.
لَيْسَتْ هذه جُمْلَةً قَصيرَةً.	جُمْلَةٌ	هذه	هذه جُمْلَةٌ قَصيرَةٌ.
المُمَثِّلَتانِ لَيْسَتا ماهِرَتينِ.	ماهِرَتانِ	المُمَثِّلَتانِ	المُمَثِّلَتانِ ماهِرَتانِ.

Vocabulary

Here some common nouns are offered. They can be used with the verbs "to want" and "to love."

self-control	ضَبْطُ النَّفْسِ	happiness	سَعادَة
prosperity	رَخاء	life	حَياة
honor	شَرَف	money	مال
dignity	كَرامَة	love	حُبّ
beauty	جَمال	joy	فَرَح
loyalty	وَلاء	peace	سَلام
forgiveness	غُفْران	patience, forbearance	صَبْر
truth	حَقّ	kindness, gentleness	لُطْف
reality	حَقيقَة	goodness	صَلاح
mercy	رَحْمة	faithfulness	إخْلاص
radiance, magnificence	بَهاء	giving	عَطاء
glory	مَجْد	generosity	كَرَم
survival, endurance	بَقاء	generosity	سَخاء

Lesson Seventeen

Exercises

Exercise 17.1

Negate the following sentences in two different ways.

1. عَلي صَعَدَ إلى الجبلِ.

2. ناهِد دَرَسْتْ مَوضوعاً.

3. عَرَفنا رَجُلاً.

4. الجُنْدي سَمِعَ عِظَةً.

5. دَخَلا إلى الفُنْدُقِ.

6. سحبوا المالَ من البنكِ.

7. الطّالِبَتانِ ضَرَبتا المِنْضَدَةَ.

Exercise 17.2

Negate the following sentences.

1. دَخَلَ الطّالِبُ الفُنْدُقَ.

2. أنا أُحِبُّ الخَطيئَةَ.

3. أنا سأعْمَلُ في البَنْكِ.

4. سنَدْرُسُ المَقالَ.

5. الرَّجُلُ هُنا.

6. المُؤمِناتُ طَبَخْنَ الوَجْبَةَ.

7. يَسْمَعُ الفَنّانونَ الأُغْنيةَ.

8. المُهَنْدِسُ نَشيطٌ.

9. سَيَسْمَعُ الفَنّانونَ الأُغْنيةَ.

10. دَفَعوا الفاتورَةَ.

11. تَدْفَعانِ الفاتورَةَ.

12. هُما مِنْ العِراقِ.

13. سوف تَلْبِسينَ الفُسْتانَ.

Exercise 17.3

Write the following sentences in Arabic.

1. They (fp) love this life.

2. Mohammad wants to love mercy.

3. Nadia loves peace, joy, and patience.

4. Aisha wants to cook in order to go to her mother.

5. They (md) want to know the teacher's name.

6. The policeman wants to know the truth.

7. The husband wants to sit with his wife.

8. I would love to hear your (ms) sermon.

9. I will not want the book.

Exercise 17.4

Parse the following verbs.

1. سَتَذْهَبُ

2. فَرِحوا

3. تَدْخلَ

4. أذْهَبَ

5. سَيَذْهَبْنَ

6. تُرِيدُ

7. يَدْرُسْنَ

Exercise 17.5

Each of the following sentences has one error. Highlight it.

1. أَذْهَبُ إلى المَدْرَسَةِ.

2. لَنْ أَذْهَبُ إلى البَيْتِ.

3. الطُّلَّابُ لَنْ يَسْمَعُونَ المُحاضَرَةَ.

4. هِيَ تَفْتَحُ البَوَّابَةَ كَي تَدْخلُ المَنْزِلَ.

5. الرَّجُلُ وزَوجَتُهُ يَرْكَعونِ في المَسْجدِ.

6. أنا أريدَ أنْ أَدْرُسَ التّاريخَ.

7. تُريدُ أنْ تَطْبُخُ؟

8. أنا أَذْهَبُ إلى الجامِعَةِ حَتَّى أَدْرُسُ.

Exercise 17.6

Negate the following sentences.

1. الفَنّانُ جَيِّدٌ.

2. عائشةُ مُهَنْدِسَةٌ.

3. العامِلانِ كسولانِ.

4. أنتَ طالبٌ.

5. نَحْنُ مُسْلِمونَ.

Lesson Eighteen
ثَمَانِيَةَ عَشَرَ

The Imperative Verb (فِعْلُ الأمرِ)

In previous lessons we grouped الأفعال (verbs) based on their tenses into ماضي (past), مُضارع (present), and مُستَقْبَل (future). In this lesson the focus is on the imperative, which is called الأَمْر (al-amr). It is the order or command. It should be noted that Arabic categorizes verbs into past, present (including future), and imperative, while in English the imperative is usually considered a mood which expresses commands or requests.

The conjugations of الأَمْر are built on the active present tense, particularly its jussive forms. The command uses only the second-person conjugations. Thus, there are six forms to conjugate.

Consider the command of the verb دَرَسَ يَدْرُسُ. To help you compare forms, we will place المَرفوع (the present indicative), المَجْزوم (present jussive), and الأَمْر (imperative) next to each other. Examine the chart, before studying the following remarks.

	الأَمْر	المجزوم	المَرفوع	الضّمائر	
مُفْرَد		أَدْرُسْ	أَدْرُسُ	أَنَا	
	أُدْرُسْ	تَدْرُسْ	تَدْرُسُ	أَنْتَ	
	أُدْرُسِي	تَدْرُسِي	تَدْرُسِينَ	أَنْتِ	
		يَدْرُسْ	يَدْرُسُ	هُوَ	
		تَدْرُسْ	تَدْرُسُ	هِيَ	
مُثَنَّى		نَدْرُسْ	نَدْرُسُ	نَحْنُ	
	أُدْرُسَا	تَدْرُسَا	تَدْرُسَانِ	أَنْتُما (مُذَكَّر)	
	أُدْرُسَا	تَدْرُسَا	تَدْرُسَانِ	أَنْتُما (مؤَنَّث)	
		يَدْرُسَا	يَدْرُسَانِ	هُما (مُذَكَّر)	
		تَدْرُسَا	تَدْرُسَانِ	هُما (مؤَنَّث)	

	نَدْرُسْ	نَدْرُسُ	نَحْنُ	جَمْع
أُدْرُسُوا	تَدْرُسُوا	تَدْرُسُونَ	أَنْتُمْ	
أُدْرُسْنَ	تَدْرُسْنَ	تَدْرُسْنَ	أَنْتُنَّ	
	يَدْرُسُوا	يَدْرُسُونَ	هُمْ	
	يَدْرُسْنَ	يَدْرُسْنَ	هُنَّ	

To form the imperative, we begin with the jussive form, replace the prefix with a هَمْزَة (which appears here as an *alif*), and add a vowel. The vowel here is ضَمَّة. Note that the dual forms of the masculine and feminine are identical, which leaves us with only five imperative forms in total.

To make a command in Arabic we do not begin with the pronoun or include it at all. So instead of أَنْتَ أُدْرُسْ, we simply say أُدْرُسْ. When you say أُدْرُسْ, you command a male, "Study!" If you state أُدْرُسْنَ, you command a group of females, "Study!"

There is an important matter which does not appear in this table but requires explanation. It is related to the vowel above the initial *hamzah* (which, again, appears here as an *alif*). This هَمْزَة usually takes either ضَمَّة or كَسْرَة. The rule is simple: Look at the root's second letter (here, it is رُ). If it has ضَمَّة, then give the هَمْزَة a ضَمَّة, but if it has فَتْحَة or كَسْرَة, the هَمْزَة takes كَسْرَة. Thus, the vowel of the هَمْزَة depends on the vowel of the second radical of the root.

This initial *hamzah* can be confusing, as it is not explicitly written. This is understandable. This هَمْزَة has three features: (1) it is not explicitly written, (2) it needs an *alif* to carry it, and (3) it is called "a connecting *hamzah*," which we will study in more depth in the following section.

Let's study several verbs in their imperative conjugations and examine whether the initial *hamzah* receives ضَمَّة or كَسْرَة:

							الضّمائر
أُشْكُرْ	اِشْرَبْ	أُقْتُلْ	اِضْرِبْ	اِسْمَعْ	اِذْهَبْ	اِفْعَلْ	أَنْتَ
أُشْكُرِي	اِشْرَبِي	أُقْتُلِي	اِضْرِبِي	اِسْمَعِي	اِذْهَبِي	اِفْعَلِي	أَنْتِ
أُشْكُرَا	اِشْرَبَا	أُقْتُلَا	اِضْرِبَا	اِسْمَعَا	اِذْهَبَا	اِفْعَلَا	أَنْتُمَا
أُشْكُرُوا	اِشْرَبُوا	أُقْتُلُوا	اِضْرِبُوا	اِسْمَعُوا	اِذْهَبُوا	اِفْعَلُوا	أَنْتُمْ
أُشْكُرْنَ	اِشْرَبْنَ	أُقْتُلْنَ	اِضْرِبْنَ	اِسْمَعْنَ	اِذْهَبْنَ	اِفْعَلْنَ	أَنْتُنَّ

In this table are seven verbs in their imperative forms. All of them are built on their jussive forms after replacing the imperfect prefix with a هَمْزَة. In the verbs, اِفْعَلْ، اِذْهَبْ، اِسْمَعْ، اِشْرَبْ, the second letter of the root has فَتْحَة, so the initial هَمْزَة will take كَسْرَة. In the verb اِضْرِبْ, the second radical of the root has a كَسْرَة; thus, the هَمْزَة receives كَسْرَة. As for اُقْتُلْ and اُشْكُرْ, the vowel on the second radical is ضَمَّة, so the initial هَمْزَة receives a ضَمَّة.

Cutting and Connecting *Hamzah* (هَمْزَةُ الْقَطْعِ وهَمْزَةُ الْوَصْلِ)

Undoubtedly, the Arabic هَمْزَة (*hamzah*) is a complicated letter. We studied it in an earlier lesson, but we omitted one aspect until this lesson as it can be confusing to explore it initially. At the outset, this section only discusses the initial *hamzah*, i.e., that which comes at the beginning of a word. There are two kinds of this هَمْزَة in Arabic.

The first is distinct, explicitly written above or under an *alif*, and sounds like a "cutting" glottal stop, i.e., you can hear it clearly. This is one reason why the Arabs call it هَمْزَةُ الْقَطْعِ, meaning "a cutting *hamzah*," e.g, أَحْمَد، أَنْتَ، إِبْراهِيم، إِيمان، أُمّ. It is written above the *alif* when it is associated with a ضَمَّة or فَتْحَة and under the *alif* when it has كَسْرَة.

The second kind of *hamzah* is not as easy to discern, particularly when it is pronounced. Arabic linguists call it هَمْزَةُ الْوَصْلِ, meaning "a connecting *hamzah*." As a general rule, the هَمْزَةُ الْوَصْلِ is never written. It is also never pronounced unless it occurs at the very beginning of speech. In the middle of a sentence, this *hamzah* is not pronounced at all—it weaves words together without the distinction of a glottal stop. In the previous section, some examples of the connecting *hamzah* appeared in the imperatives of triliteral verbs, e.g, اِفْعَلْ، اِذْهَبْ، اِسْمَعْ، اِشْرَبْ, in addition to the definite article (الـ).

Study the following words. All of them begin with a *hamzah*:

Group B	Group A
ٱلْمُدَرِّسِ	أَنَا
الْجَامِعَة	أَيْنَ
ٱبْنُ	أَنْتِ، أَنْتَ
ٱسْمُ	إِسلام
اِمْرَأَة	أَحْمَد، إِبْراهِيم، إِسْماعِيل

Lesson Eighteen

إِسْحاق، أُمَيْمَة	ابْنَة
إِلى، أَنْ، إِنْ	الْوَصْل
أُمّ، أَب، أَخ	الْقَطْع

In Group A there are examples of هَمْزَةُ الْقَطْعِ. As a rule, it occurs at the beginning of the vast majority of human names and particles, in addition to pronouns.

In Group B there are examples of هَمْزَةُ الْوَصْلِ. It always occurs with the definite article—no exception. It also has a few nouns: اِمْرَأة، ابْن، ابْنَة، اِسْم. Note that this is simply a phonetic rule, related to how Arabs pronounce it.

It is important to note that there are some cases when هَمْزَةُ الْوَصْلِ must be deleted. By this, we mean deleting the *alif*, upon which the *hamzah* is supposedly carried. The most common example is when it is preceded by the preposition لِـ. So, in order to say "to the man," we need to add لِـ to الرَّجُل. We will take off the هَمْزَةُ الْوَصْلِ (which is on the definite article), and, thus, we have لِـلرَّجُل.

Similarly, to write "the woman," we add الـ to امْرَأة. We will delete the هَمْزَةُ at the beginning of امْرَأة and end with الْمَرْأة. Thus, if you want to write "to the woman," add لِـ to الْمَرْأة. Delete the هَمْزَةُ of the definite article, and the result will be لِـلْمَرْأة. In pronunciation, however, note the difference between امْرَأة and الْمَرْأة.

Identify the kind of every هَمْزَة in the following passage from the Gospel of John 3:10–16:

إِنْجيلُ يوحَنّا

أَجابَ يَسوعُ: «أَنْتَ مُعَلِّمُ إِسْرائيلَ وَلَسْتَ تَعْلَمُ هَذا! اَلْحَقَّ الْحَقَّ أَقولُ لَكَ: إِنَّنا إِنَّما نَتَكَلَّمُ بِما نَعْلَمُ وَنَشْهَدُ بِما رَأَيْنا وَلَسْتُمْ تَقْبَلونَ شَهادَتَنا. إِنْ كُنْتُ قُلْتُ لَكُمُ الأَرْضِيّاتِ وَلَسْتُمْ تُؤْمِنونَ فَكَيْفَ تُؤْمِنونَ إِنْ قُلْتُ لَكُمُ السَّماوِيّاتِ؟ وَلَيْسَ أَحَدٌ صَعِدَ إِلَى السَّماءِ إِلاَّ الَّذي نَزَلَ مِنَ السَّماءِ ابْنُ الإِنْسانِ الَّذي هُوَ في السَّماءِ. «وَكَما رَفَعَ موسَى الْحَيَّةَ في الْبَرِّيَّةِ هَكَذا يَنْبَغي أَنْ يُرْفَعَ ابْنُ الإِنْسانِ لِكَيْ لا يَهْلِكَ كُلُّ مَنْ يُؤْمِنُ بِهِ بَلْ تَكونُ لَهُ الْحَياةُ الأَبَدِيَّةُ. لِأَنَّهُ هَكَذا أَحَبَّ اللهُ الْعالَمَ حَتَّى بَذَلَ ابْنَهُ الْوَحيدَ لِكَيْ لا يَهْلِكَ كُلُّ مَنْ يُؤْمِنُ بِهِ بَلْ تَكونُ لَهُ الْحَياةُ الأَبَدِيَّةُ. لِأَنَّهُ لَمْ يُرْسِلِ اللهُ ابْنَهُ إِلَى الْعالَمِ لِيَدينَ الْعالَمَ بَلْ لِيَخْلُصَ بِهِ الْعالَمُ.

The هَمْزَةُ الْقَطْعِ can be found in many words in this passage, including the following:

أَجَابَ

أَنْتَ

إِسْرَائِيلَ

As for هَمْزَةُ الْوَصْلِ, there are several:

اَلْحَقَّ

السَّمَاوِيَّاتِ

الَّذِي

السَّمَاءِ

ابْنُ

Identify the kind of each remaining هَمْزَة in the passage.

Similarly, attempt to do the same with the following passage, which is the entire chapter 1 from the Quran.

بِسمِ اللهِ الرَّحمٰنِ الرَّحيمِ

الحَمدُ لِلّهِ رَبِّ العالَمينَ

الرَّحمٰنِ الرَّحيمِ

مالِكِ يَومِ الدّينِ

إِيّاكَ نَعبُدُ وَإِيّاكَ نَستَعينُ

اهدِنَا الصِّراطَ المُستَقيمَ

صِراطَ الَّذينَ أَنعَمتَ عَلَيهِم غَيرِ المَغضوبِ عَلَيهِم وَلَا الضّالّينَ

Now we will study a special feature of some Arabic *un-nunated* nouns where we cannot use *tanwīn*.

Un-nunated Nouns (الْمَمْنُوعُ مِنْ الصَّرْفِ)

In previous chapters, we called the inflection of a noun "declension," and the inflection of a verb "conjugation." We also used different ending vowels—the little markings, which we called حَرَكات—to determine the function of a word in a sentence. We further studied the important feature of a declinable item (مُعْرَب) and an indeclinable one (مَبْنِي). A مُعْرَب item changes its ending form (or final vowel) to indicate a change in grammatical roles. We concluded that all particles are

Lesson Eighteen

indeclinable. All verbs, too, are indeclinable, except some forms of the present tense. As for nouns, we stated that most are declinable, except for the demonstratives, interrogatives, and pronouns. The three cases of a declinable noun are مَرْفوع (nominative), مَجْرور (genitive), and مَنْصوب (accusative). When a noun is indefinite, we use تَنْوين (tanwīn), i.e., doubling the ending vowel (e.g., بَيْتٌ، بَيْتٍ، بَيْتاً).

There is a feature in Arabic which prevents using the تَنْوين at the end of some nouns. The nouns in this case are un-nunated. Linguists categorize these nouns under the title مَمْنوع مِنْ الصَّرْف (mamnūʿ min al-ṣarf). The title literally means "banned, forbidden, prohibited from nunation" (i.e., tanwīn). Some call a noun of this sort "a diptote," identifying it as "restricted from change." By this label, grammarians indicate two main characteristics: These nouns cannot receive تَنْوين and, when genitive, they will receive فَتْحَة instead of كَسْرَة.

So, what makes a noun prohibited from nunation, i.e., مَمْنوعٌ مِنْ الصَّرْفِ؟

First, female names with more than three letters are among the مَمْنوع مِنْ الصَّرْف. Here are a few examples:

ماجِدة، خَديجَة، صَفِيَّة، زَيْنَب، سُعاد.

All of these nouns are feminine, and they each include more than three letters. They cannot receive تَنْوين, and, when their case is genitive, they will receive فَتْحَة instead of كَسْرَة. So, you write ذَهَبَتْ زَيْنَبُ instead of ذَهَبَتْ زَيْنَبٌ and مَعَ زَيْنَبَ instead of مَعَ زَيْنَبِ.

Second, nouns ending with ألِفٌ مَقْصورَة, hamzah preceded by alif, or tāʾ marbūṭah as a sign of femininity cannot receive تَنْوين. Examples of feminine nouns ending with ألِفٌ مَقْصورَة include مُنَى، ذِكْرَى، قَتْلَى. As for those ending with hamzah preceded by alif, this is called ألِفٌ مَمْدودَة (alif mamdūda). These include عُظَماء، عُلَماء، صَحَراء، أصدقاء، أطِبّاء. None of these receive تَنْوين.

Consider this example: ذَهَبَ إبْراهيمُ إلى صَحَراءَ (Ibrahim went to a desert). The noun صَحَراءَ is un-nunated; it is genitive with a فَتْحَة. In the sentence ذَهَبَ عُلَماءُ عُظَماءُ إلى بَيْتٍ (great scientists went to a home), the indefinite nouns عُلَماءُ and عُظَماءُ do not receive تَنْوين. Similarly, in the sentence شَكَرْنا شُعَراءَ وأطِبّاءَ (we thanked poets and physicians), the indefinite direct object شُعَراءَ takes only one فَتْحَة, as it cannot receive تَنْوين. Moreover, the feminine forms of colors (they are adjectives) usually end with ألِفٌ مَمْدودَة (alif mamdūda) and are among the مَمْنوع مِنْ الصَّرْف. They include خَضْراء (green), حَمْراء (red), سَوداء (black), زَرْقاء (blue), شَقْراء (blonde), and سَمْراء (brown). None of these forms receives تَنْوين. Finally, regarding feminine nouns ending with tāʾ marbūṭah, Arabic linguists call this tāʾ "the feminine tāʾ." There are many names which have this feature, including the name of Muhammad's daughter, فاطِمَة, and that of his wife, عائِشَة; this is also true for the city names of جِدّة and مَكّة.[1]

Third, non-Arabic names with more than three letters are in the list of مَمْنوع مِنْ الصَّرْف, and إِبْراهيم، إِسْحاق، يَعْقوب، إِسْرائيل، يوسُف، داوود، ماركو، رَمْسيس. This includes نابُلْيون. All are originally non-Arabic names with more than three letters. So, we say مِنْ إِبْراهيمَ إلى إِسْحاقَ and سَمِعَ إِبْراهيمُ. Note how a genitive noun receives فَتْحَة, because it is مَمْنوعٌ مِنْ الصَّرْفِ.

Fourth, every name that consists of two words is مَمْنوع مِنْ الصَّرْف. Examples include بَيْت لَحْم (Bethlehem in Palestine), بَعْلبك (Baalbek in Lebanon), and حَضْرَمَوْت (Hadramaut in Yemen). These are comparable to hyphenated names in other languages. Thus, we write ذَهَبوا إلى حَضْرَمَوْتَ. An example from the United States would be the name نيويورك (New York), which is also a non-Arabic name and thus un-nunated. We write هو مِن نيويوركَ.

Fifth, every name that takes the form of a verb is مَمْنوع مِنْ الصَّرْف. Most common among these names are nouns and adjectives on the pattern of أَفْعَل, such as the names أَحْمَد، أَصْغَر، أَكْمَل، أَكْبَر. All of them are human names, built on verbs such as حَمَدَ، صَغُرَ، كَمُلَ، كَبُرَ, respectively, and following the pattern أَفْعَل. This is also the case with the masculine forms of some colors, such as أَزْرَق، أَحْمَر، أَخْضَر. All of them are adjectives on the pattern أَفْعَل. None of these names (nouns and adjectives) receive تَنْوين.

Sixth, every broken plural noun on the pattern فَعائِل، مَفاعِل or مَفاعيل is مَمْنوعٌ مِنْ الصَّرْفِ. For instance, nouns on the pattern مَفاعِل include مَساجِد (mosques) and مَدارِس (schools); nouns on the pattern فَعائِل include كَنائِس (churches); nouns on the pattern مَفاعيل include مَفاتيح (keys) and عَصافير (birds).

Seventh, and finally, names or adjectives ending with an additional ان to their initial form are مَمْنوع مِنْ الصَّرْفِ. Consider the adjectives عَطْشان (thirsty), شَبْعان (satisfied), سَكْران (drunk), and غَضْبان (angry). All of them are built on triliteral roots with the addition of ان. They are masculine forms, and their feminine counterparts, عَطْشَى، شَبْعَى، سَكْرَى، غَضْبَى end with ألفٌ مَقْصورَة and are, therefore, also among the مَمْنوع مِنْ الصَّرْف.

---

1. There are some names of men that end with *tā' marbūṭah*. Grammarians label them as "feminine in pronunciation," due to the final *tā'*, and they are un-nunated. For example, the Muslim names أُمَيّة، مُعاوِية، حَمْزَة، طَلْحَة are all for men who were contemporary to Muhammad. Their names end with a *tā' marbūṭah* and thus do not receive تَنْوين.

Lesson Eighteen

With these seven points, we have explored the major aspects of un-nunated nouns الْمَمْنوعُ مِنْ الصَّرْفِ. Of course, there are exceptions and irregularities, but these points are introductory and aimed at helping students address this reoccurring feature of Arabic nouns.

There is one particular exception which should be mentioned here, as it often occurs with names. In the case of a three-letter feminine noun where the middle letter has a سُكون, there is liberty to use تَنوين or not. Both cases are correct. So, the country name مِصْر (Egypt) and the city name حِمْص (Homs) can appear with or without تَنوين. The sentences ذَهَبْتُ إلى مِصْرَ and ذَهَبْتُ إلى مِصْرٍ are both correct. The same goes for the sentences أنا مِن حِمْصَ and أنا مِن حِمْصٍ. As for the female names هِنْد and شَمْس, it is correct to write دَرَسَتْ هِنْدُ في الفَصْلِ or دَرَسَتْ هِنْدٌ في الفَصْلِ, as well as سَمِعْتُ شَمْسَ or سَمِعْتُ شَمْساً. Similarly, it is correct to state دَرَسَتْ مَعَ هِنْدَ, where we treat هِنْد as an un-nunated noun which receives فَتْحَة as a genitive noun (object of preposition). It is also correct to write دَرَسَتْ مَعَ هِنْدٍ, where هِنْد is treated as a nunated noun which accepts تَنوين. As an object of preposition, it takes double كَسْرَة.

There are two situations in which all rules about الْمَمْنوعُ مِنْ الصَّرْفِ will be irrelevant and inapplicable: the definiteness and the *iḍāfah* construct.

Recall that in all these abovementioned cases nouns without the definite article were used. If a definite article is added to that noun, we do not need تَنوين. Once a definite article is used, the regular rules for nouns are applied. Consider these two sentences: دَرَسَتْ في الْمَدارِسِ and دَرَسَتْ في مَدارِسَ. Both are correct. The former has the un-nunated noun مَدارِسَ, while the latter uses the definite noun الْمَدارِسِ. Both nouns are in the genitive case. The former took فَتْحَة, and the latter كَسْرَة.

Like with the addition of the definite article, if the noun is placed in an *iḍāfah* construct, it no longer adopts the rules for the un-nunated nouns. For example, in the sentence أنا عَبَدْتُ في كَنائِسَ (I worshipped in churches), the noun كَنائِسَ is an un-nunated noun in the genitive case and takes a فَتْحَة. However, in the sentence أنا عَبَدْتُ في كَنائِسِ القاهِرةِ (I worshipped in the churches of Cairo), the same noun كَنائِسِ is *muḍāf* and القاهِرةِ *muḍāf ilayhi*. Since كَنائِسِ is in an *iḍāfah* construct, the rules of الْمَمْنوعُ مِنْ الصَّرْفِ do not apply. Thus, كَنائِسِ takes كَسْرَة.

Determine الْمَمْنوعُ مِنْ الصَّرْفِ in the following list of words, and state the reason for its un-nunated status:

Translation	Group B	Translation	Group A
yellow (m)	أصْفَر	a young man	شَاب
yellow (f)	صَفْراء	a young lady	شَابة

sun (also a feminine name, Shams)	شَمْس	a young lady	فَتاة
Majida (a feminine name)	ماجِدة	able	قادِر
brunette	سَمْراء	angry	غاضِب
small (f)	صُغْرى	beautiful	جَميل
pregnant	حُبْلى	deep	عَميق
names (also a feminine name, Asmaa)	أَسْماء	different	مُخْتَلِف
Tehran	طَهْران	wrong	غَلَطْ
Lebanon	لُبْنان	general, public	عام
Adnan (a masculine name)	عَدْنان	money	مال
wounded (fp)	جَرْحى	high	عال
Ajman	عَجْمان	stiff, hard	صَلْب
green (m)	أَخْضَر	wide	واسِع
green (f)	خَضْراء	cutter	قاطِع
churches	كَنائِس	tight, narrow	ضَيِّق
mosques	مَساجِد	seller	بائِع
synagogues	مَجامِع	maker	صانِع
in a daze (also a masculine name, Sarhan)	سَرْحان	few, little	قَليل
red (m)	أَحْمَر	patient, sick	مَريض
lame (m)	أَعْرَج	right, healthy	صَحيح
lame (f)	عَرْجاء	conqueror, winner	غالِب
virgin	عَذراء	weak, vulnerable	ضَعيف

Lesson Eighteen

All words in Group B are مَمْنوع مِنْ الصّرْف. In Group A all of the words can be inflected. They are not un-nunated.

Try another exercise. State whether these sentences are correct or incorrect. Correct the incorrect sentences:

دَرَسَتْ هِنْدٌ في الفَصْلِ.

سَمِعْتُ هِنْدَ في الحَديقَةِ.

سَمِعْتُ هِنْداً في الحَديقَةِ.

أنا عَبَدْتُ في مَساجِدَ جَميلَةٍ.

أنا عَبَدْتُ في مَساجِدِ القاهِرةِ.

All are correct. Now, consider these two incorrect sentences. Attempt to locate the errors before checking the explanation below:

أحْمَدُ جَلَسَ مع إبْراهيمِ.

ذَهَبَتْ مُنَى إلى لُبْنانِ في شَهْرِ رَمَضانِ.

The first sentence أحْمَدُ جَلَسَ مع إبْراهيمِ (Ahmad sat with Ibrahim) is inaccurate in the noun إبْراهيم, particularly in its final vowel. The name إبْراهيم is the object of the preposition and مَمْنوع مِنْ الصّرْف. It must receive a فَتْحَة when genitive. Thus, the correct sentence should be هو جَلَسَ مع إبْراهيمَ.

The second sentence ذَهَبَتْ مُنَى إلى لُبْنانِ في شَهْرِ رَمَضانِ (Mona went to Lebanon in the month of Ramadan) has two mistakes. The noun لُبْنان is the object of the preposition إلى and must be genitive, but it is مَمْنوع مِنْ الصّرْف. It should receive فَتْحَة not كَسْرَة. The other mistake is in رَمَضان, which is also مَمْنوع مِنْ الصّرْف. Since it is مُضاف إليهِ, it must be genitive, which requires a فَتْحَة. Thus, the correct sentence should be أحْمَدُ جَلَسَ مع إبْراهيمَ. One final note on this sentence is worth mentioning. The noun مُنَى is the subject of the verb ذَهَبَتْ. Therefore, مُنَى must be in the nominative and should receive a ضَمّة. The noun مُنَى ends with an *alif maqṣūrah*, which causes the problem of pronouncing ضَمّة after an *alif*. While مُنَى is in the nominative case and should receive a ضَمّة, we do not place it at the end as it makes the pronunciation difficult.

Arabic Adverbs

In English, adverbs qualify verbs, nouns, or adjectives. Adverbs tell us something about the verb and its subject: the cause, intensity, time, or frequency of the action. Think of some adverbs: usually, always, sometimes, often, yesterday, and very. They modify verbs by conveying when, why, how, where, and how often in relation to the action being discussed.

In Arabic there are many adverbial expressions. They describe a verb and its subject. They take various forms. Sometimes they are adverbs with no other use; other times they are variations of nouns, yet serving as adverbs. Here, the discussion will focus on the most common Arabic adverbs, specifically explaining how they function in sentences.

One of the most common ways adverbs appear in a sentence is the circumstantial accusative, which is called الحال (al-ḥāl). It means "the being," "the state," or "the appearance." This is understandable, especially considering that الحال reveals something about the "being" of what it modifies, which is usually the verb and its subject. If subjects and predicates (of nominal sentences), as well as verbs and subjects (of verbal sentences), are primary items of the Arabic sentence, the adverbs are not. They serve as secondary elements in a sentence and sometimes can be removed without affecting the overall meaning. More importantly, the حال is an indefinite noun and is always accusative. Thus, we usually find الحال with تَنوين فَتْحَة, following the verb it modifies.

Consider the following sentences. All include adverbs:

Adverb	Translation	Sentence
جداً	I love my mother very much.	أنا أُحِبُّ أُمّي جداً.
جداً	Ali loves the falafel very much.	علي يُحِبُّ الفَلافِلَ جداً.
عادَةً	You usually kneel at the mosque.	أَنْتُما تَرْكَعانِ عادَةً في المَسْجِدِ.
عادَةً	You usually worship at church.	أنتم تَعبُدونَ عادَةً في الكَنيسةِ.
فَقَطْ	He only studies to succeed.	هو يَدْرُسُ فَقَطْ لِيَنْجَحَ.
فَقَطْ	She only cooks at her home.	هي تَطْبُخُ فَقَطْ في بَيتِها.
أَحْياناً	We worship (bow) sometimes at home.	نَسْجُدُ أَحْياناً في البيتِ.
أَحْياناً	They dance sometimes at their home.	هُنَّ يَرْقُصْنَ أَحْياناً في مَنْزِلِهِن.
دائِماً	She always listens to music.	هي تَسْمَعُ الموسيقى دائِماً.
دائِماً	They always thank God.	هُما يَشْكُرانِ الله دائِماً.
أَبَداً	I will never go to the bank.	أنا لَنْ أَذْهَبَ أَبَداً إلى البَنْكِ.

Lesson Eighteen

أَبَداً	You will never go up to the tower.	أَنْتَ لَنْ تَطْلُعَ أَبَداً إلى البُرْجِ.
قَطُّ	I never went to the bank.	أنا ما ذَهَبْتُ قَطُّ إلى البَنْكِ.
قَطُّ	You never went up to the tower.	أَنْتَ ما طَلَعْتُ قَطُّ إلى البُرْجِ.

In this table notice that all the adverbs are indefinite. They modify verbs. The vast majority of the adverbs are clearly in the accusative case, except قَطُّ which appears nominative. Arabic linguists parse قَطُّ as *mabnī* in the nominative instead of the accusative, because it needs the تَنوين ضَمَّة at the end. You should also note how أَبَداً and قَطُّ are comparable in meaning. One general difference is that قَطُّ deals with past tense, while أَبَداً deals mostly with future tense.

Adverbs can be built upon adjectives or nouns. Often we begin with an adjective (e.g., كَثير، قَليل، بَطيء، سَريع، نَشيط، سَعيد، شَمال) or a noun (e.g., نَهار، لَيْل، فَجْر، صَباح، مَساء، يَمين), then add تَنوين فَتْحَة to produce an adverb. Study the following examples:

Adverb	Translation	Sentence
كَثيراً	I drink water often.	أنا أَشْرَبُ الماءَ كَثيراً.
قَليلاً	We mention death a little.	نَحْنُ نَذْكُرُ المَوْتَ قَليلاً.
بَطيئاً	Go slowly!	اِذْهَبْ بَطيئاً.
سَريعاً	She exits the house quickly.	هي تَخْرُجُ سَريعاً من البيتِ.
نَشيطاً	He plays soccer energetically.	يَلْعَبُ الكُرَةَ نَشيطاً.
سَعيداً	I work happily.	أَعْمَلُ سَعيداً.
نَهاراً	I work during the day.	أَعْمَلُ نَهاراً.
لَيْلاً	I sleep at night.	أنامُ لَيْلاً.
فَجْراً	I worship (bow) at dawn.	أَسْجُدُ فَجْراً.
صَباحاً	I study in the morning.	أَدْرُسُ صَباحاً.
مَساءً	I play in the evening.	أَلْعَبُ مَساءً.
يَميناً	She crossed over to the right.	عَبَرَتْ يَميناً.
شَمالاً	We went right then left.	ذَهَبْنا يَميناً ثم شَمالاً.

There are still many other adverbs in Arabic. Here are more examples, which will help us learn how adverbs work and also increase our vocabulary:

Adverb	Translation	Sentence
هُنا	Come here.	أُحْضُرْ هُنا.
هُنا	You (f) are coming here.	أَنتِ تَحْضُرِينَ هُنا.
هُنا	He lives here.	هو يَسْكُنُ هُنا.
هُناكَ	She grinds over there.	هي تَطْحَنُ هُناكَ.
هُناكَ	We will live over there forever.	سَنَسْكُنُ هُناكَ إلى الأَبَدِ.
مَعاً	We played together.	لَعِبْنا مَعاً.
وَحْدي	I played by myself.	لَعِبْتُ وَحْدي.
عَمْداً	They rang the bell deliberately.	ضَرَبُوا الجَرَسَ عَمْداً.
أَمْسِ	They returned yesterday.	رَجَعُوا أَمْسِ.
أَمْسِ	I withdrew the money yesterday.	سَحَبْتُ المالَ أَمْسِ.
الآنَ	Wash this (f) now.	اِغْسِلْ هَذِهِ الآنَ.
الآنَ	The moon appeared now.	القَمَرُ ظَهَرَ الآنَ.
بَعْدُ	He did not write yet.	لَمْ يَكْتُبْ بَعْدُ.
بَعْدُ	You (dual) did not study yet.	لَمْ تَدْرُسا بَعْدُ.
أَخيراً	We finally closed the door.	غَلَقْنا البابَ أَخيراً.
حَديثاً	They researched the project recently.	بَحَثْنا المَشْروعَ حَديثاً.
غَداً	We will carry the box tomorrow.	سَنَحْمِلُ الصُّنْدُوقَ غَداً.
غَداً	You will plant the tree tomorrow.	سَتَزْرَعانِ الشجرةَ غَداً.
سَنَوِياً	Plant annually.	اِزْرَعْ سَنَوِياً.
يَوماً	You sat down one day.	أَنْتُما جَلَسْتُما يَوماً.
أَيضاً	They researched as well (or also).	هُمْ بَحَثُوا أَيضاً.

Lesson Eighteen

كَذَلِكَ	They researched as well (or also).	هُمْ بَحَثُوا كَذَلِكَ.
أوّلاً	They saw the sun firstly.	هما نَظَرَا الشمسَ أوّلاً.
أوّلاً	Firstly, they (md) thank God.	أوّلاً، شَكَرَا الله.
ثانياً	Secondly, they (md) worshiped the Creator.	ثانياً، عَبَدَا الخالِقَ.
ثالثاً	Thirdly, they (md) kneeled in the church.	ثالثاً، سَجَدَا في الكَنيسةِ.
تَحْتَ	We sat under the palm tree.	جَلَسْنا تَحْتَ النَخْلةِ.
تَحْتَ	The fish swims under the water.	السَمَكةُ تَسْبَحُ تَحْتَ الماءِ.
أمامَ	He drank in front of the door.	شَرِبَ أمامَ البابِ.
خَلْفَ	She laughed behind the desk.	ضَحِكَتْ خَلْفَ المَكْتَبِ.
قَبْلَ	He hit the enemy a year ago.	ضَرَبَ العَدوَ قَبْلَ سَنَةٍ.

Adverbs in Arabic receive many names and labels. Some classify adverbs as those of time, manner, place, degree, while others identify them as locative and causative, among others. It suffices in this introductory course to understand adverbs in general and to learn their meanings in sentences.

Finally, you might be surprised to know that some of the most frequently used Arabic words, including شُكْراً (thank you), عَفْواً (you're welcome), and أَهْلاً وسَهْلاً (welcome) are adverbs for implied verbs.

Since we are now familiar with more adverbs than before, in the following lesson we will focus on unique verbs and their conjugations, such as those whose roots include long vowels, *hamzah*, or doubled letters, among others.

Vocabulary

yellow (m)	أصْفَر	a young man	شاب
yellow (f)	صَفْراء	a young lady	شابة
sun (also a feminine name, Shams)	شَمْس	a young lady	فَتاة
Majida (a feminine name)	ماجِدة	able	قادِر

brunette	سَمْراء	angry	غاضِب
smallest, youngest (f)	صُغْرى	beautiful	جَميل
small, young (f)	صَغيرَة	deep	عَميق
pregnant	حُبْلى	different	مُخْتَلِف
names (also a feminine name, Asmaa)	أَسْماء	wrong	غَلَطْ
Tehran	طَهْران	general, public	عام
Lebanon	لُبْنان	money	مال
Adnan (a masculine name)	عَدْنان	high	عال
wounded (mp/fp)	جَرْحى	stiff, hard	صَلْب
Ajman	عَجْمان	wide	واسِع
green (m)	أَخْضَر	cutter	قاطِع
green (f)	خَضْراء	tight, narrow	ضَيِّق
churches	كَنائِس	seller	بائِع
mosques	مَساجِد	maker	صانِع
synagogues	مَجامِع	few, little	قَليل
in daze (also a masculine name, Sarhan)	سَرْحان	patient, sick	مَريض
red (m)	أَحْمَر	right, healthy	صَحيح
lame (m)	أَعْرَج	conqueror, winner	غالِب
lame (f)	عَرْجاء	weak, vulnerable	ضَعيف
virgin	عَذراء	very much	جداً
falafel	فَلافِل	usually	عادَةً
often, a lot	كَثيراً	only	فَقَطْ

Lesson Eighteen

a little	قَليلاً	sometimes	أَحْياناً
slowly	بَطيئاً	always listens to music	دائِماً
quickly	سَريعاً	never	أَبَداً
energetically	نَشيطاً	never	قَطْ
happily	سَعيداً	here	هُنا
during the day	نَهاراً	there	هُناكَ
at night	لَيْلاً	together	مَعاً
at dawn	فَجْراً	by myself	وَحْدي
in the morning	صَباحاً	deliberately	عَمْداً
in the evening	مَساءً	yesterday (adverb)	أَمْسِ
to the right	يَميناً	now	الآنَ
to the left	شَمالاً	yet	بَعْدُ
firstly	أَوَّلاً	finally	أَخيراً
secondly	ثانِياً	recently	حَديثاً
thirdly	ثالِثاً	tomorrow	غَداً
under	تَحْتَ	annually	سَنَوِياً
in front of	أَمامَ	one day (adverb)	يَوْماً
behind	خَلْفَ	also	أَيْضاً
a year ago	قَبْلَ سَنَةٍ	also, as well	كَذَلِكَ

Exercises

Exercise 18.1

Read the following passage from Genesis 12:1–4. Circle the un-nunated nouns and each *hamzah*, stating whether it is cutting or connecting.

وَقالَ اللهُ لِأَبْرامَ: «اتْرُكْ بَلَدَكَ وَشَعبَكَ وَعائِلَةَ أَبِيكَ، واذهَبْ إلى الأرضِ الَّتِي سَأُرِيها أنا لَكَ. وَأنا سَأَجْعَلُ مِنْ نَسلِكَ أُمَّةً عَظيمَةً. وَسَأُبارِكُكَ، وَسَأَجْعَلُ لَكَ اسماً شَهيراً، فَتَكُونَ بَرَكَةً لِلآخَرِينَ. سَأُبارِكُ مَنْ يُبارِكُونَكَ، وَسَأَلْعَنُ مَنْ يَحتَقِرُونَكَ. وَبِكَ تَتَبارَكُ كُلُّ عَشائِرِ الأرضِ.» فَذَهَبَ أَبْرامُ كَما أَمَرَهُ اللهُ. وَرافَقَهُ لُوطُ. وَكانَ أَبْرامُ فِي الخامِسَةِ وَالسَّبْعِينَ مِنْ عُمْرِهِ عِنْدَما تَرَكَ حاران.

Exercise 18.2

Examine the Genesis passage in the previous exercise. Identify two imperative verbs, four future tense verbs, and four nouns with possessive pronouns.

Exercise 18.3

State whether these sentences are correct or incorrect. Correct the incorrect sentences.

1. جَلَسَ مع إبْراهيمِ.
2. دَرَسْتُ في المَدارِسِ.
3. أنا مِن نيويوركَ.
4. ذَهَبَ إبْراهيمُ إلى صَحَراءَ.
5. سَمِعَتْ هِنْدٌ المُحاضرةَ.
6. أنا سَمِعْتُ هِنْدَ في الجامعةِ.
7. أَنْتِ سَمِعْتِ هِنْداً في الحَديقَةِ.
8. أنا رَكَعْتُ في كنائسَ كَبيرةٍ.

Lesson Eighteen

9. هُمْ عَبَدُوا في كنائِسِ القاهرةِ.

10. دَرَسْنا مع فاطمةَ.

11. ذَهَبنا في رِحْلَةٍ إلى طَهْرانَ، في إيرانَ، في شَهْرِ رَمَضانَ.

Exercise 18.4

Translate the following sentences into English.

1. تَسْمَعُ العِظاتَ دائِماً.

2. أنا أَعْمَلُ نَهاراً وأنامُ لَيْلاً.

3. أَحْمَدُ يَدْرِسُ فَقَطْ لِيَنْجَحَ.

4. أنا أَشْرَبُ القهوةَ كَثيراً.

5. جَلَسْنا تَحْتَ الشجرةِ مَعاً.

Exercise 18.5

Translate the following sentences into Arabic.

1. We finally opened the gate.

2. Wash (ms) the shirt now!

3. Firstly, I would love to thank my father.

4. Secondly, I want to sit on a new chair.

5. We will cross the river tomorrow.

Lesson Nineteen
تِسْعَةَ عَشَرَ

Sound and Weak Verbs

In Arabic, there are 28 letters. These letters are divided into two groups: sound and weak. All letters are "sound" except three: ا (*alif*), و (*wāw*), and ي (*yā'*). Whether these three letters are consonants or vowels, they are called "weak" because they alter their forms quite often between paradigms, tenses, and voices.

For example, the verb قَالَ means "he said," يَقُول "he says," and قِيلَ "it was said." Notice how the letter ا in the past tense becomes و in the present and ي in the passive. This is a rough introductory example to demonstrate how a "weak" letter switches its form. Sometimes these weak letters not only switch forms but even disappear. The imperative of the verb قَالَ is قُلْ, where the ا is completely gone.

This is why the three letters ا و ي are called "weak," while the rest of the letters in the alphabet are "sound." A sound letter is called صَحِيح (*saḥīḥ*) and a weak letter مُعْتَلّ (*muʿtall*). The former literally means "healthy" or "healthful," while the latter "weak," "sick," or "ill."

Similarly, the terminology of "weak" and "sound" are applied to verbs. You recall that a root usually has three radicals, i.e., three base letters. If one of these root letters is weak, then the verb is considered a weak verb: مُعْتَلّ. If the verb's root does not include any weak letters, then it is a sound verb: صَحِيح.

Surprisingly, the letter *alif* (ا) is never a root letter. If you see it in a basic verb form (e.g., قَالَ), it is actually an *alif* that was originally a *wāw* (و) or *yā'* (ي). As a rule of thumb, when you see an *alif* in a conjugation, it is usually an additional letter or a *wāw* or *yā'* turned into an *alif*.

Finally, we should pay attention not to conflate the *alif* and the *hamzah*. The former is مُعْتَلّ, while the latter is صَحِيح. For instance, consider the two verbs قَالَ (he said) and سَأَلَ (he asked). The former verb is weak, while the latter is sound. The *hamzah* is not a weak letter; the *alif* is. We call the verb سَأَلَ a *hamzated* verb, since its root includes a *hamzah*. We will study it shortly.

Basic Categories in Sound and Weak Verbs

A sound verb is called فِعْل صَحيح. It is a verb whose root does not include any weak letters. A sound verb can take one of three forms:

1. A regular sound verb, which does not include in its root any *hamzah* or doubled letters. We studied many examples of this verb, including دَرَسَ, خَلَقَ, جَلَسَ, and صَنَعَ.

2. A *hamzated* verb, in which the root has a *hamzah* in one of its three radicals, which are also called "base letters" or "root letters." For example, أَخَذَ (he took), أَكَلَ (he ate), سَأَلَ (he asked), and بَدَأَ (he began) are all *hamzated* verbs.

3. A geminate verb, in which the root includes two identical letters, most likely in the form of a *shaddah*. Some call it a doubled verb. For example, مَرَّ (he passed by), رَدَّ (he answered, responded), دَقَّ (he knocked, hammered), and شَقَّ (he split, slit) are all geminate verbs.

A weak verb is called فِعْل مُعْتَلّ. It is a verb whose root includes any of the three weak letters ا و ي, although—by now—we know that ا is not actually a root letter, but is originally a و or ي. The verb is "weak" because one of its radicals is altered or completely disappearing in one or more of the verb's conjugations. A weak verb can take one of three forms:

1. An assimilated verb, in which the root's first letter is weak. For example, وَقَفَ (he stood), وَرَدَ (he arrived, came), and يَبِسَ (it withered, dried up) are weak assimilated verbs, because their first radicals are weak letters.

2. A hollow verb, in which the root's second letter is weak. For instance, عادَ (he returned), صامَ (he fasted), قالَ (he said), and باعَ (he sold) are all hollow verbs, because their root's middle letter is مُعْتَلّ.

3. A defective verb, in which the root's third radical is weak. For instance, دَعا (he summoned, called out), غَزا (he invaded), مَشَى (he walked), رَمَى (he threw) are weak defective verbs. Each of them has a weak letter as the third radical.

Thus, there are six categories within triliteral verbs; three sound and three weak. The sound verbs are usually predictable in their conjugations, unlike the weak verbs, which are more complex. The sound verbs, with only a few exceptions, follow the patterns we explained while discussing the conjugations of regular verbs (e.g., دَرَسَ، خَلَقَ، جَلَسَ).

In what follows, we will study examples of sound (*hamzated* and geminate) and weak (assimilated, hollow, and defective) verbs. At the outset, you must remember that these five categories are often unpredictable, especially to beginners. Their conjugations are irregular. They do not necessarily follow the common patterns we discussed earlier when we studied the triliteral sound verbs. Since this is an introductory course, we will explore some forms within these five categories in order to make you familiar with their major conjugations.

Hamzated Verbs

These verbs have *hamzah* in one of their three radicals. Here are some *hamzated* verbs.

	Group 3		Group 2		Group 1
he got healed	بَرَأَ	he asked	سَأَلَ	he took	أَخَذَ
he read	قَرَأَ	he roared	زَأَرَ	he ate	أَكَلَ
he started	بَدَأَ	he saw	رَأَى	he captured	أَسَرَ
he rejoiced	هَنَأَ	he had mercy	رَأَفَ	he ordered	أَمَرَ
he filled	مَلَأَ			he allowed	أَذِنَ
he sought refuge	لَجَأَ			he became sorry	أَسِفَ
				he became safe	أَمِنَ

Group 1 represents *hamzated* verbs, in which the *hamzah* is found in the first radical. Group 2 lists verbs where the *hamzah* is in the second radical, while in Group 3 the *hamzah* is in the final letter of the root. These verbs will operate for the most part as regular sound verbs which we previously studied, particularly in the past and present conjugations. However, they will vary significantly in the imperative and when two *hamzah*s occur consecutively.

In order to study the major conjugations of these *hamzated* verbs, let's examine the forms of هُوَ and أَنَا in both the perfect and imperfect tenses, in addition to the singular imperative. We will begin with Group 1, then reflect on Groups 2 and 3.

Lesson Nineteen

		Group 1					Tense	Pronoun
أَمِنَ	أَسِفَ	أَذِنَ	أَمَرَ	أَسَرَ	أَكَلَ	أَخَذَ	Past	هُوَ
يَأْمَنُ	يَأْسَفُ	يَأْذَنُ	يَأْمُرُ	يَأْسِرُ	يَأْكُلُ	يَأْخُذُ	Present	هُوَ
اِئْمَنْ	اِئْسَفْ	اِئْذَنْ	اُؤْمُرْ	اِئْسِرْ	كُلْ	خُذْ	Imperative	أَنْتَ
أَمِنْتُ	أَسِفْتُ	أَذِنْتُ	أَمَرْتُ	أَسَرْتُ	أَكَلْتُ	أَخَذْتُ	Past	أَنَا
آمَنُ	آسَفُ	آذَنُ	آمُرُ	آسِرُ	آكُلُ	آخُذُ	Present	أَنَا

Examine the table above. These verbs are generally irregular in their conjugations, but we can still make some helpful observations.

First, the past tense conjugations of the *hamzated* verbs follow the regular paradigms as explained in previous chapters. This is because past tense conjugations use only suffixes and these suffixes do not change, so the existence of a *hamzah* will not affect the conjugation. This is good news.

Second, the present tense conjugations are a bit more sophisticated, as they use prefixes and suffixes. This is significant in particular when we have two *hamzah*s occurring consecutively: a *hamzah* of the prefix followed by another as the first letter in the *hamzated* verb. However, there are still some patterns. It suffices to mention a general rule: change the initial *hamzah* into *maddah*.[1] For example, consider using the pronoun أَنَا with the verb أَخَذَ يَأْخُذُ in the present. Adding a prefix أ to أْخُذُ results in آخُذُ, since a *hamzah* followed by a long *alif* forms *alif maddah* (Lesson Three).[2]

---

1. For some inquiring minds, the rule is more complex than that: When there are two *hamzah*s in a row in a conjugation, keep the first *hamzah* as it is, and switch the second *hamzah* into a long vowel matching the short vowel of the first *hamzah*. For example, in the present conjugation with the pronoun أَنَا, we need to add a prefix أ to the verb's root. If the first radical of the verb is a *hamzah* (in the present conjugation, it is associated with a *sukūn*), then we will have two *hamzah*s in a row. In this case, the first *hamzah* (of the suffix) remains unchanged, while the second *hamzah* (the *hamzah* of the verb's root) changes to a long vowel matching the short vowel of the first radical (in this case a *fathah*). The result is a *maddah*.

2. For advanced students, the details of this change are as follows: We add a prefix أ to ءْخُذُ. In this case, the prefix and its short vowel will remain the same. The *hamzah* at the beginning of ءْخُذُ will change to a long *alif*, because there is a *fathah* associated with the *hamzah* of the prefix. Thus, we have أ followed by اْخُذُ. Because a *hamzah* followed by a long *alif* forms *alif maddah*, the conjugation becomes أَنَا آخُذُ.

Third, the imperative conjugations of *hamzated* verbs are more advanced. In most cases, if the first radical of the root is a *hamzah*, drop it off. However, the matter is more complex than it appears, and a detailed explanation of these conjugations would extend beyond the scope of this book. It suffices to note that the comparison of the imperative conjugations in the table above suggests two major directions: In the case of خُذْ and كُلْ, the *hamzah* is dropped, while in اِنْسِرْ, أُوْمُرْ, اِئْذَنْ, اِنْسَفْ, and اِئْمَنْ, the rule of two *hamzah*s in a row is somewhat applied. Recall that the conjugations of the imperative are built on the active present tense, particularly its jussive forms.[3]

Now explore the following examples from Group 2 and Group 3 of the *hamzated* verbs. The former has the *hamzah* in its second radical, while the latter has it in the third radical.

	Group 2			Tense	Pronoun
رَأَفَ	رَأَى	زَأَرَ	سَأَلَ	Past	هُوَ
يَرْأَفُ	يَرَى	يَزْأَرُ	يَسْأَلُ	Present	هُوَ
اِرْأَفْ	رَ	اِزْأَرْ	اِسْأَلْ	Imperative	أَنْتَ
رَأَفْتُ	رَأَيْتُ	زَأَرْتُ	سَأَلْتُ	Past	أَنَا
أَرْأَفُ	أَرَى	أَزْأَرُ	أَسْأَلُ	Present	أَنَا

---

3. The rules of the imperative are complex and sophisticated. However, some details can be provided for inquiring students. For instance, take a straightforward sound verb تَذْكُرُ as active present tense for the pronoun أَنْتَ. Its jussive form is تَذْكُرْ, while أُذْكُرْ is its imperative. However, ذَكَرَ يَذْكُرُ is not a *hamzated* verb. In the case of the *hamzated* verb أَكَلَ, the active present conjugation is تَأْكُلُ with the pronoun أَنْتَ. Its jussive form is تَأْكُلْ, while its imperative conjugation is formed by using أ instead of the prefix تَ in تَأْكُلْ. Remember that أ is actually a connecting *hamzah*. If the تَ is removed, we are left with ءكُلْ prefixed with أ. But the *hamzah* in the ءكُلْ will drop off in the imperative. Thus, we are left with كُلْ prefixed with a connecting *hamzah* أ. The connecting *hamzah* is only necessary when its following letter has a *sukūn*. In the case of كُلْ, the letter has a *ḍammah*. Thus, the connecting *hamzah* is not needed and is removed. The final result is كُلْ. This is the imperative form of the verb أَكَلَ.

Pronoun	Tense	Group 3					
هُوَ	Past	بَرَأَ	قَرَأَ	بَدَأَ	هَنَأَ	مَلَأَ	لَجَأَ
هُوَ	Present	يَبْرَأُ	يَقْرَأُ	يَبْدَأُ	يَهْنَأُ	يَمْلَأُ	يَلْجَأُ
أَنْتَ	Imperative	اِبْرَأْ	اِقْرَأْ	اِبْدَأْ	اِهْنَأْ	اِمْلَأْ	اِلْجَأْ
أَنَا	Past	بَرَأْتُ	قَرَأْتُ	بَدَأْتُ	هَنَأْتُ	مَلَأْتُ	لَجَأْتُ
أَنَا	Present	أَبْرَأُ	أَقْرَأُ	أَبْدَأُ	أَهْنَأُ	أَمْلَأُ	أَلْجَأُ

In these two tables notice that the perfect conjugations are straightforward as regular sound verbs, and the imperfect ones follow the same rule mentioned for Group 1. Still, imperative conjugations are more sophisticated and will not be covered in this introductory course. Now we will turn to the second category of sound verbs: geminate verbs.

Geminate Verbs

A geminate verb is a doubled verb, in which the root includes two identical letters (often second and third radicals). They are most likely to appear in the form of a *shaddah*. Earlier some examples of geminate verbs were mentioned. Examine their perfect conjugations:

		الفِعْل مَرَّ	الفِعْل رَدَّ	الفِعْل دَقَّ	الفِعْل شَقَّ
مُفْرَد	أَنَا	مَرَرْتُ	رَدَدْتُ	دَقَقْتُ	شَقَقْتُ
	أَنْتَ	مَرَرْتَ	رَدَدْتَ	دَقَقْتَ	شَقَقْتَ
	أَنْتِ	مَرَرْتِ	رَدَدْتِ	دَقَقْتِ	شَقَقْتِ
	هُوَ	مَرَّ	رَدَّ	دَقَّ	شَقَّ
	هِيَ	مَرَّتْ	رَدَّتْ	دَقَّتْ	شَقَّتْ

		الفِعْل شَقَّ	الفِعْل دَقَّ	الفِعْل رَدَّ	الفِعْل مَرَّ	
	نَحْنُ	مَرَرْنا	رَدَدْنا	دَقَقْنا	شَقَقْنا	
	أَنْتُما (مُذَكَّر)	مَرَرْتُما	رَدَدْتُما	دَقَقْتُما	شَقَقْتُما	مُثَنَّى
	أَنْتُما (مؤنَّث)	مَرَرْتُما	رَدَدْتُما	دَقَقْتُما	شَقَقْتُما	
	هُما (مُذَكَّر)	مَرَّا	رَدَّا	دَقَّا	شَقَّا	
	هُما (مؤنَّث)	مَرَّتا	رَدَّتا	دَقَّتا	شَقَّتا	
	نَحْنُ	مَرَرْنا	رَدَدْنا	دَقَقْنا	شَقَقْنا	
	أَنْتُمْ	مَرَرْتُم	رَدَدْتُم	دَقَقْتُم	شَقَقْتُم	
	أَنْتُنَّ	مَرَرْتُنَّ	رَدَدْتُنَّ	دَقَقْتُنَّ	شَقَقْتُنَّ	جَمْع
	هُمْ	مَرُّوا	رَدُّوا	دَقُّوا	شَقُّوا	
	هُنَّ	مَرَرْنَ	رَدَدْنَ	دَقَقْنَ	شَقَقْنَ	

From these past tense conjugations it is clear that the two identical radicals sometimes appear in a *shaddah* form, and at other times they split and appear next to each other in the conjugation. Notice that in the case of third-person (singular, dual, or plural) masculine conjugations, the identical letters appear as a *shaddah*. However, in the case of first and second person, the two identical letters appear side by side. It is also important to note that the vowels of the perfect conjugations follow the common paradigm we previously studied for the sound regular verbs.

Consider the imperfect conjugations of the same verbs:

		الفِعْل يَشُقُّ	الفِعْل يَدُقُّ	الفِعْل يَرُدُّ	الفِعْل يَمُرُّ	
	أَنا	أَمُرُّ	أَرُدُّ	أَدُقُّ	أَشُقُّ	
	أَنْتَ	تَمُرُّ	تَرُدُّ	تَدُقُّ	تَشُقُّ	
	أَنْتِ	تَمُرِّينَ	تَرُدِّينَ	تَدُقِّينَ	تَشُقِّينَ	مُفْرَد
	هُوَ	يَمُرُّ	يَرُدُّ	يَدُقُّ	يَشُقُّ	
	هِيَ	تَمُرُّ	تَرُدُّ	تَدُقُّ	تَشُقُّ	

Lesson Nineteen

		نَشُقُّ	نَدُقُّ	نَرُدُّ	نَمُرُّ	نَحْنُ
مُثَنَّى		تَشُقَّانِ	تَدُقَّانِ	تَرُدَّانِ	تَمُرَّانِ	أَنْتُما (مُذَكَّر)
		تَشُقَّانِ	تَدُقَّانِ	تَرُدَّانِ	تَمُرَّانِ	أَنْتُما (مؤَنَّث)
		يَشُقَّانِ	يَدُقَّانِ	يَرُدَّانِ	يَمُرَّانِ	هُما (مُذَكَّر)
		تَشُقَّانِ	تَدُقَّانِ	تَرُدَّانِ	تَمُرَّانِ	هُما (مؤَنَّث)
جَمْع		نَشُقُّ	نَدُقُّ	نَرُدُّ	نَمُرُّ	نَحْنُ
		تَشُقُّونَ	تَدُقُّونَ	تَرُدُّونَ	تَمُرُّونَ	أَنْتُمْ
		تَشْقُقْنَ	تَدْقُقْنَ	تَرْدُدْنَ	تَمْرُرْنَ	أَنْتُنَّ
		يَشُقُّونَ	يَدُقُّونَ	يَرُدُّونَ	يَمُرُّونَ	هُمْ
		يَشْقُقْنَ	يَدْقُقْنَ	يَرْدُدْنَ	يَمْرُرْنَ	هُنَّ

In these present tense conjugations note that the two identical radicals always appear in a *shaddah* form, except in the feminine plural forms of second and third person where the identical letters appear next to each other. Still, the same vowels we previously studied in the paradigm of the imperfect regular sound verbs are used here.

As an exercise, form the past and present tense paradigms of the following geminate verbs: كَفَّ يَكُفُّ (to stop short, refrain), دَبَّ يَدِبُّ (to creep on earth), and سَبَّ يَسُبُّ (to insult, cuss).

In this section the introductory matters of sound verbs were covered. The focus was on *hamzated* verbs and geminate verbs, since regular sound verbs were studied in previous chapters. Now, we turn our focus to weak (assimilated, hollow, and defective) verbs.

Assimilated Verbs

An assimilated verb has a و (*wāw*) or ي (*yāʾ*) as its first radical. The و occurs as the first radical more frequently than the ي.

Here are some verb examples:

Translation	المضارع	الماضي	
to stand up	يَقِفُ	وَقَفَ	1
to inherit	يَرِثُ	وَرِثَ	2
to promise	يَعِدُ	وَعَدَ	3
to weigh	يَزِنُ	وَزَنَ	4
to trust	يَثِقُ	وَثِقَ	5
to arrive, come	يَرِدُ	وَرَدَ	6
to brand, mark, stamp	يَسِمُ	وَسَمَ	7
to find	يَجِدُ	وَجَدَ	8
to jump	يَثِبُ	وَثَبَ	9
to fall, to happen	يَقَعُ	وَقَعَ	10
to grant (freely), bestow	يَهَبُ	وَهَبَ	11
to place, put	يَضَعُ	وَضَعَ	12
to wither, become dry	يَيْبَسُ	يَبِسَ	13
to give up, despair	يَيْأَسُ	يَئِسَ	14
to be awake	يَيْقَظُ	يَقِظَ	15

This table shows the past and present conjugations of the singular third-person masculine هُوَ of some weak verbs. Most of them have و as the first radical.

Before we examine a sample of the full paradigm of assimilated verbs, there is a basic observation from the table above. For verbs with an initial و weak letter (1–12), most of their present conjugations have a *kasrah* with the second radical (e.g., 1–10), although a few still use a *fatḥah* (e.g., 11–12). One can also notice that these verbs drop off the weak letter و in the present conjugations with هُوَ. The final three examples (13–15) have a weak letter ي as their first radical. In their conjugations, as we shall see, they almost entirely follow the regular sound verbs.

Lesson Nineteen

Consider the past and present paradigms of the verb وَقَفَ in order to examine what changes occur in assimilated verbs' conjugations:

	الضَّمائِر	الماضي	المضارع
مُفْرَد	أَنَا	وَقَفْتُ	أَقِفُ
	أَنْتَ	وَقَفْتَ	تَقِفُ
	أَنْتِ	وَقَفْتِ	تَقِفِينَ
	هُوَ	وَقَفَ	يَقِفُ
	هِيَ	وَقَفَتْ	تَقِفُ
مُثَنَّى	نَحْنُ	وَقَفْنَا	نَقِفُ
	أَنْتُما (مُذَكَّر)	وَقَفْتُمَا	تَقِفَانِ
	أَنْتُما (مُؤَنَّث)	وَقَفْتُمَا	تَقِفَانِ
	هُما (مُذَكَّر)	وَقَفَا	يَقِفَانِ
	هُما (مؤَنَّث)	وَقَفَتَا	تَقِفَانِ
جَمْع	نَحْنُ	وَقَفْنَا	نَقِفُ
	أَنْتُمْ	وَقَفْتُم	تَقِفُونَ
	أَنْتُنَّ	وَقَفْتُنَّ	تَقِفْنَ
	هُمْ	وَقَفُوا	يَقِفُونَ
	هُنَّ	وَقَفْنَ	يَقِفْنَ

From this table you notice that the past tense conjugations of this weak assimilated verb follow patterns similar to those we used with regular verbs. This is good news. With present tense conjugations the matter is different: the weak letter (first radical of the root) disappears. In general, most Arabic assimilated verbs follow this twofold rule: there is no change in the patterns in the past tense, while in the present tense the weak letter is dropped off.

Examine the paradigms of two more assimilated verbs وَعَدَ and وَجَدَ in past and present forms:

		يَجِدُ	وَجَدَ	يَعِدُ	وَعَدَ
	أَنَا	أَجِدُ	وَجَدْتُ	أَعِدُ	وَعَدْتُ
	أَنْتَ	تَجِدُ	وَجَدْتَ	تَعِدُ	وَعَدْتَ
مُفْرَد	أَنْتِ	تَجِدِينَ	وَجَدْتِ	تَعِدِينَ	وَعَدْتِ
	هُوَ	يَجِدُ	وَجَدَ	يَعِدُ	وَعَدَ
	هِيَ	تَجِدُ	وَجَدَتْ	تَعِدُ	وَعَدَتْ
	نَحْنُ	نَجِدُ	وَجَدْنَا	نَعِدُ	وَعَدْنَا
	أَنْتُما (مُذَكَّر)	تَجِدَانِ	وَجَدْتُمَا	تَعِدَانِ	وَعَدْتُمَا
مُثَنَّى	أَنْتُما (مؤَنَّث)	تَجِدَانِ	وَجَدْتُمَا	تَعِدَانِ	وَعَدْتُمَا
	هُما (مُذَكَّر)	يَجِدَانِ	وَجَدَا	يَعِدَانِ	وَعَدَا
	هُما (مؤَنَّث)	تَجِدَانِ	وَجَدَتَا	تَعِدَانِ	وَعَدَتَا
	نَحْنُ	نَجِدُ	وَجَدْنَا	نَعِدُ	وَعَدْنَا
	أَنْتُمْ	تَجِدُونَ	وَجَدْتُمْ	تَعِدُونَ	وَعَدْتُمْ
جَمْع	أَنْتُنَّ	تَجِدْنَ	وَجَدْتُنَّ	تَعِدْنَ	وَعَدْتُنَّ
	هُمْ	يَجِدُونَ	وَجَدُوا	يَعِدُونَ	وَعَدُوا
	هُنَّ	يَجِدْنَ	وَجَدْنَ	يَعِدْنَ	وَعَدْنَ

In order to practice, follow the table above, and chart the past and present conjugations of وَثَبَ, وَهَبَ, وَقَعَ, وَسَمَ, and وَثَبَ.

Lesson Nineteen

Let's now examine an assimilated verb that begins with a ي. Here is the paradigm of past and present conjugations:

	الضَّمائِر	الماضي	المُضارِع
مُفْرَد	أنَا	يَبِسْتُ	أيْبَسُ
	أنْتَ	يَبِسْتَ	تَيْبَسُ
	أنْتِ	يَبِسْتِ	تَيْبَسِينَ
	هُوَ	يَبِسَ	يَيْبَسُ
	هِيَ	يَبِسَتْ	تَيْبَسُ
مُثَنّى	نَحْنُ	يَبِسْنَا	نَيْبَسُ
	أنْتُما (مُذَكَّر)	يَبِسْتُما	تَيْبَسانِ
	أنْتُما (مؤَنَّث)	يَبِسْتُما	تَيْبَسانِ
	هُما (مُذَكَّر)	يَبِسَا	يَيْبَسانِ
	هُما (مؤَنَّث)	يَبِسَتَا	تَيْبَسانِ
جَمْع	نَحْنُ	يَبِسْنَا	نَيْبَسُ
	أنْتُمْ	يَبِسْتُم	تَيْبَسُونَ
	أنْتُنَّ	يَبِسْتُنَّ	تَيْبَسْنَ
	هُمْ	يَبِسُوا	يَيْبَسُونَ
	هُنَّ	يَبِسْنَ	يَيْبَسْنَ

Unlike assimilated verbs that begin with a و, those beginning with a ي follow almost the same patterns as sound verbs. They do not drop off the weak letter in present conjugations. In past tense conjugations they adopt the regular suffixes we use with sound verbs.

Hollow Verbs

A verb is hollow when its second radical is weak. Here are some examples:

	الماضي	المضارع	Translation
1	نامَ	يَنامُ	to sleep
2	خافَ	يَخافُ	to fear
3	هابَ	يَهابُ	to dread, fear
4	صامَ	يَصومُ	to fast (from food)
5	عادَ	يَعودُ	to return
6	قالَ	يَقولُ	to say
7	قامَ	يَقومُ	to get up
8	زارَ	يَزورُ	to visit
9	دارَ	يَدورُ	to revolve
10	ثارَ	يَثورُ	to rebel, revolt against
11	تابَ	يَتوبُ	to repent
12	باعَ	يَبيعُ	to sell
13	سارَ	يَسيرُ	to walk, march
14	زادَ	يَزيدُ	to increase

Hollow verbs are a bit more advanced. Their conjugations can be tricky for beginners, especially due to the necessity of determining whether an *alif* of the second radical is actually a و or ي. This requires practice and can usually be achieved by speaking with Arabic-speaking people or, of course, the use of a dictionary. Nonetheless, there are hollow verbs with و or ي as their second radical.

Hollow verbs are complex for other various reasons, including the various changes to the weak letter—it is sometimes completely dropped off, replaced by a short vowel, or switched to a long vowel. This extends beyond the scope of this introductory course; however, some general features can be noted.

The past tense conjugations are often straightforward. They use only suffixes and are unusually predictable, as there is no irregularity when compared to the suffixes used with sound verbs. The only unexpected feature with hollow verbs appears in the behavior of the weak letter in the middle, as it may disappear or switch to another vowel. In fact, the same can be *almost* said concerning the present tense conjugations, especially in relation to their prefixes, which appear unchanged. Sometimes, however, the suffixes can be tricky and inconsistent.

For our introductory purposes, examine two hollow verbs in their full past and present paradigms.

Here are the verbs: صَامَ يَصُومُ and قَالَ يَقُولُ:

		يَقُولُ	قَالَ	يَصُومُ	صَامَ	
مُفْرَد	أَنَا	أَقُولُ	قُلْتُ	أَصُومُ	صُمْتُ
	أَنْتَ	تَقُولُ	قُلْتَ	تَصُومُ	صُمْتَ
	أَنْتِ	تَقُولِينَ	قُلْتِ	تَصُومِينَ	صُمْتِ
	هُوَ	يَقُولُ	قَالَ	يَصُومُ	صَامَ
	هِيَ	تَقُولُ	قَالَتْ	تَصُومُ	صَامَتْ
مُثَنَّى	نَحْنُ	نَقُولُ	قُلْنَا	نَصُومُ	صُمْنَا
	أَنْتُما (مُذَكَّر)	تَقُولَانِ	قُلْتُمَا	تَصُومَانِ	صُمْتُمَا
	أَنْتُما (مُؤَنَّث)	تَقُولَانِ	قُلْتُمَا	تَصُومَانِ	صُمْتُمَا
	هُما (مُذَكَّر)	يَقُولَانِ	قَالَا	يَصُومَانِ	صَامَا
	هُما (مُؤَنَّث)	تَقُولَانِ	قَالَتَا	تَصُومَانِ	صَامَتَا
جَمْع	نَحْنُ	نَقُولُ	قُلْنَا	نَصُومُ	صُمْنَا
	أَنْتُمْ	تَقُولُونَ	قُلْتُمْ	تَصُومُونَ	صُمْتُمْ
	أَنْتُنَّ	تَقُلْنَ	قُلْتُنَّ	تَصُمْنَ	صُمْتُنَّ
	هُمْ	يَقُولُونَ	قَالُوا	يَصُومُونَ	صَامُوا
	هُنَّ	يَقُلْنَ	قُلْنَ	يَصُمْنَ	صُمْنَ

In past tense forms the suffixes are unchanged. The third-person conjugations (except feminine plural) are identical to those in sound verbs. The weak letter disappears in all conjugations with first and second person (in addition to feminine plural).

In present tense forms the prefixes and suffixes are unchanged. The weak letter in the middle of قَالَ or صَامَ is apparently a و, as the forms are يَصُومُ and يَقُولُ. So, the present conjugations use قول and صوم instead of قال and صام, respectively. By and large, in all present conjugations of these two hollow verbs—with the exception of conjugations with أَنْتُنَّ and هُنَّ—the forms follow those of sound verbs. With أَنْتُنَّ and هُنَّ, the weak letter is dropped. While the matter of hollow verbs is complex, these introductory observations suffice for our purposes.

To practice, form the paradigms of عَادَ يَعودُ and زَارَ يَزورُ before you check the answer below:

		يَزورُ	زَارَ	يَعودُ	عَادَ
مُفْرَد	أَنَا	أَزورُ	زُرْتُ	أَعودُ	عُدْتُ
	أَنْتَ	تَزورُ	زُرْتَ	تَعودُ	عُدْتَ
	أَنْتِ	تَزورِينَ	زُرْتِ	تَعودِينَ	عُدْتِ
	هُوَ	يَزورُ	زَارَ	يَعودُ	عَادَ
	هِيَ	تَزورُ	زَارَتْ	تَعودُ	عَادَتْ
مُثَنَّى	نَحْنُ	نَزورُ	زُرْنَا	نَعودُ	عُدْنَا
	أَنْتُمَا (مُذَكَّر)	تَزورَانِ	زُرْتُمَا	تَعودَانِ	عُدْتُمَا
	أَنْتُمَا (مؤَنَّث)	تَزورَانِ	زُرْتُمَا	تَعودَانِ	عُدْتُمَا
	هُما (مُذَكَّر)	يَزورَانِ	زَارَا	يَعودَانِ	عَادَا
	هُما (مؤَنَّث)	تَزورَانِ	زَارَتَا	تَعودَانِ	عَادَتَا

نَزُورُ	زُرْنَا	نَعُودُ	عُدْنَا	نَحْنُ		
تَزُورُونَ	زُرْتُمْ	تَعُودُونَ	عُدْتُمْ	أَنْتُمْ		
تَزُرْنَ	زُرْتُنَّ	تَعُدْنَ	عُدْتُنَّ	أَنْتُنَّ	جَمْع	
يَزُورُونَ	زَارُوا	يَعُودُونَ	عَادُوا	هُمْ		
يَزُرْنَ	زُرْنَ	يَعُدْنَ	عُدْنَ	هُنَّ		

In this table the verbs عَادَ يَعودُ and زَارَ يَزورُ follow the same patterns as discussed above with the other hollow verbs. These examples are meant to be only a sample from this sophisticated group of verbs.

Defective Verbs

Defective verbs are the third and final group of weak verbs. Their third radical is a weak letter. This category of verbs is by far the most irregular and complex among the weak verbs. They sometimes require the disappearance or switching of the weak letter. Since the radical letter immediately precedes the suffixes in the conjugations, sometimes the third radical and the suffix assimilate. This makes the recognition of the conjugations more difficult for beginners. The goal in this section is not to master defective verbs but rather to observe how they appear in a few examples. A thorough study of defective verbs would extend beyond the scope of this introductory course.

Consider the paradigms of two defective verbs: دَعَا (he summoned or called out) and غَزَا (he invaded).

يَغْزُو	غَزَا	يَدْعُو	دَعَا		
أَغْزُو	غَزَوْتُ	أَدْعُو	دَعَوْتُ	أَنَا	
تَغْزُو	غَزَوْتَ	تَدْعُو	دَعَوْتَ	أَنْتَ	
تَغْزُوِينَ	غَزَوْتِ	تَدْعُوِينَ	دَعَوْتِ	أَنْتِ	مُفْرَد
يَغْزُو	غَزَا	يَدْعُو	دَعَا	هُوَ	
تَغْزُو	غَزَتْ	تَدْعُو	دَعَتْ	هِيَ	

نَغْزُو	غَزَوْنَا	نَدْعُو	دَعَوْنَا	نَحْنُ	
تَغْزُوَانِ	غَزَوْتُمَا	تَدْعُوَانِ	دَعَوْتُمَا	أَنْتُمَا (مُذَكَّر)	
تَغْزُوَانِ	غَزَوْتُمَا	تَدْعُوَانِ	دَعَوْتُمَا	أَنْتُمَا (مُؤَنَّث)	مُثَنَّى
يَغْزُوَانِ	غَزَوَا	يَدْعُوَانِ	دَعَوَا	هُما (مُذَكَّر)	
تَغْزُوَانِ	غَزَتَا	تَدْعُوَانِ	دَعَتَا	هُما (مؤَنَّث)	
نَغْزُو	غَزَوْنَا	نَدْعُو	دَعَوْنَا	نَحْنُ	
تَغْزُونَ	غَزَوْتُم	تَدْعُونَ	دَعَوْتُم	أَنْتُمْ	
تَغْزُونَ	غَزَوْتُنَّ	تَدْعُونَ	دَعَوْتُنَّ	أَنْتُنَّ	جَمْع
يَغْزُونَ	غَزَوْا	يَدْعُونَ	دَعَوْا	هُمْ	
يَغْزُونَ	غَزَوْنَ	يَدْعُونَ	دَعَوْنَ	هُنَّ	

In these defective verbs one will notice several irregularities, but we should leave examining them to an advanced course.

To conclude, in this lesson various irregular verbs were examined. We explored sound verbs, including *hamzated* and geminate verbs, as well as three kinds of weak verbs. The goal of this lesson was to introduce you to the various groups of sound and weak verbs and to demonstrate the general outline for conjugating them. Now we turn our attention to studying more verb forms as a concluding lesson of the book.

Vocabulary

he took	أَخَذَ	he asked	سَأَلَ
he ate	أَكَلَ	he roared	زَأَرَ
he captured	أَسَرَ	he saw	رَأَى
he ordered	أَمَرَ	he had mercy	رَأَفَ
he allowed	أَذِنَ	he got healed	بَرَأَ
he became sorry	أَسِفَ	he read	قَرَأَ
he became safe	أَمِنَ	he started	بَدَأَ

he passed by	مَرَّ	he rejoiced	هَنَأَ
he answered, responded	رَدَّ	he filled	مَلَأَ
he knocked, hammered	دَقَّ	he sought refuge	لَجَأَ
he split, slit	شَقَّ	he stood up	وَقَفَ
he summoned, called out	دَعا	he inherited	وَرِثَ
he invaded	غَزا	he promised	وَعَدَ
he walked	مَشَى	he weighed	وَزَنَ
he threw	رَمَى	he trusted	وَثِقَ
he stood	وَقَفَ	he arrived, came	وَرَدَ
he arrived, came	وَرَدَ	he branded, marked	وَسَمَ
he/it withered, dried up	يَبِسَ	he found	وَجَدَ
he slept	نامَ	he jumped	وَثَبَ
he feared	خافَ	he fell, it happened	وَقَعَ
he dreaded, feared	هابَ	he granted, bestowed	وَهَبَ
he fasted (from food)	صامَ	he placed	وَضَعَ
he returned	عادَ	it withered, become dry	يَبِسَ
he said	قالَ	he gave up, despaired	يَئِسَ
he got up	قامَ	he became awake	يَقِظَ
he visited	زارَ	he repented	تابَ
he revolved	دارَ	he sold	باعَ
he rebelled, revolted against	ثارَ	he walked, or marched	سارَ
		he increased	زادَ

Exercises

Exercise 19.1

Translate the following sentences into English.

1. ما أَخَذَ السَّيّارةَ.

2. قد رَأى النورَ.

3. مَلأَ الصُنْدوقَ.

4. سَأَلَ سؤالاً.

5. يَسْأَلُ الأستاذَ في الفصلِ.

6. مَرَرْتُ بِهِ.

7. وَقَفَ على السَجّادةِ.

8. وَزَنّا العَرَبَةَ معاً.

9. نامَ في البيتِ.

10. صُمْتُ رَمَضانَ.

Exercise 19.2

Translate the following sentences into Arabic.

1. They said to him: Peace.

2. He is asking his teacher.

3. He saw the moon.

4. We will pass by the church tomorrow.

5. He promised his sister, and she promised a policeman.

6. He found the pen.

7. The child slept at night.

8. He fears God.

9. He walked to the car.

10. You (md) are fasting in Ramadan?

11. I returned from Lebanon a year ago.

12. The king summoned the thief.

Exercise 19.3

In the following table, circle each sound verb and underscore every weak verb.

آكُلُ	صامَ	تَزورُ	يَبِسَ	يَقولُ	مَرَّتا
شَقَقْتُما	سَبَّ	تَعُدْنَ	مَشَى	باعَ	يَقولُ
مَرَرْتُنَّ	يَرِدُ	نَغْزو	لَجَأ	صُمْتَ	دَرَسَ
تَجِدانِ	وَثَبَ	دَعَوْتُنَّ	يَأْمَنُ	تَقولانِ	سَأَلَ
خافَ	يَهَبُ	رَأى	أَسِفْتُ	صُمْتُنَّ	شَقَّ

Exercise 19.4

The following verbs were studied and conjugated in the lesson. Parse them.

1. أَذِنَ

2. خُذْ

3. سَأَلَ

4. مَرَرْتُم

5. شَقَقْنَ

6. يَيْأَسُ

7. خافَ

8. هابَ

9. صامَتْ

10. دَعَوْتُ

Lesson Twenty
عِشْرُونَ

Verbs Forms

In this lesson our focus is to study a unique feature in Arabic related to verbs. As explained previously, the root is the most basic form of a verb. We can expand this basic form through various modifications in order to change the notion expressed by the verb and its root. For example, if the verb كَسَرَ means "he broke," the verb كَسَّرَ means "he broke into pieces" or "he crushed." Similarly, if غَلَقَ means "he closed," the verb غَلَّقَ indicates "he firmly locked" or "securely closed" something. The emphatic forms كَسَّرَ and غَلَّقَ are created by doubling the second radical, i.e., adding a *shaddah* on the root's second letter. The result is called a verb form, which conveys an intensification of the notion initially expressed by the basic verbs كَسَرَ and غَلَقَ.[1]

At the outset it should be noted that the various verb forms are created by adding letters or vowels to the basic root. There are fifteen different verb forms in Arabic, including the most basic form فَعَلَ, which is the first possible form. Some of the forms are rarely used. Since this course is introductory, we will focus on the most frequently used ten forms. We will examine them, highlight their unique notions, and inspect their major conjugations. Following is the list of the most frequent verb forms and their patterns:

Form Pattern		Form Pattern	
تَفاعَلَ	Form 6	فَعَلَ	Form 1
اِنْفَعَلَ	Form 7	فَعَّلَ	Form 2
اِفْتَعَلَ	Form 8	فاعَلَ	Form 3
اِفْعَلَّ	Form 9	أَفْعَلَ	Form 4
اِسْتَفْعَلَ	Form 10	تَفَعَّلَ	Form 5

---

1. In this lesson I relied on the exceptional work of Professor William Wright (1830–1889), *A Grammar of the Arabic Language*. The book has been reprinted several times in various impressions. Wright's work is monumental and serves as an outstanding reference of Classical Arabic. His analysis of the verb forms is exhaustive. See Wright, *A Grammar of The Arabic Language*, 1:29ff.

Form 1 فَعَلَ

This form فَعَلَ is the most basic verb form in Arabic. It consists of the root and three short vowels. This is the verb form we have studied in several of the previous chapters, as we focused on triliteral sound and weak verbs. This verb form is for the most part transitive, i.e., it accepts and requires a direct object (or more); however, it can also be intransitive. Consider the following verbs: قَتَلَ (he killed), شَكَرَ (he thanked), and ضَرَبَ (he hit). All are transitive and follow the pattern فَعَلَ. This is not the case with جَلَسَ (he sat) and ذَهَبَ (he went away). Both are intransitive, yet they are still on the pattern فَعَلَ. Finally, note that the alternative patterns فَعِلَ and فَعُلَ are part of this verb form, with the exception of the vowel associated with the second radical. These alternative patterns usually produce intransitive verbs. The verbs تَعِبَ (he got tired), فَرِحَ (he rejoiced), and مَرِضَ (he got sick) follow the pattern فَعِلَ, while صَغُرَ (it became small), كَبُرَ (it became big), سَهُلَ (it became easy), and صَعُبَ (it became difficult) follow the pattern فَعُلَ.

Form 2 فَعَّلَ

This form is built on Form 1 by doubling the second radical using a *shaddah*. The form is emphatic in nature. It conveys intensiveness and sometimes exaggeration.

See the following examples:

Translation	Form 2	Translation	Form 1
to cut into pieces	قَطَّعَ	to cut	قَطَعَ
to wash thoroughly	غَسَّلَ	to wash	غَسَلَ
to slaughter, massacre	قَتَّلَ	to kill	قَتَلَ
to beat intensively	ضَرَّبَ	to hit	ضَرَبَ
to break into pieces (smash)	كَسَّرَ	to break	كَسَرَ
to lock firmly	غَلَّقَ	to close	غَلَقَ

Notice that the verbs of Form 2 not only double the second radicals from Form 1 but also convey meanings comparable to those of Form 1 except with an intensive notion.

Lesson Twenty

Form 2 not only conveys intensiveness but also a causative connotation. Consider the following examples:

Translation	Form 2	Translation	Form 1
to cause someone to write (i.e., teach writing)	كَتَّبَ	to write	كَتَبَ
to remind (someone of something)	ذَكَّرَ	to recall	ذَكَرَ
to cause someone to understand	فَهَّمَ	to understand	فَهِمَ
to gladden	فَرَّحَ	to rejoice	فَرِحَ
to inform	عَرَّفَ	to know	عَرَفَ
to teach	عَلَّمَ	to realize	عَلِمَ
to cause someone to drink	شَرَّبَ	to drink	شَرِبَ
to cause someone to laugh	ضَحَّكَ	to laugh	ضَحِكَ
to ease, soften	سَهَّلَ	to become easy	سَهُلَ

This table shows not only how Form 2 is built on Form 1 but also how Form 2 provides the notion of causation for verbs of Form 1. Pay particular attention to the vowel of the second radical as you create Form 2 from Form 1. If the second radical of the verb in Form 1 is كَسْرَة or ضَمَّة, it switches to فَتْحَة in Form 2. Moreover, when a verb of Form 1 is intransitive, it becomes transitive in Form 2.

Form 3 فَاعَلَ

This form is built on Form 1 by replacing the short vowel of the first radical with a long one. The فَتْحَة of the first radical switches to an *alif*. In essence, this form simply lengthens the vowel of the first radical of the first form. Form 3 is transitive. It denotes a reciprocal relationship between parties or the interaction between the subject and object of the verb. See the following examples:

Translation	Form 3	Translation	Form 1
to sit with someone	جَالَسَ	to sit down	جَلَسَ
to correspond (with someone)	كَاتَبَ	to write	كَتَبَ
to enter into exchange	دَاخَلَ	to enter	دَخَلَ
to discuss (with someone)	بَاحَثَ	to search	بَحَثَ
to run a race (with someone)	سَابَقَ	to outrun	سَبَقَ
to live (with someone)	سَاكَنَ	to live, reside	سَكَنَ
to fight (someone)	قَاتَلَ	to kill	قَتَلَ
to dance (with someone)	رَاقَصَ	to dance	رَقَصَ

Compare Form 3 to Form 1. The third form describes the verb as an action executed within a reciprocal interaction. For instance, consider جَلَسَ and جَالَسَ in sentences. The sentence الرَّجُلُ جَلَسَ في مَكْتبِهِ (the man sat in his office) has no sense of reciprocal interaction, while الرَّجُلُ جَالَسَ المَلِكَ (the man sat with the king) conveys a reciprocal interaction.

Similarly, contrast the verb رَقَصَ to رَاقَصَ. The sentence الفَنَّانُ رَقَصَ في الحَفْلِ means "the [male] artist danced at the party," while الفَنَّانُ رَاقَصَ المرأة في الحَفْلِ reads, "the [male] artist danced with the woman at the party." Of course, one can rewrite the former sentence to reflect the latter, by stating الفَنَّانُ رَقَصَ مَعَ المَرْأَةِ في الحَفْلِ, which means "the [male] artist danced with the woman at the party." However, Form 3 uses fewer words than the first form and, more importantly, is more poetic in Arabic.

Form 4 أَفْـعَـلَ

The fourth form is built on the first form by adding the prefix هَمْزَة with a فَتْحَة and removing the vowel on the first radical. The result is a سُكون on the first radical and the addition of the prefix أ. This form is primarily causative. For instance, if كَتَبَ means "he wrote," أَكْتَبَ would convey "he caused someone to write" or "he dictated." If جَلَسَ means "he sat down," أَجْلَسَ would reflect "he caused (or forced) someone to sit down." Notice that the first form جَلَسَ is intransitive, while the fourth form أَجْلَسَ is transitive.

This fourth verb form is causative, as was Form 2. One may wonder, If the second and fourth verb forms are causative, are there any differences? The answer is yes and no. Sometimes there is no significant difference, such as in the case of جَلَّسَ (second form) and أَجْلَسَ (fourth form). Both reflect the notion that "he caused someone to sit down," although the former is more intense and indicates force. Similarly, the verb سَمِعَ means "he listened," while سَمَّعَ and أَسْمَعَ mean "he caused someone to listen."

However, in other cases the causative connotation offered by Form 2 is clearly different from that of Form 4. Consider the verb عَلِمَ, which means "he realized" or "he knew." In its second form it becomes عَلَّمَ, which means "to cause someone to know" or "to make someone learn." It simply means "to teach." In its fourth verb form, it becomes أَعْلَمَ, which indicates "to let someone know (of something)" or simply "to inform (someone of something)." Consider another example of the verb خَرَجَ (to exit). Its second form is خَرَّجَ, which means "to cause [or get someone] to exit." In its fourth form, أَخْرَجَ, it means "to let someone (or something) out," "get someone out," or simply "to evict" or "to expel." The differences between the second and fourth forms become clearer with practice and using Arabic dictionaries.

Here are some more examples of Form 4 verbs:

Translation	Form 4	Translation	Form 1
to bid one to enter	أَدْخَلَ	to enter	دَخَلَ
to have someone listen (to something)	أَسْمَعَ	to hear	سَمِعَ
to house (someone)	أَسْكَنَ	to live, reside	سَكَنَ
to have someone to dance	أَرْقَصَ	to dance	رَقَصَ
to make (something) good (i.e., to fix)	أَصْلَحَ	to be good	صَلَحَ
to enter into the morning time	أَصْبَحَ	to be morning	صَبَحَ
to (set someone) free	أَعْتَقَ	to liberate	عَتَقَ

Form 5 تَفَعَّلَ

Like the others, this form is built on the first form. However, it is better to view it as formed from the second form فَعَّلَ by adding the prefix تَ, which is a short syllable in itself. This prefix تَ provides the precise notion of this form, distinguishing it from the second form. In Arabic this prefix is reflexive; therefore, Form 5 is reflexive, too.

By "reflexive," we mean that the subject and object of the verb are the same. When translating this form into English, passive voice is the best choice.

See examples of Form 5 as we build them from Form 2:

Translation	Form 5	Translation	Form 2
to be cut into pieces	تَقَطَّعَ	to cut into pieces	قَطَّعَ
to be washed thoroughly	تَغَسَّلَ	to wash thoroughly	غَسَّلَ
to be slaughtered, massacred	تَقَتَّلَ	to slaughter, massacre	قَتَّلَ
to be beaten intensively	تَضَرَّبَ	to beat intensively	ضَرَّبَ
to be broken into pieces	تَكَسَّرَ	to break into pieces	كَسَّرَ
to be locked firmly	تَغَلَّقَ	to lock firmly	غَلَّقَ

Form 6 تَفاعَلَ

Here the reflexive prefix تَ is also found. If the fifth form is built on the second with the addition of the prefix تَ, this sixth form is built on Form 3 with the addition of the same prefix. If the third form describes an action executed within a reciprocal interaction, Form 6 makes it reflexive. Translating the sixth form is best done by using reflexive terms, including "oneself," "one's," "each other," or "with others." If the third form is transitive and reciprocal, the sixth is reflexive and *decisively* reciprocal.

Consider several examples to clarify the meaning of Form 6. If جَلَسَ means "he sat down," then جَلَّسَ means "he caused someone to sit down," while الرَّجُلُ جالَسَ المَرأةَ reads "the man sat down with the woman," and تَجالَسا "they sat down (with each other)." Note how one Arabic word تَجالَسا conveys an entire English sentence. Arabs consider this to be one of the beautiful aspects of their language; namely, the ability to convey a detailed meaning using few words.

Note the slight difference between the rendition of the third form جالَسَهَ (he sat with him) and the sixth form تَجالَسا (they sat down together). Similarly, if the third form قاتَلَه means "he fought him," the sixth form تَقاتَلا reads "they [both] fought each other," and تَقاتَلوا "they [all] fought together." Thus, قاتَلَه indicates the act going in one direction, while تَقاتَلا reflects reciprocal action.

Lesson Twenty

Moreover, if the third form سابَقَ indicates "he ran (against someone)," the sixth form تَسابَقَ conveys "he raced (with others)," as in هُوَ تَسابَقَ مَعهم, which means "he raced them" or "he ran a race against them." Furthermore, if تَسابَقا means "the two raced" or "the two ran a race," the verb تَسابَقوا indicates "they [all] raced." The aspect of reciprocity is clear in the sixth form.

The notion conveyed by the third form ساكَنَ is more reflective of "he lived (with someone)," while that of the sixth form تَساكَنَ indicates that the act of "living" was accomplished by various actors. The verb تَساكَنا suggests "the two lived together," while تَساكَنتا means "the two [females] lived with one another."

Form 7 اِنْفَعَلَ

The seventh form is built on the first by adding the prefix اِنْ. This prefix consists of a *hamzah* plus a *nūn* with a سُكون. Note that the *hamzah* is of the وَصْل kind (Lesson Eighteen) and is never written. This prefix transforms the notion of the first form into passive. So if the first form عَمِلَ means "he did," the seventh form اِنْعَمَلَ indicates "it was done." If the first form شَرِبَ means "he drank," the seventh form اِنْشَرَبَ reads "it was drunk." Pay attention to the behavior of the vowel on the second radical of عَمِلَ and شَرِبَ when you form the seventh forms. If the second vowel is كَسْرة in the first form, it turns to فَتْحة in the seventh.

See some examples of Form 7:

Translation	Form 7	Translation	Form 1
he/it was cut off	اِنْقَطَعَ	he cut	قَطَعَ
he/it was washed	اِنْغَسَلَ	he washed	غَسَلَ
he/it was killed	اِنْقَتَلَ	he killed	قَتَلَ
he/it was beaten	اِنْضَرَبَ	he hit	ضَرَبَ
he/it was broken	اِنْكَسَرَ	he broke	كَسَرَ
it was locked	اِنْغَلَقَ	he closed	غَلَقَ
it was planted	اِنْزَرَعَ	he planted	زَرَعَ
he was left (alone)	اِنْتَرَكَ	he left	تَرَكَ
it was paid	اِنْدَفَعَ	he paid	دَفَعَ
it was discussed	اِنْبَحَثَ	he discussed	بَحَثَ

Form 8 اِفْتَعَلَ

This form is built on the first form by inserting the letter ـتـ between the first and second radicals and adding the prefix *hamzah* (again, it is of the وَصْلِ kind, i.e., connecting). Recall that the letter ـتـ—in forms 5 and 6—brings forth the reflexive notion. This is true here, too. It is reflexive and sometimes reciprocal.

For instance, if the first form سَمِعَ indicates "he heard," the eighth form اِسْتَمَعَ suggests "he put himself into hearing (something)" or simply "he listened (carefully)." If the first form كَتَبَ suggests "he wrote," the eighth form اِكْتَتَبَ provides a reflexive notion, and means "he was registered." As for the first form نَصَرَ, it translates "he made victorious." In its eighth form, اِنْتَصَرَ means "he overcame (or won)." Similarly, if فَتَحَ means "he opened," اِفْتَتَحَ indicates "he inaugurated." Also, if عَرَفَ means "he knew," اِعْتَرَفَ translates "he made known," "declared," "acknowledged," or "confessed."

Form 9 اِفْعَلَّ

This form is the least common among the ten discussed in this lesson. It is built on the first form and is formed by doubling the third radical and placing the initial *hamzah*. The vowel on the first radical should change from فَتْحَة to سُكون. This form is used mostly with colors. It reflects intensity and the changing of colors. So, when we say اِسْوَدَّ, we mean "it became black," while اِحْمَرَّ means "it became red."

Form 10 اِسْتَفْعَلَ

This form is common. It is formed by prefixing the first form with اِسْتَـ. This prefix forces the change of the vowel on the first radical from فَتْحَة to سُكون. Form 10 is descriptive, demonstrative, expressive, and sometimes possessive. If the first form simply indicates an action, the tenth form describes the quality of desiring, longing, demanding, or requiring that action.

For instance, if the first form سَلِمَ means "he became safe," the tenth form اِسْتَسْلَمَ reflects the quality of desiring safety or to avoid harm, which literally translates "he surrendered." If غَفَرَ means "he forgave," its tenth form اِسْتَغْفَرَ indicates the quality of seeking forgiveness, which translates as "he sought pardon." The verb حَضَرَ means "he became present" or "he came." Its tenth form is اِسْتَحْضَرَ, which highlights the quality of desiring someone's presence and literally translates "he required (someone's) presence." So, the verb اِسْتَحْضَرَها can be rendered "he sought her presence." Also, the verb اِسْتَغْفَرَهُ means "he sought his pardon," while اِسْتَغْفَرَهُم means "he asked for their pardon."

Lesson Twenty

As a general note after exploring these ten verb forms, a student should be careful not to assume that every form can work with each triliteral verb. The examples provided here are only meant to explain how verb forms operate; however, the matter is sophisticated and more complex than it might appear. This introductory discussion is meant to give students a general understanding of the verb forms.

Since we have now completed the major verb forms, we will turn our attention to another aspect of Arabic verbs, particularly as they relate to nouns. In what follows we focus on how to build a noun from a verb.

Verbal Noun (المَصْدَر)

A verbal noun is a noun derived from a verb. In Arabic it is called المَصْدَر (al-maṣdar), which literally means "the source," indicating the point where "everything originates." It is also called اسْمُ الفِعْل, because it is اسْمُ derived from فِعْل. Grammatically, المَصْدَر is a noun which describes the action of the verb. Think of the English words "walk" and "walking." The former is a verb, and the latter is a noun that describes that act of the verb. We say, "I walk" and "walking is a good exercise." Similarly, consider "listen, listening," "work, working," "drink, drinking," "read, reading," and so forth.

At the outset, forming المَصْدَر is not straightforward at all. Sometimes a verbal noun of one verb can take two forms with slightly different meanings. Additionally, there is no specific rule for forming the verbal nouns, although we have many patterns to follow. These patterns are helpful to form المَصْدَر, but not every form fits every verb.

Here our focus is to study the five most common patterns of verbal nouns:

Pattern	Verbal Noun	Translation	Verb	Translation
فَعْل	مَجْد	glory	مَجَدَ	to glory (magnify)
	زَرْع	planting	زَرَعَ	to plant
	قَتْل	killing	قَتَلَ	to kill
	غَزْو	invasion	غَزَا	to invade
	ضَرْب	beating	ضَرَبَ	to beat
	قَوْل	saying	قال	to say
	حَمْل	pregnancy	حَمَلَ	to carry
	جَمْع	collection	جَمَعَ	to collect
	سَمْع	hearing	سَمِعَ	to hear
	فَهْم	understanding	فَهِمَ	to understand
فَعَلْ	عَمَلْ	work (business)	عَمِلَ	to work
	مَرَضْ	sickness	مَرِضَ	to get sick
	سَهَرْ	watchfulness	سَهِرَ	to stay up late
	فَرَحْ	rejoicing	فَرِحَ	to rejoice
	طَلَبْ	requesting	طَلَبَ	to request
	كَرَمْ	generosity	كَرُمَ	to be generous

Lesson Twenty

Pattern	Verbal Noun	Translation	Verb	Translation
فَعال	صَلاح	goodness	صَلَحَ	to be good
	نَجاح	success	نَجَحَ	to succeed
	فَلاح	success	فَلَحَ	to succeed
	سَماح	allowance	سَمَحَ	to allow
	ذَهاب	the act of going	ذَهَبَ	to go
	سَباب	insulting	سَبَّ	to insult
	شَراب	drink	شَرِبَ	to drink
	فساد	corruption	فَسَدَ	to spoil
فِعالة	عِبادَة	worship	عَبَدَ	to worship
	زِراعَة	agriculture	زَرَعَ	to plant
	دِراسَة	studying	دَرَسَ	to study
	تِجارَة	commerce	تَجَرَ	to do business
	قِراءَة	reading	قَرَأَ	to read
	كِتابَة	writing	كَتَبَ	to write
فُعولَة	سُهولَة	easiness	سَهُلَ	to be easy
	صُعوبَة	difficulty	صَعُبَ	to be difficult

In this table, each verbal noun follows one of the following common five patterns:

فَعْل

فَعْل

فَعال

فِعالَة

فُعولَة

To form the مَصْدَر, we start with the verb, follow the pattern, and then create the corresponding noun. Notice that the مَصْدَر holds the basic notion of the verb, e.g., "to read" becomes "reading." It should be reiterated that the pattern we use to create the verbal noun of a specific verb does not necessarily work with other verbs. For example, from the verb دَرَسَ the verbal noun دِراسَة is created by using the pattern فِعالَة. No other pattern can be used to create the verbal noun from the verb دَرَسَ. Hypothetically, if the pattern فُعولَة is used instead, the result will be an imaginary verbal noun دُروسَة, which is incorrect.

However, sometimes a specific verb can have more than one verbal noun. Usually, these different verbal nouns provide slightly different meanings, but they always carry the same basic notion in the root of the verb. For instance, consider the verb زَرَعَ in the table above. There are two verbal nouns: زَرْع and زِراعَة. The noun زَرْع conveys "planting," while زِراعَة means the business itself, "agriculture."

In conclusion, the five abovementioned patterns should suffice as an introduction to understanding the way verbal nouns are built in Arabic and provide students with some of the common examples.

Vocabulary

to cause someone to write (i.e., teach writing)	كَتَّبَ	to cut into pieces	قَطَّعَ
to remind (someone of something)	ذَكَّرَ	to wash thoroughly	غَسَّلَ
to cause someone to understand	فَهَّمَ	to slaughter, massacre	قَتَّلَ
to gladden	فَرَّحَ	to beat intensively	ضَرَّبَ
to inform	عَرَّفَ	to break into pieces	كَسَّرَ
to teach	عَلَّمَ	to lock firmly	غَلَّقَ
to cause someone to drink	شَرَّبَ	to sit with someone	جالَسَ
to cause someone to laugh	ضَحَّكَ	to correspond (with someone)	كاتَبَ

to ease, soften	سَهَّلَ	to enter into exchange	داخَلَ
to bid one to enter	أَدْخَلَ	to discuss (with someone)	باحَثَ
to have someone listen (to something)	أَسْمَعَ	to run a race (with someone)	سابَقَ
to house/accommodate (someone)	أَسْكَنَ	to live (with someone)	ساكَنَ
to have someone to dance	أَرْقَصَ	to fight (someone)	قاتَلَ
to make (something) good, i.e., to fix	أَصْلَحَ	to dance (with someone)	راقَصَ
to enter into the morning time	أَصْبَحَ	to be cut into pieces	تَقَطَّعَ
to (set someone) free	أَعْتَقَ	to be washed thoroughly	تَغَسَّلَ
he/it was cut off	اِنْقَطَعَ	to be slaughtered, massacred	تَقَتَّلَ
he/it was washed	اِنْغَسَلَ	to be beaten intensively	تَضَرَّبَ
he/it was killed	اِنْقَتَلَ	to be broken into pieces	تَكَسَّرَ
he/it was beaten	اِنْضَرَبَ	to be locked firmly	تَغَلَّقَ
he/it was broken	اِنْكَسَرَ	he was left (alone)	اِنْتَرَكَ
it was locked	اِنْغَلَقَ	it was paid	اِنْدَفَعَ
it was planted	اِنْزَرَعَ	it was discussed	اِنْبَحَثَ
to glory (magnify)	مَجَدَ	glory	مَجْد
to plant	زَرَعَ	planting	زَرْع
to kill	قَتَلَ	killing	قَتْل

to invade	غَزَا	invasion	غَزْو
to beat	ضَرَبَ	beating	ضَرْب
to say	قال	saying	قَوْل
to carry	حَمَلَ	pregnancy	حَمْل
to collect	جَمَعَ	collection	جَمْع
to hear	سَمِعَ	hearing	سَمْع
to understand	فَهِمَ	understanding	فَهْم
to work	عَمِلَ	work (business)	عَمَل
to get sick	مَرِضَ	sickness	مَرَض
to stay up late	سَهِرَ	watchfulness	سَهَر
to rejoice	فَرِحَ	rejoicing	فَرَح
to request	طَلَبَ	requesting	طَلَب
to be generous	كَرُمَ	generosity	كَرَم
to be good	صَلَحَ	goodness	صَلاح
to succeed	نَجَحَ	success	نَجاح
to succeed	فَلَحَ	success	فَلاح
to allow	سَمَحَ	allowance	سَماح
to go	ذَهَبَ	the act of going	ذَهاب
to insult	سَبَّ	insulting	سَباب
to drink	شَرِبَ	drink	شَراب
to spoil	فَسَدَ	corruption	فَساد
to count	حَسِبَ	worship	عِبادَة
to write	كَتَبَ	agriculture	زِراعَة
to hide	حَجَبَ	studying	دِراسَة

Lesson Twenty

to worship	عَبَدَ	commerce	تِجارَة
to plant	زَرَعَ	reading	قِراءَة
to study	دَرَسَ	writing	كِتابَة
to do business	تَجَرَ	bandage	ضِمادَة
to read	قَرَأَ	maintenance	صِيانَة
to write	كَتَبَ	easiness	سُهولَة
to tie around	ضَمَدَ	difficulty	صُعوبَة
to be easy	سَهُلَ	to maintain	صانَ
		to be difficult	صَعُبَ

Exercises

Exercise 20.1

Use the examples given in the lesson to translate the following sentences into Arabic.

1. He cut the bread into pieces.

2. She washed the dress thoroughly.

3. They (md) massacred the enemy.

4. He locked the door firmly.

5. He taught his son writing.

6. She reminded her mother to rejoice.

7. The artist (f) danced with the man at the party.

8. He fixed the problem.

9. The bread was cut into pieces.

10. The man was beaten.

11. The gate was locked.

12. He inaugurated the new school.

Exercise 20.2

Follow the examples given earlier on verb forms and verbal nouns in order to translate the following sentences into English. This exercise should help you deal with various verb forms. You will need some vocabulary from previous lessons.

1. الفَرَحُ إلى العَالَمِ.
2. أريدُ النجاحَ.
3. أُحِبُّ الدِّراسَةَ والقِراءةَ.
4. أنا لا أريدُ السَّهَرَ.
5. اللِّصُّ اِسْتَسْلَمَ.
6. إمامُ المسجدِ اِسْتَغْفَرَ الله.
7. اِعْتَرَفَ بالخَطيئَةِ.
8. هي اِسْتَمَعَتْ للمحاضرةِ.
9. الكَلْبُ اِنْتَرَكَ وَحْدَهُ.
10. اِنْبَحَثَ المَقالَ في المَكْتَبَةِ.
11. اِنْزَرَعَتْ شَجَرَةً.
12. الزُجاجُ تَكَسَّرَ.
13. الوالِدُ أَدْخَلَ البنتَ إلى المَدْرَسَةِ.
14. المَلِكُ أَعْتَقَ القاتِلَ.
15. الزَوْجُ كاتَبَ زَوْجَتَهُ.
16. خَبَرُ النجاحِ فَرَّحَ البِنْتَ.
17. الأمُّ عَرَّفَتْ اِبنَها الطَّريقَ.
18. المُدَرِّسُ ضَحَّكَ المُدَرِّسَةَ.
19. اللهُ سَهَّلَ لَهُم المَشْروعَ.
20. الفاتورةُ اِنْدَفَعَتْ.

GLOSSARY OF VOCABULARY AND EXPRESSIONS

١

father	أب
never	أَبَداً
son	ابْن
daughter	ابْنة
doors	أبْواب
white (m)	أبْيَض
relating to white	أبْيَضيّ
two	اثْنان
I love/like	أُحِبُّ
Ahmed	أحْمَد
red (m)	أحْمَر
relating to Red	أحْمَريّ
sometimes	أحْياناً
brother	أخ
sister	أُخْت
exam	اخْتِبار
he took	أخَذَ
green (m)	أخْضَر
faithfulness	إخْلاص
finally	أخيراً
to bid one to enter	أدْخَلَ
I study	أدرُسُ

smart people	أذْكِياء
he allowed	أذِنَ
ear	أُذُن
I go	أذْهَبُ
four (m)	أرْبَع
Wednesday	الأرْبِعاء
Jordan	الأُرْدُن
to have someone to dance	أرْقَصَ
I want to	أريد أن
couch	أريكة
Spain	إسْبانيا
professor	أسْتاذ
Australia	أسْتِراليا
he captured	أسَرَ
Israel	إسْرائيل
he became sorry	أسِفَ
to live with someone	أسْكَنَ
Alexandria	الإسْكَنْدَريَّة
noun, name	اسْم
nouns, names	أسْماء
demonstratives	أسْماء الإشارَة
fish (p)	أسْماك
to have someone listen (to something)	أسْمَعَ
sign, signal	إشارَة

279

I want ...	أَنَا أُرِيدُ ...	Thank God!	أَشْكُرُ اللهَ!
I think ...	أنا أَظُنُّ أن ...	to enter into the morning time	أَصْبَحَ
I guess that ...	أنا أَعْتَقِدُ أن ...	yellow (m)	أَصْفَر
I am fine!	أنا تَمام!	to make (something) good, to fix or repair	أَصْلَحَ
I am hungry	أنا جَوعان	dishes	أَطْباق
I am happy	أنا سَعيد	children	أَطْفال
I am thirsty	أنا عَطْشان	to (set someone) free, to release	أَعْتَقَ
I am okay	أنا على ما يُرام	lame (m)	أَعْرَج
I have	أنا عِنْدي	I seek refuge in God!	أعوذُ بالله
It was discussed	اِنْبَحَثَ	song	أُغْنِيّة
you	أَنْتَ	the mighty ones	أَقْوِياء
it was left (alone)	اِنْتَرَكَ	he ate	أَكَلَ
you (mp)	أَنْتُمْ	big eater	أَكول
you (md/fd)	أَنْتُما	god	إله
you (fp)	أَنْتُنَّ	mother	أُمّ
female	أُنْثى	in front of	أمام
the gospel (Injil)	الإنجيل	imam	إمام
it was paid	اِنْدَفَعَ	exam	اِمْتِحان
Andalus	الأَنْدَلُس	he ordered	أَمَرَ
it was planted	اِنْزَرَعَ	America	أَمْريكا
man (human)	إنسان	yesterday (adverb)	أَمْسِ
he/it was beaten	اِنْضَرَبَ	he became safe	أَمِنَ
it was washed	اِنْغَسَلَ	prince (also a masculine name, Amir)	أَمير
it was locked	اِنْغَلَقَ	now	الآنَ
nose	أنف	God willing	إن شاءَ الله
he was killed	اِنْقَتَلَ	I (am)	أنا
he/it was cut off, chopped off	اِنْقَطَعَ	I love ...	أنا أُحِبُّ ...
it was broken	اِنْكَسَرَ		
hello, welcome	أَهْلاً وسَهْلاً		

far, remote	بَعيد	Jerusalem	أُورْشَليم (القُدْس)
unpleasant	بَغيض	firstly	أوّلاً
survival, endurance	بَقاء	those (mp/fp)	أُولائِكَ
cow	بَقَرَة	which of?	أيُّ
Bakr (masculine name)	بَكْر	also, as well	أيضاً
girls	بَنات	where	أيْنَ
girl	بِنْت		
bank	بَنْك		ب
radiance, magnificence	بَهاء		
gates	بَوّابات	door	باب
gate	بَوّابَة	daddy	بابا
home or house	بَيت	courtyard	باحَة
actor's house	بيتُ المُمَثِّل	to discuss with someone	باحَثَ
Beirut	بَيروت	cold	بارِد
white (f)	بَيْضاء	he sold	باعَ
homes, houses	بُيوت / مَنازِل	seller	بائِع
		he searched, discussed	بَحَثَ
	ت	he started	بَدَأ
		beginning	بِدايَة
he repented	تابَ	he got healed	بَرَأ
seller, merchant	تاجِر	Portugal	البُرْتُغال
crown	تاج	blessing	بَرَكَة
history	تاريخ	lake	بِرْكَة
those (fd)	تانِكَ	Britain	بريطانيا
to do business	تَجَرَ	a smiling one	بَسّام
under	تَحْتَ	humans	بَشَر
he left (something)	تَرَكَ	champion	بَطَل
pleased to meet you	تَشَرَّفْنا	slow	بَطيء
to be beaten intensively	تَضَرَّبَ	slowly	بَطيئاً
she cooks	تَطْبُخُ	yet	بَعْدُ

Glossary of Vocabulary and Epressions

English	Arabic		English	Arabic
wealth	ثَرْوَة		he got tired	تَعِبَ
serpent	ثُعْبان		to be washed thoroughly	تَغَسَّلَ
fox	ثَعْلَب		to be locked firmly	تَغَلَّقَ
heavy	ثَقيل		please, come on in here (for a male)	تَفَضَّل هُنا
three (m)	ثَلاث		please, come on in (for a group)	تَفَضَّلوا
snow	ثَلْج		Please, come on in (for a female)	تَفَضَّلي
eight (m)	ثَمانٍ		Please, come on in (for a male)	تَفَضَّل
dress	ثَوب		to be slaughtered or massacred	تَقَتَّلَ

ج

	to be cut into pieces	تَقَطَّعَ
he came	جاءَ	report	تَقْرير
to sit with someone	جالَسَ	to be broken into pieces	تَكَسَّرَ
sitter	جالِس	dirt, dust	تُراب
university	جامِعَة	Turkey	تُرْكيا
mountain	جَبَل	apples	تُفّاح
grandfather	جَدّ	alligator	تِمْساح
very	جِدّاً	commerce	تِجارَة
wall	جِدار	nine (m)	تِسْع
new	جَديد	that (f)	تِلْكَ
root	جَذْر	Tunisia	تونِس
wounded (mp/fp)	جَرْحى	Tunisian	تونِسيّ
bell	جَرَس		
newspaper	جَريدة		
part (of something)	جُزْء		
Algeria	الجَزائِر		

ث

he sat down	جَلَسَ	he rebelled or revolted against	ثارَ
beauty (also a masculine name)	جَمال	thirdly	ثالِثاً
he collected	جَمَعَ	secondly	ثانِياً
camel	جَمَل		

Aleppo	حَلَب	sentence	جُملة
to shave	حَلَقَ	beautiful (also a masculine name)	جَميل
milk	حَليب	south	جَنوب
donkey	حِمار	southern	جَنوبيّ
porter	حَمَّال	weather	جَوّ
bathroom	حَمّام		
he praised, thanked (God)	حَمِدَ	## ح	
Thank God!	الحَمدُ للهِ!	hot/cold	حار / بارد
red (f)	حَمْراء	God forbid!	حاشا لله!
he carried	حَمَلَ	bus	حافِلَة / أتوبيس
praiseworthy one	حَميد	pub	حانَة
life	حَياة	love	حُبّ
		pregnant	حُبْلى
## خ		beloved	حَبيب
		hijab (veil)	حِجاب
servant	خادِم	to hide	حَجَبَ
he feared	خافَ	room	حُجْرَة
uncle (mother's side)	خال	it occurred	حَدَثَ
Khalid	خالِد	recently	حَديثاً
creator	خالِق	sad	حَزين
news	خَبَر	calculus, calculation	حِساب
death's news	خَبَرُ الوَفاةِ	he counted	حَسِبَ
bread	خُبزَ	envious	حَسود
expert	خَبير	party	حَفْلَة
he served	خَدَمَ	truth	حَقّ
he exited	خَرَجَ	reality	حَقيقَة
Khartoum	الخُرْطوم	government	حُكومَة
lamb	خَروف	wise	حَكيم
map	خَريطَة	swearer (repeatedly)	حَلّاف
loss	خَسارَة		

Glossary of Vocabulary and Epressions

خَضْراء	green (f)
خِطاب	letter, speech
خَطيب	fiancé (also orator)
خَطيئة	sin
خَفيف	light (not heavy)
خَلفَ	behind
خَلَقَ	he created
خَمْس	five (m)
خَوف	fear

د

داخَل	to enter into exchange
دار	he revolved
دائماً	always
دُبّ	bear (animal)
دَخَلَ	he entered
دَرّاجَة	bicycle
دِراسَة	studying
دَرَج	stairs
دَرَسَ	he studied
دَعا	he summoned, called out
دَعْوَة	invitation
دَفَعَ	he paid, pushed
دَقَّ	he knocked, hammered
دَلو	bucket
دِمَشْق	Damascus
الدِّنْمارْك	Denmark
ديك	rooster

ذ

ذانِكَ	those (md)
ذُباب	flies (insects)
ذَكَرَ	he mentioned, recalled
ذَكَر	male
ذَكَّرَ	to remind (someone of something)
ذَكي	smart (m)
ذَلِكَ	that (m)
ذَهاب	going (the act of)
ذَهَبَ	he went

ر

راديو	radio
رَأس	head
رَأفَ	he had mercy
راقَصَ	to dance (with someone)
راكِع	kneeler (worshiper)
رَأى	he saw
رَجاء	hope
رِجال	men
رَجُل	man
رَجُلُ الشُرْطَةِ	policeman
رِحْلَة	trip, journey
رَحْمة	mercy
رَحيم	merciful
رَخاء	prosperity
رَخيص	cheap
رَدَّ	he answered, responded

س

سابَقَ	to run a race (with someone)
ساجِد	prostrater (in worship)
ساخِن	hot
سارَ	he walked
سارة	Sarah
سارِق	thief
ساعَة	hour, clock
سافَرَ	he traveled
ساكَنَ	to live (with someone)
سَأَلَ	he asked
سامِع	listener
سائِق	driver
سَبَّ	he insulted
سَباب	insult
سَبْع	seven (m)
سَبَقَ	he outran
سِتّ	six (m)
سَجّادَة	carpet
سَجَدَ	he worshiped
سَحابَة	cloud
سَحَبَ	he withdrew
سَحَرَ	he bewitched
سَخاء	generosity
سَرْحان	in daze (also a masculine name, Sarhan)
سَرَقَ	he stole
سَرير	bed

رِداء	gown, dress
رَديء	bad
رِسالَة / رسائِل	message, messages
رَسول	messenger
رَعَدَ	to thunder
رَقَصَ	he danced
رَقْم / أَرْقام	number, numbers
رَكِبَ	he rode
رَكْض	running (sport)
رَكَعَ	he kneeled
رَمَى	he threw
رِياضَة	sport

ز

زادَ	he increased
زارَ	he visited
زَأَرَ	he roared
زُجاج	glass
زِراعَة	agriculture
زَرَعَ	he planted (a tree)
زَرْقاء	blue (f)
زِلزال	earthquake
زَمان	age, time
زَميل / زُملاء	fellow/fellows (also, classmate/classmates)
زَهْرَة	flower
زَوْج	husband
زَوجَة	wife
زورق	boat

Glossary of Vocabulary and Epressions

he/it became easy	سَهُلَ
easy	سَهْل
easiness	سُهولَة
question	سُؤال
black (f)	سَوْداء
Sudan	السّودان
Syria	سوريا
Sweden	السّويد
car, cars	سيّارة / سيّارات
engineer's car	سيّارةُ المُهَندِسِ
lady	سَيِّدة

ش

young man	شَاب
young lady	شابة
window/windows	شُبّاك / شَبابيك
tree	شَجَرة
drink	شَراب
drinker	شَرّاب
sail	شِراع
he caused someone to drink	شَرَّبَ
he drank	شَرِبَ
policeman	شُرْطِيّ
he commenced	شَرَعَ
honor	شَرَف
east	شَرْق
eastern	شَرْقِيّ
hair	شَعْر
poem	شِعْر

fast	سَريع
quickly, soon	سَريعاً
Souad (a feminine name)	سُعاد
happiness	سَعادة
happy	سعيد
happily	سَعيداً
serial killer, slaughterer	سَفّاح
blood-shedder	سفّاك
ship	سَفينة
he lived, resided, settled	سَكَنَ
peace	سَلام
peace be upon you	السَّلامُ عَلَيْكُم
fine (not sick)	سَليم
sky, heaven	سَماء
allowance	سَماح
earphone	سَمّاعة
doctor's stethoscope	سَمّاعةُ الطَّبيبِ
he allowed	سَمَحَ
brunette	سَمراء
he heard	سَمِعَ
hearing	سَمْع
listener (often and repeatedly)	سَميع
year	سَنَة
Sunna	سُنّة
Senegal	السِّنغال
annually	سَنَوِيّاً
watchfulness	سَهَر
to stay up late	سَهِرَ
to ease, soften	سَهَّلَ

cockroach	صُرصور	lip	شَفَة
he spent (money)	صَرَفَ	he split, slit	شَقَّ
it became hard, difficult	صَعُبَ	apartment	شَقّة
hard, difficult	صَعْب	he thanked	شَكَرَ
difficulty	صُعوبَة	thank you	شُكْراً
it became small	صَغُرَ	thankful person	شَكور
smallest, youngest (f)	صُغْرى	north	شَمال
small (m)	صَغير	to the left	شَمالاً
page	صَفْحَة	northern	شَماليّ
yellow (f)	صَفْراء	sun (also a feminine name, Shams)	شَمْس
adjective/adjectives	صِفة / صِفات		
goodness	صَلاح	witnesses	شُهود
stiff or hard	صَلْب	demon	شَيْطان
it became good	صَلَحَ	Shiite/Shiites	شيعيّ / شيعَة

ص

cross	صَليب		
he made	صَنَعَ	honest	صادِق
voice	صَوت	he fasted (from food)	صامَ
photo/photos	صورَة / صُوَر	he maintained	صانَ
fasting	صَوْم	maker	صانِع
maintenance	صيانَة	good morning (greeting)	صَباحُ الخَيْرِ
China	الصّين	good morning (response)	صَباحُ النّورِ
		in the morning	صَباحاً

ض

		patience	صَبْر
		patient (enduring) one	صَبور
hitter	ضارِب	boy	صبيّ
self-control	ضَبْطُ النَّفْسِ	desert	صَحَراء
to cause someone to laugh	ضَحَّكَ	dishes	صُحون
he laughed	ضَحِكَ	right (correct)	صَحيح
huge (f)	ضخمة	friend	صَديق
he beat	ضَرَبَ		
to beat intensively	ضَرَّبَ		

Glossary of Vocabulary and Epressions

hitting	ضَرْب	he appeared	ظَهَرَ
blind	ضَرير		
weak	ضَعيف	## ع	
bandage	ضِمادَة	he returned	عادَ
pronouns	ضَمائِر	usually (adverb)	عادَةً
he tied around	ضَمَدَ	just (fair)	عادِل
narrow	ضَيّق	high	عال
## ط		world	عالَم
		year	عام
student	طالِب	worker	عامِل
table	طاوِلَة	Aisha	عائِشَة
chef	طَبّاخ	worship	عِبادَة
he cooked	طَبَخَ	he worshiped, adored	عَبَدَ
doctor, physician	طَبيب	he crossed over	عَبَرَ
he crushed	طَحَنَ	Ajman	عَجْمان
road	طَريق	wondrous, marvelous	عَجيب
food	طَعام	Adnan (a masculine name)	عَدْنان
child	طِفل	enemy	عَدوّ
he requested, demanded	طَلَبَ	virgin	عَذراء
requesting	طَلَب	Iraq	العِراق
he went up, appeared	طَلَعَ	cart, trolley	عَرَبَة
Tehran	طَهْران	Arabic (the language)	العَرَبِيَّة
long (m)	طَويل	lame (f)	عَرْجاء
kind	طَيِّب	he informed	عَرَّفَ
## ظ		he knew	عَرَفَ
		bride	عَروس
envelope	ظَرْف	bridegroom	عَريس
darkness	ظَلام (ظُلْمَة)	dinner	عَشاء
noon	ظُهْر	ten (m)	عَشْر

288   Glossary of Vocabulary and Epressions

tithes	عُشور
giving	عَطاء
perfume seller	عَطّار
sermon/sermons	عِظَة / عِظات
great	عَظيم
you're welcome, or sorry	عَفْواً
all knowing	عَلّام
he taught	عَلَّمَ
he realized, knew	عَلِمَ
science/sciences	عِلْم / عُلوم
on or upon	عَلَى
Ali	عَلي
all knowing	عَليم
uncle (father's side)	عَمّ
Amman	عَمّان
intentionally, deliberately	عَمْداً
Umar	عُمَر
work	عَمَل
he made	عَمِلَ
deep	عَميق
grapes	عِنَب
eye/eyes	عَين / عُيون

غ

angry	غاضِب
winner	غالِب
expensive	غالي
stupid	غَبي
tomorrow	غَداً
lunch	غَداء
west	غَرب
western	غَربيّ
room	غُرْفَة
he conquered, invaded	غَزا
invasion	غَزْو
he washed	غَسَلَ
he washed thoroughly	غَسَّلَ
he got angry	غَضِبَ
all forgiving	غَفّار
forgiveness	غُفْران
all forgiving	غَفور
he defeated, won	غَلَبَ
wrong	غَلَط
he closed	غَلَقَ
rich	غَني

ف

bill	فاتورَة
knight	فارِس
Fatima	فاطِمَة
girl	فَتاة
opener	فَتّاح
he opened	فَتَحَ
at dawn	فَجْراً
to gladden	فَرَّحَ
rejoicing	فَرَح
he rejoiced	فَرِحَ
horse	فَرَس

قَاطِع	cutter	فُرْصَة	chance, opportunity
قال	he said	فُرْصَة سعيدة!	Nice to meet you! (literally, happy chance!)
قامَ	he rose	فَرَنْسا	France
القاهِرة	Cairo	فساد	corruption
قَبِلَ	he accepted	فَسَدَ	it spoiled
قَبْلَ سَنَةٍ	a year ago	فَشِلَ	he failed
قَبيح	ugly	فَصْلِ / صَفّ	classroom
قَتّال	a murderous one	فضاء	space (universe)
قَتَل	he killed	فَعَلَ	he did
قَتَّل	he slaughtered, massacred	فَقَط	only
قَتْل	killing	فَقير	poor
قُدّوس	holy	فلاح	farmer
قَدير	powerful, mighty	فَلافِل	falafel
قَديم	old	فَلَحَ	to succeed
قَذِر (وَسِخ)	dirty	فَلَسْطين	Palestine
قَرَأ	he read	فَلَسْطينيّ	Palestinian (m)
قِراءَة	reading	فَنّان	artist
قَرار	decision	فندق	hotel
القُرْآن	the Quran	فَهَّم	to cause someone to understand
القُرْآنُ الكَريم	the Noble Quran	فَهِم	he understood
قَريب	near, a relative	فَهْم	understanding
قَرية	village	في المَسيحِ	in Christ
قَسّ	reverend	في حَياةٍ ومَوتٍ	in life and death
قِسّيسُ الكَنيسَةِ	church's pastor		
قِصّة	story		
قَصير	short (m)	**ق**	
قَطّ	never	قاتَلَ	he fought (someone)
قِطار	train	قادِر	able
قَطَعَ	he cut	قارِب	boat

he cut into pieces	قَطَعَ	also, as well	كَذَلِكَ
he sat down	قَعَدَ	liar (repeatedly)	كَذوب
heart	قَلب	dignity, honor	كَرامَة
pen	قَلَم	chair	كُرسِيّ
few or little	قَليل	generosity	كَرَم
little (adverb)	قَليلاً	he became generous	كَرُمَ
moon	قَمَر	generous	كَريم
shirt	قَميص	robe, clothes	كِساء
he conquered or defeated	قَهَرَ	he broke into pieces (smashed)	كَسَّرَ
coffee	قَهْوَة	lazy (m)	كَسول
saying	قَوْل	words, speech	كلام
		dog	كَلْب
		how much or many?	كَمْ
		church/churches	كَنيسَة / كَنائِس
		how (is)	كَيْفَ
		how is it going?	كَيْفَ الحالُ؟
		how are you (for a male)?	كَيْفَ حَالُكَ؟
		how are you (for a female)?	كَيْفَ حَالُكِ؟
		how are you (for a mixed group)?	كَيْفَ حَالُكُمْ؟

ك

to correspond (with someone)	كاتَبَ
writer	كاتِب
liar	كاذِب
priest	كاهِن
church's priest	كاهِنُ الكَنيسَةِ
it became big (or he grew)	كَبُرَ
large (m)	كَبير
book/books	كِتاب / كُتُب
the Holy Bible	الكِتابِ المُقَدَّسِ
writing	كِتابَة
he wrote	كَتَبَ
he caused someone to write (i.e., taught writing)	كَتَّبَ
shoulder	كَتِف
often, much	كَثيراً
liar/liars	كَذّاب / كَذّابون

ل

no	لا
I do not like (or love)	لا أُحِبُّ
theology	لاهوت
he wore	لَبِسَ
Lebanon	لُبْنان
Lebanese (m)	لُبْنانِيّ
he sought refuge	لَجَأَ

to a university	لِجامِعَةٍ
I have	لَدَيّ
delicious	لَذيذ
thief	لِص
kindness	لُطْف
nice, kind (m)	لَطيف
he played	لَعِبَ
game	لُعْبَة
meeting	لِقاء
why?	لِماذا
to/for a school	لِمَدْرَسَةٍ
not here	لَيسَ هُنا
not there	لَيسَ هُناكَ
night (m/f)	لَيل / لَيلَة
at night	لَيْلاً

م

what?	مَا / مَاذا
what God willed, O my God!	ما شاءَ اللهُ!
water	ماء
Majida (a feminine name)	ماجِدة
money	مال
Mom	ماما
clever	ماهِر
exaggeration	مُبالَغَة
Congratulations!	مَبْروك!
abandoned	مَتْروك
when?	مَتى
for example	مَثَلاً

dual	مُثَنّى
to glory	مَجَدَ
glory	مَجْد
synagogue/synagogues	مَجْمَع / مَجامِع
passive voice (also unknown)	مَجْهول
accountant	مُحاسِب
lecture	مُحاضَرَة
beloved	مَحْبوب
court	مَحْكَمَة
Muhammed	مُحَمَّد
Mahmood (a masculine name)	مَحْمود
laboratory	مُخْتَبَر
different	مُخْتَلِف
teacher	مُدَرِّس
school	مَدْرَسَة
school teacher (f)	مُدَرِّسةُ المَدْرَسَةِ
manager	مُدير
city	مَدينَة
masculine	مُذَكَّر
he passed by	مَرَّ
woman	مَرْأة
Hello!	مَرْحَباً!
stage, phase	مَرْحَلَة
illness	مَرَض
he got sick, became ill	مَرِضَ
boat	مَرْكِب
patient (sick)	مَريض
plant (planted thing)	مَزْروع

active voice (also known)	مَعْلوم	in the evening	مَساءً
laboratory	مَعْمَل	Good evening (greeting)!	مَساءُ الخَيْرِ!
a made thing	مَعْمول	Good evening (response)!	مَساءُ النّورِ!
Morocco	المَغْرِب	Good evening (literally, evening of flowers)!	مَساءُ الوَرْدِ!
keys	مَفاتيح	mosques	مَساجِد
open	مَفْتوح	an outrun person (loser)	مَسْبوق
singular	مُفْرَد	mosque	مَسْجِد / جامِع
article (f)	مَقالَة	theater	مَسْرَح
a killed person	مَقْتول	Muslim	مُسْلِم
an adventurous person	مِقْدام	an allowed matter (permissible)	مَسْموح
a cut item	مَقْطوع	a heard one (audible)	مَسْموع
office, or desk	مَكْتَب	an anointed one, Christ	مَسيح
library	مَكْتَبة	Christians	مَسيحيّون
he filled	مَلَأَ	drink	مَشْروب
angel	مَلاك	project	مَشْروع
king	مَلِك	problem	مُشْكِلَة
excellent	مُمْتاز	he walked	مَشَى
actor	مُمَثِّل	Egypt	مِصْر
actresses	مُمَثِّلات	a spent (money), allowance	مَصْروف
from	مِنْ	Egyptian	مِصْريّ
Please!	مِن فَضْلِكَ!	Mustafa (a masculine name)	مُصْطَفى
house	مَنْزِل	kitchen	مَطْبَخ
table	مِنْضَدَة / طاوِلَة	cooked (meal)	مَطْبوخ
district/districts	مِنْطَقَة / مَناطِق	rain	مَطَر
Maha (a feminine name)	مَها	together	مَعاً
a humorist joker	مِهْذار	miracle	مُعْجِزَة
engineer	مُهَنْدِس	teacher	مُعَلِّم
death	مَوْت		
banana	مَوْز		

Glossary of Vocabulary and Epressions

God's grace	نِعْمَةُ الله	topic, subject	مَوضوع
during the day	نَهاراً	believer	مُؤْمِن
end	نِهايَة	feminine	مؤَنَّث
light	نور		
sleep	نَوْم	**ن**	

ه

		Nazareth	النّاصِرَة
		window	نافِذة
he dreaded, feared	هابَ	he slept	نامَ
phone	هاتِف	Nahid (a feminine name)	ناهِد
these (md)	هَاتَانِ	prophet	نَبي
gift	هَدِيَّة	success	نَجاح
this (m)	هَذا	carpenter	نَجّار
these (md)	هَذانِ	he succeeded	نَجَحَ
this (f)	هذِهِ	we	نَحْنُ
plateau	هَضَبَة	we are well	نَحْنُ بِخَيْرٍ
do, is, are (questions)?	هَلْ	we love	نَحْنُ نُحِبُّ
they (mp)	هُمْ	we want	نَحْنُ نُريدُ
they (md/fd)	هُما	warner	نَذير
they (fp)	هُنَّ	he went down, or descended	نَزَلَ
he rejoiced	هَنَأَ	Nisrin (a feminine name)	نِسرين
here	هُنا	Thank God!	نَشْكُرُ الله!
over there	هُناكَ	energetic	نَشيط
Hind (a feminine name)	هِنْد	energetically	نَشيطاً
he (is)	هُوَ	he supported, made victorious	نَصَرَ
he wants to	هوَ يُريدُ أن		
air	هَواء	he looked	نَظَرَ
these (mp/fp)	هَؤُلاءِ	clean (m)	نَظيف
she (is)	هِيَ	yes	نَعَم
she needs	هي تَحْتاجُ	grace	نِعْمَة

she wants	هِيَ تُرِيدُ	he promised	وَعَدَ
she wants to	هِيَ تُرِيدُ أن	he fell, it happened	وَقَعَ
		he stood up	وَقَفَ

و

And peace be upon you!	وَعَلَيْكُم السَّلامُ	an agent	وَكيل
one (m)	واحِد	loyalty	وَلاء
wide	واسِع	boy	وَلَد
father/mother	والِد / والِدة	he granted, bestowed	وَهَبَ
by Allah (oath)	واللهِ		

ي

Japan	اليابان
he/it withered, dried up	يَبِسَ
Jesus	يَسوع
Jesus Christ	يَسوعُ المَسيح
he works	يَعْمَلُ
he became awake	يَقِظَ
to the right	يَميناً
Yusuf (or Joseph)	يوسُف
today	اليَوم
day	يَوْم
one day	يَومٌ واحِدٌ
one day (adverb)	يَوماً
Greece	اليونان
he gave up, despaired	يَئِسَ

he jumped	وَثَبَ
he trusted	وَثِقَ
meal	وَجْبَة
he found	وَجَدَ
face	وَجْه
by myself	وَحْدي
he inherited	وَرِثَ
he arrived, came	وَرَدَ
rose/roses	وَرْدَة / وُرود
sheet of paper	وَرَقَة
he weighed	وَزَنَ
he branded, marked	وَسَمَ
he placed	وَضَعَ
container	وِعاء